# AMEDEO

# GVILLET

# AMEDEO

*A True Story of*
*Love and War*
*in Abyssinia*

SEBASTIAN O'KELLY

HarperCollins*Publishers*

HarperCollins *Publishers*,
77–85 Fulham Palace Road,
Hammersmith, London W6 8JB

www.**fireandwater**.com

Published by HarperCollins 2002
1 3 5 7 9 8 6 4 2



ISBN 0 00 2572192

Maps by John Gilkes

Set in PostScript Linotype Janson with Spectrum display
by Rowland Phototypesetting Ltd, Bury St Edmunds, Suffolk

Printed and bound in Great Britain by
The Bath Press, Bath

To Emily and Anna
'Le due figliole'

# CONTENTS

# LIST OF ILLUSTRATIONS

*All pictures without credits are from the private collection of Amedeo Guillet and the author*

'On 19 January the 4th and 5th Indian Divisions crossed the frontier north of the Blue Nile . . . they met little resistance, though at one point a force of local horsemen, the Amharic Cavalry Band led by an Italian officer on a white horse, attempted a death-or-glory charge against their machine-guns.'

John Keegan, *The Second World War*

# INTRODUCTION

In 1995 when I was a magazine editor, I asked the great Bill Deedes of the *Daily Telegraph* to go to Milan to interview Indro Montanelli. In Italian journalism Montanelli, who died in July 2001, was a figure of similar stature and, like Lord Deedes, he had served in the Abyssinian war, although as a volunteer officer rather than as a newsman. I decided that I would go along too, acting as a *consigliere*–translator, but really to eavesdrop on their conversation.

The founder-editor of *Il Giornale*, Montanelli had split with his proprietor, Silvio Berlusconi, over his political ambitions – the tycoon had just become prime minister for the first time – and, at eighty-eight, was about to launch a daily newspaper. He and Bill Deedes were well matched. Bill, the inspiration for William Boot in Evelyn Waugh's *Scoop*, had risen to become a cabinet minister, editor of the *Telegraph* and the most illustrious figure in our trade. Montanelli, who became a pressman after the conquest of Abyssinia, was purged from the Fascist Corporation of Journalists for writing with insufficient fervour about the Italian victories during the Spanish Civil War. He moved to Helsinki, to teach Italian literature, and was therefore conveniently on hand to cover the start of the Second World War. He interviewed Hitler after the fall of Poland and reported on the Finnish war from the Russian front. Back in Milan in 1944–5, he was sentenced to death for his critical writing by Mussolini's Social Republic, but was saved by the war's end. By the Seventies, he was equally unpopular with Italy's extreme left, and was shot in the legs by the Red Brigades as he walked along a Milan street.

'I won't mention the mustard gas they used in '35 until last,' said Bill conspiratorially, while we waited outside Montanelli's office. A few minutes later, the Italian appeared, tall, donnish and a little stiff, in contrast to Bill who, at eighty-two, was a sprightly, irrepressible figure. After greeting us cordially, for he had long known of 'Milord Deedes', Montanelli sat back behind his typewriter, lit a cigarette and waited for what he imagined would be an amiable chat to begin.

'Now, about the gas you used on the Abyssinians . . .' Bill began, astonishing us all (and pronouncing it, to my glee, as 'gash').

'*Basta con il gas!*' Montanelli groaned, having heard quite enough about it in the preceding sixty years. 'We are guilty. Guilty. Now let's talk of something else.'

Forty minutes later, having made himself understood without any help from me, Bill was satisfied that he had got enough from the interview: a handful of telling facts about the new newspaper, a bit of background and a quote or two from 'your man', as he insisted on calling Montanelli. 'Just like filling a punnet of strawberries,' confided the indefatigable reporter.

We adjourned to a restaurant Montanelli suggested beside the Castello Sforzesco, where the two old men reminisced happily, and they trumped each other's stories. When Montanelli remembered his friend Kim Philby, an apparently lazy and drunken correspondent during the Spanish Civil War – until the spy's death a jar of caviar used to be sent from Moscow to Milan every Christmas – Bill recalled his bringing Mrs Philby back from Beirut to London after her husband's defection. A government minister at the time, he was returning from the colonial handover in Singapore when he was ordered to detour to the Middle East to pick up the traitor's wife, who sat at the back of the plane behind curtains, in purdah.

On my prompting, the talk then returned to Ethiopia in the Thirties, and the two began recalling such figures as Marshal Badoglio, Graziani, the Duke of Aosta and Haile Selassie. Both spoke lyrically of the country, its peoples, ancient culture and the beautiful women (about whom, writing in *Scoop*, Evelyn Waugh had caused Bill some difficulties in regard to Mrs Deedes). Also at lunch was the writer Vittorio Dan Segre, who the year before had published a brilliant, semi-novelised account of Amedeo Guillet's guerrilla exploits, aimed at young Italians who knew almost nothing of their country's colonial past.

'What a magnificent man,' said Montanelli, who had been a friend of Amedeo for many years, and about whose adventures he, too, had written in the early sixties. I was intrigued, and for a while they indulged my interest. At last, however, Montanelli raised himself unsteadily to his feet to return to the office.

'If you want to know more,' said the great editor. 'You must go to Ireland . . .'

# ONE

# *The Prisoner*

DECEMBER 1941. HODEIDA, THE YEMEN

It was in the early afternoon when the prisoners could expect to be fed. At that time of day, a little light penetrated the subterranean gloom, while outside every living creature abandoned the cauldron of the streets. The grating rumble of a cart, the cries of bartering tradesmen and even the ululating calls of the muezzin fell silent as the sun lingered at its zenith. It was then that some women in the town gathered up scraps saved from their meal of the night before and made their way through the labyrinth of foetid passageways to the little square in front of the dungeon. From where they were, below the level of the street outside, the prisoners could not hear their approach, but they knew that their only meal of the day would shortly arrive.

All of a sudden vegetables, crusts of bread, bits of fish and fruit showered down from the bars high above, caught like motes of dust in a shaft of light. With clanking chains, the fettered men surged forward to fall on the debris, pushing each other out of the way. Some of those giving food were wives or relatives, others were responding to the Koran's injunction to show compassion to the imprisoned. Apart from these charitable offerings, and a communal bowl of boiled rice every two or three days, the prisoners received no food, for the fact of their being where they were was proof that they had somehow transgressed, and the task of the guards was to keep them locked up, but not necessarily alive.

One prisoner was slower than the others. He limped painfully towards the food on the floor, holding up the chains linking his feet with a piece of rope. Around his left ankle, below the fetters he was supporting, was a dirty bandage, caked in dried blood and pus. Although he was always the last, he still managed to find something: a fish head, a torn corner of pitta or a broken cake of rice, which he would pick methodically from the floor of beaten earth. The seven or eight other prisoners – murderers, smugglers, petty thiefs, crooked traders, perhaps even the odd innocent man – had nothing to do with the stranger who called himself Ahmed Abdullah al Redai. Too much interest was taken in him by the authorities for that to be prudent. Not that he looked important or dangerous, dressed as he was in filthy clothes which fell away from his emaciated frame. But even in the depths of their oubliette they had heard about Ahmed Abdullah. While his Arabic was fluent, the accent was strong and foreign, and they knew that he was not, as his name professed, a Yemeni from the town of Reda. Some said he was a soldier from the war between the Nazarenes; while others had heard that he was a spy in the pay of the British in Aden, to the south. There were even those who believed he was a Christian.

For hours, the prisoner sat motionless in a corner of the cell, resting his back against the stone wall. Every so often he slowly raised himself and shuffled over to the communal water vat, lifting to his lips a ladle fashioned from an old tin can. A festering bucket served the prisoners' other physical needs and he would approach it suppressing his lingering feelings of disgust. He felt bitter now, when recalling his hopes on first seeing the cloud-covered mountains of the Yemen from the sambuk which had brought him across the Red Sea from Eritrea. As the vessel beached at Hodeida, an old mufti with a white beard had been carried through the waves by two fishermen and hauled aboard. He had stood on the prow, and before the passengers could wade ashore they had been required to make the Muslim profession of faith: There is no other god but God and Mohammed is his prophet. The stranger had repeated the familiar words without feeling fraudulent, for he recited his Arabic prayers five times a day and did so sincerely.

The senior port official, an elegant young man in robes of white silk, sat under a lean-to on the beach, where he questioned the new arrivals. He acknowledged their responses with a bored nod, and then waved them through. The stranger waited until he was the last before he approached. He stood before the low writing table, looking down at the young man, who sat on cushions and a carpet laid over the sand. He was neither a Yemeni nor a Muslim, he announced, but an Italian officer who had been fighting against the British. He was the equivalent of an *amir al-alai*, a colonel, who had commanded eight hundred horsemen, and he now sought refuge from his enemies in the Yemen. The official silently studied the figure in front of him. Dressed in miserable clothes with no possessions, or proof of identity, he looked like thousands of other desperate Arabs along the coast struggling to survive in difficult times. The hands were rough and callused, the weatherbeaten face scarred down the right cheek and, though his blue-grey eyes shone brightly, the whites were yellowed with malaria. But something about him, perhaps the quiet intensity with which he spoke or the levelled eyes which held his own with no sign of fear, made the young official hesitate to dismiss him. He invited the stranger to sit and tell him more, and ordered an underling to bring them tea.

To the prisoner, that interview felt like months ago, although he knew it could not have been more than two or three weeks. But for all the outside world would be aware, he could remain in the dungeon for years. All his efforts to evade the British seemed so futile now. Had he surrendered with the others, at least the enemy would have recognised his rank and kept him alive. But fortune had abandoned him and every day in the semi-darkness he was growing weaker. The glands of his groin were swollen from coping with the suppurating bullet wound to his ankle. It would not be long before gangrene set in. He had often faced death before, and he was resigned to it. In his pain and misery, it was not even unwelcome.

During the long, uninterrupted hours in the stifling cell, the prisoner's mind wandered back to the years before the war. Already they had the unreality of a dream. Receptions and balls in Rome and Turin, Budapest and Berlin merged one with the other in a blur of shimmering silks and assorted uniforms. Loud, laughing faces of half-remembered friends – well-born army officers like himself, society women and some of Italy's new movie stars – flashed past as though taunting him. He had been fêted then as one of Italy's star sportsmen; the great hope of the Italian riding team in the Berlin Olympics of 1936. The prisoner's fevered mind lurched again and he felt as giddy and nauseous as he had once in Budapest when the champagne had flowed and he had been carried around the mess of the Hadek Hussars, hailed as the 'Conqueror of Abyssinia'. And then suddenly he was standing before the diminutive figure of the Italian king at one of those awkward royal receptions for carefully chosen young people at the Villa Savoia in Rome. Vittorio Emanuele III, who had known him since childhood, was explaining in his hesitant, didactic manner the origin of the term steeplechase 'when English lords used to gallop madly across fields from one village *campanile* to another'. The next moment he was being led by the arm through the scented gardens of the Castello in Tripoli by Italo Balbo, the governor of Libya, who was worried that the Duce's new alliance with Nazi Germany would be the ruin of them all . . .

The odour of the shared bucket assailed the prisoner's senses, ending his reverie and the hours of waiting in the semi-darkness resumed. His past life in fashionable society, once the fulfilment of all his ambitions, had long since been left behind, and he looked back on it now, feeling nothing, almost as though it were someone else's.

Deeper emotions welled up inside him when his mind turned,

as it always did, to the two women who loved him. Guilt mingled with longing when he thought of Khadija. He closed his eyes and saw her again standing uncertainly at the entrance to his tent, the kerosene lamp highlighting her features and casting deep dark shadows in the folds of the white *shammah* wrapped around her head and shoulders against the night cold. He had buried many men that day, including some of those who were closest to him. Through reddened eyes, he watched as Khadija approached his bed and, saying nothing, she pulled off his riding boots. In that moment of tenderness, when happiness and life itself seemed so fleeting, he had taken her into his arms.

He was her chief, Khadija used to tell him, and in those days he had been the all-powerful *comandante*, one of the most promising young officers of the Duke of Aosta, the viceroy of Africa Orientale Italiana. But after the British had defeated the Italians, extinguishing the Duce's African empire, he had had nothing to offer her, yet she had stayed at his side. He became just a *shifta*, a bandit, inexplicably fighting on with a handful of his *ascari* after the rest of the Italian army had surrendered. Khadija was seldom far from his side, firing her ancient Austro-Hungarian carbine at the British lorries as they heaved their way up the mountain roads of Eritrea. '*Ay zosh! Ay zosh!* Up! Up!' she would shout in Tigrinian, as the ragged band closed in to loot and kill. Her fighting with the men brought them good fortune, she would say as she curled up beside him on the straw mat of their tukul. He would watch her fall asleep, covering her naked shoulders with an old blanket and then kiss the intricate braids in which she wore her hair. In the darkness of the dungeon, the prisoner's eyes filled with tears.

He had always tried to be honest with her, he would convince himself. From the beginning, she had known that one day they would part and that at home waiting for him was another woman; a woman whom he also loved and had asked to be his wife. Khadija would bow her head and say that she understood, but in her heart she did not stop hoping that he would never leave.

The prisoner had no idea what Beatrice Gandolfo's feelings were for him now: whether she was still waiting for him to return, or had found someone else, or even married, he had no idea. His name had not been among those killed in action, but nor had it been on the lists the British passed to the Red Cross of Italian officers interned in prison camps throughout India, Kenya and South Africa. He was simply missing – *disperso* – in the void left by the collapse of Africa Orientale Italiana. Whatever Beatrice – Bice – had decided, he would not, could not, reproach her. They had known each other all their lives and the bond between them, cousins as well as lovers, was too strong to be broken.

Bice's older sisters had always made more fuss of him than she ever did, when he stayed with them in Naples or went bathing at the Gandolfos' summer house at Vietri. It was they who demanded to know the latest scandalous gossip surrounding Edda Ciano, the Duce's chrome-blonde daughter, or what the royal princesses were wearing or whether he was really stepping out with the movie star Elsa Merlini, as the magazines reported. Still only in her teens, Bice would follow him intently with her dark brown eyes, smiling slightly but saying little. And when she did speak, it was as though she were gently teasing him, as if she were ten years his senior and not the reverse.

No one seemed to understand and accept his weaknesses and absurdities quite as she did. And he remembered the day, while they were sailing a little boat off the Amalfi coast, when he realised – and the thought had appalled him at first – that he was falling in love with his young cousin. Bice had swum over to the sheer rockface of the shore and, ignoring his words of caution, had climbed up to a high ledge. She looked down at him in the boat, smiled and then dived into the sea, and her long, reddish blonde hair, so unusual in a southern Italian, streamed towards him under the water.

Had fate been different, they would have shared their lives and had children, and together grown old. That she would never know what had happened to him was his saddest thought. When the fighting between the British and Italians finally came to an end, someone in Eritrea, maybe even one of the enemy officers who had pursued him, would confirm that he had still been alive several months after the fall of Asmara. But nothing more. She would never know of the dungeon on the other side of the Red Sea, which had cost him so much to cross. Here he would die and be buried and quickly forgotten as the crazed Ahmed Abdullah al Redai. And then no trace in this world would remain of the man he had been.

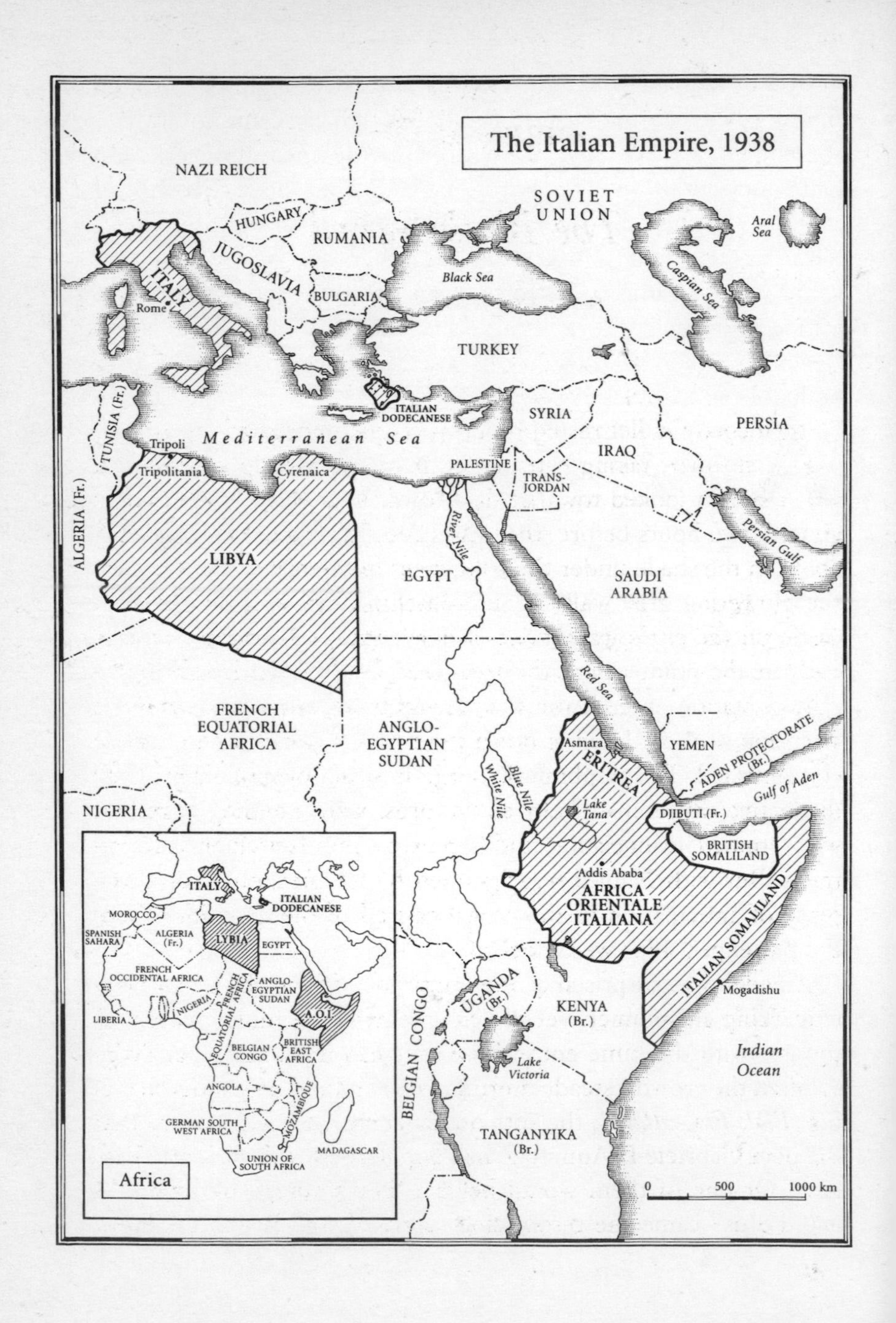
The Italian Empire, 1938
NAZI REICH
SOVIET UNION
HUNGARY
RUMANIA
JUGOSLAVIA
ITALY
Rome
BULGARIA
Black Sea
Caspian Sea
Aral Sea
TURKEY
ITALIAN DODECANESE
SYRIA
PERSIA
IRAQ
Mediterranean Sea
TUNISIA (Fr.)
Tripoli
Tripolitania
Cyrenaica
PALESTINE
TRANS-JORDAN
Persian Gulf
ALGERIA (Fr.)
LIBYA
EGYPT
River Nile
SAUDI ARABIA
Red Sea
FRENCH EQUATORIAL AFRICA
ANGLO-EGYPTIAN SUDAN
Asmara
ERITREA
YEMEN
ADEN PROTECTORATE (Br.)
Gulf of Aden
White Nile
Blue Nile
Lake Tana
DJIBUTI (Fr.)
NIGERIA
BRITISH SOMALILAND
Addis Ababa
AFRICA ORIENTALE ITALIANA
ITALIAN SOMALILAND
Mogadishu
BELGIAN CONGO
UGANDA (Br.)
KENYA (Br.)
Lake Victoria
Indian Ocean
TANGANYIKA (Br.)
0
500
1000 km
Africa
ITALY
ITALIAN DODECANESE
MOROCCO
SPANISH SAHARA
ALGERIA (Fr.)
LYBIA
EGYPT
FRENCH OCCIDENTAL AFRICA
ANGLO-EGYPTIAN SUDAN
A.O.I.
LIBERIA
NIGERIA
FRENCH EQUATORIAL AFRICA
BELGIAN CONGO
BRITISH EAST AFRICA
ANGOLA
MOZAMBIQUE
GERMAN SOUTH WEST AFRICA
MADAGASCAR
UNION OF SOUTH AFRICA

# TWO

# *The Black Sword*

NAPLES, AUGUST 1935

Amedeo Guillet rested his arms on the railings of the ancient steamer, taking care not to mark his olive-grey uniform, and looked towards the crowd. Ever since he had come aboard, two hours before, they had been slowly gathering, milling about in the shade under the palm trees in the piazza and beneath the glowering grey walls of the Maschio Angioino, the Angevin castle on the city's waterfront. A dense mass was waiting expectantly at the point where the tree-lined avenue that led from the railway station entered the square, and it was there, too, that the attention of those looking down from the balconies seemed to be concentrated. Tall carabinieri, in full dress uniform of bicorn hats, distinctive white cross belts and swords, were standing together, with studied insouciance, indifferent to the excitement around them. But with Naples reinvigorated by its afternoon siesta, the sense of anticipation in the crowd carried to the quayside where the passenger ships were docked.

Amedeo was surprised at the multitude. Troop ships had been embarking all summer, yet the city seemed determined to see off the last with the same enthusiasm as it had done the first. Every so often the crowd's steady murmur was ruptured by youths chanting '*Eià!*, *Eià!*, *Alalà!*', the supposedly ancient Greek war cry that the poet Gabriele D'Annunzio had popularised with the early Fascists. Or one of them would bellow: 'For whom, Abyssinia?' '*A noi!* To us!' came the resounding reply. '*A noi!*' It was the latest gimmicky catchphrase put about by the propagandists of the regime. All of a sudden, a ripple spread through the crowd. A second later a roar greeted the arrival of a column of marching men. Amedeo watched as figures began scurrying across the piazza towards them, drawn like iron filings to a magnet. Flowers were thrown to the soldiers or pressed into their hands, and amid the waving and the sea of faces could be seen little flags with the green, white and red of the Italian tricolour. It must have been something like this in May 1915, Amedeo felt, when his father and uncles had gone to war.

The column was mid-way through the throng when the sound seemed to change to a loud and delighted cheer. They were the Alpini, Amedeo could see, mountain troops from the north, whose beards and peaked felt caps made them look a little like William Tell. Children edged to the front, encouraged by smiling mothers who stooped and pointed, for behind the officers and regimental flags at the head of the column were half a dozen German shepherd dogs, leather satchels strapped to their backs. Trained to carry dispatches over frozen Alpine passes, the regiment's canine messengers were being mobilised for service on the Ethiopian *ambas*.

Then it was the turn of the Bersaglieri (literally 'marksmen') who emerged into the piazza with a fanfare of trumpets and at their customary jog, the cascades of cockerel feathers on their hats rippling through the crowd like merrymakers at carnival. It was the first time, though, that Amedeo had seen their distinctive headdress attached to tropical pith helmets. As they came through the gateway to the port, the foreground to countless paintings of the Neapolitan waterfront, a military band struck up the *Hymn of the Piave*. For the first time Amedeo, who had been watching unmoved by the scene, felt his emotions stir. No other song of the Great War had such resonance as this melancholic, but defiant morale-raiser, which had been sung to rally the Italian troops after the rout at Caporetto in 1917. Her allies had urged Italy to abandon the whole of the Veneto, as the Austrians, backed by German divisions, broke the front. But the king himself, Vittorio Emanuele III, had brought the shattered army to heal at the river: 'And the Piave murmured, "The foreigner will not pass".'

The tune changed once more and Amedeo's attention was drawn again to the piazza, cast in lengthening shadows as the sun gently expired over the Bay of Naples. A legion of Black Shirts had arrived, young volunteers determined to give victory in Africa a distinctively Fascist stamp. And they were singing as they came on. It was that idiotic, jaunty song that had been unavoidable for weeks, and it grew louder as the marching men approached the port:

*Faccetta nera, bell'Abissina,*
*Aspetta e spera: la vittoria s'avvicina . . .*
Little Black Face, beautiful Abyssinian girl,
Await and hope: victory is approaching . . .

Amedeo looked down to those gathered on the quay and caught Bice Gandolfo's eye. They smiled as the men strode past in a swaggering march, swinging their bare forearms, for a black shirt, it seemed, was always worn with the sleeves rolled up. Ethiopia's days of serfdom, they sang, would be replaced by the slavery of love. Then came the rousing finale:

Little Black Face, you will be Roman
And for a flag, you will have the Italian.
We will march past, arm-in-arm,
And parade in front of the Duce
And in front of the King!

In the cheering that followed, Bice made a dismissive little gesture with one white-gloved hand. Her father beside her, Amedeo's Uncle Rodolfo, shouted up: 'I am sure the king would be delighted to meet her!' And the three of them laughed as the column headed down the quay.

From the far end of the docks, a foghorn blasted. One of the troop ships, festooned in bunting and paper streamers, was casting off. Every available space on deck was filled with cheering men, waving their hats, hurling flowers and last minute protestations of love at their women below. On the ship's two funnels were giant, stylised, portraits of the Duce, wearing a helmet, jaw clenched in martial resolution, his head thrown back to iron out the chins. Other ships joined in the cacophony, sounding their horns, and then fireworks exploded over the city, jarring its crumbling palazzi down to their tufa foundations as they had so many times before.

It seemed more like a wedding than war, and the small cluster of friends and relatives gathered at the quay beside Amedeo's ship were the guests whom nobody knew. With half the Italian army being shipped to Eritrea and Somaliland, little fuss was being made of the old steamer that plied between Naples and Tripoli, the capital of Italian Libya. Amedeo had urged his uncle not to see him off. It would take the chauffeur at least an hour to pick his way back through the crowds to the Gandolfos' palazzo on the Via dei Mille. But the older man had insisted and Bice, to his surprise, had wanted to come too. Amedeo felt grateful now that they had done so. For although he was bound for Libya, his final destination was the same as that of the cheering men. He, too, would be going to war in Abyssinia if, as seemed inevitable, war it turned out to be.

Some acquaintances approached Uncle Rodolfo, and Amedeo watched him indulgently as he performed the courteous rituals. He was dressed in an outfit that he took to be the quintessence of an English gentleman at leisure, in yachting shoes, a white linen suit and a sailor's cap, which he doffed at absolutely the correct degree of sociable nonchalance. *Nu vero milordo*, Neapolitans called Signor Gandolfo, mixing genuine admiration with crafty flattery. Amedeo had always felt drawn to this charming relative, whose frank enjoyment of the pleasures of the Bay of Naples was mildly disapproved by the more duty-bound Guillets. And Amedeo's feelings of affection were reciprocated by the older man. Uncle

Rodolfo looked forward to his visits whenever he was competing at riding events in Naples, and he was sensitive, too, to the family bond between them. Before they had left for the port, Uncle Rodolfo had been moved to re-tell the stories of how the kinship between Gandolfos and Guillets had come about. His father and Amedeo's grandfather, both officers in the army of Piedmont, had fought side-by-side in the 1860s against the Austrians in the great battles of the Risorgimento, Italy's national resurgence. After the moribund Bourbon kingdom of Naples had been swept away, and the nation finally made, the two friends had ridden like victorious conquerors into the town of Capua, where they married the daughters of its leading citizen, one of the 'new' Italians of the south.

But whereas the Guillets had remained Piedmontese and northern in outlook, Rodolfo Gandolfo had long since been seduced by the ways of the Mezzogiorno. Wealthy and untroubled by the need to work, he nonetheless exercised his talents as an engineer to direct the great project to drain the malarial Serra Mazzoni marshes, and once built a theatre in Capua, which he then gave to the town. But his chief passion was to sail his yacht around the Bay of Naples, assisted by his crew of three daughters, of whom Bice, aged sixteen, was the youngest.

His little cousin was becoming sophisticated, Amedeo could not help thinking, as he watched Bice exchange pleasantries with the newcomers. He had been ten when he had held her in his arms as a baby, and he still thought of her as a child, calling her Bice or Bicetta, her name in endearing diminuendo, and seldom Beatrice, still less Signorina Gandolfo. For a moment he had felt self-conscious taking leave of her on the quay, kissing her cheek chastely for the first time, rather than joshing her fondly as he had always done before.

The steamer emitted a baleful sound from its horn, which interrupted his thoughts but still failed to arouse any interest in the piazza, and the sailors began slipping the moorings. Uncle Rodolfo called out a final good luck, waving his cap, and Bice raised a white hand as the steamer eased its way past the bigger ships into the harbour.

Naples had never seemed lovelier to Amedeo than on that evening, the dying sun catching the maiolica cupolas of the churches and casting the Certosa di San Martino, high above the least salubrious quarters of the city, in a warm orange glow. Sprawling and raucous, the southern metropolis grated against his northern sense of decorum, but from the safe distance of the sea, away from the chaos, the filth and the crime, it appeared magnificent. A true capital, Amedeo conceded, and the only Italian city worthy of the term. Apart from Turin, of course. It was not his Italy, which he preferred to think of as a land of neat, modest towns in the Alpine foothills, but it was undeniably the Patria. Whatever the Italians were only two generations after the nation itself had come into being – and the current view, incessantly repeated, was that they were the heirs to Imperial Rome – they would be much less, Amedeo believed, without the humanity of this ancient, suffering city of which all Italians seemed so embarrassed, and yet proud.

His eyes swept the scene, from the elegant seafront boulevards of Santa Lucia to the palace of the Bourbon kings, to the core of alleyways knotted around the mediaeval cathedral, where the poor lived crammed into cellars. And then he looked out beyond the city, to the great curve of the bay, where the land, once it emerged from the sea, was pulled upwards in a sharpening arc like a graph on paper, to the growling old man of Vesuvius himself.

For as long as he could, he fixed his gaze on the figure in white, and the pale, red-haired girl beside him, until they blurred with the others waving from the quay.

The ship's steward had unpacked Amedeo's uniforms and hung them in the wardrobe, but the sword he had carefully laid on the made-up bed. Amedeo picked it up and toyed with it in his hands for a few moments, turning it over to admire its curved shape. Every part of it was black: the steel scabbard and rings, the rather tinny hilt and the long tapering blade. His father, Baron Alfredo Guillet, when a major in the élite Mounted Carabinieri from which the Royal Bodyguard was drawn, had carried the sword in the Great War. But in the stalemate on the barren limestone hills of the Carso in Friuli, where every shellburst showered lethal fragments, men cowered in trenches, the horses disappeared and glistening cavalry sabres were dulled with acid to a matt black. Amedeo grasped the vulcanite grip, perfectly moulded to his hand, and pulled the sword free, enjoying its metallic rasp. He made a whipping cut in the air and examined the quivering blade, its point sharpened on both edges to prise through ribs and bone. It was a nineteenth-century weapon, re-fashioned for the slaughter of the twentieth.

Putting it aside, he stretched out on the narrow bed. He was going to war at last, to do what he had been training for ever since he joined the Military Academy at Modena seven years before as an eighteen-year-old cadet. But long before that he had known he would be a soldier. Arms were the family occupation of the Guillets just as others were bakers or bankers, silversmiths or peasants. His father had retired from the army a colonel, both his paternal uncles were generals, as had been his grandfather and numerous other, more remote, ancestors. Their uniformed portraits and blurred daguerreotypes hung from his father's library wall, and their dusty treatises on military strategy filled the shelves.

Amedeo had only a vague grasp of the causes of the Abyssinian crisis. The rights and wrongs behind the border clash in which several Dubats, Italian Somali troops, and many more Ethiopians had been killed, seemed too complicated to master. So it was proving for the diplomats at the League of Nations in Geneva, who for months had been poring over yellowing maps that showed the grazing rights and waterholes in the Ogaden desert. But if Italy went to war, Amedeo would have not the slightest doubt what he would be fighting for. It did not have much to do with the exhortations of Benito Mussolini, who had whipped Italians into a frenzy of indignation as though an Ethiopian horde were storming the Campidoglio. Nor were his sentiments entirely explained by the conventional patriotism that every child learned at school, revering the trinity of Mazzini, Garibaldi and Cavour, the prophet, the soldier and the statesman who had forged the united Italy. In a land where personal loyalties – to family, to friends – were far more important than abstract ones, the Guillets were bound to Italy's dynastic rulers in a bond which stretched back for generations, and Amedeo fully shared the sense of obligation.

He had always been proud of his Savoyard name. In the southern cities of Bari and Messina, where his father had been posted and Amedeo spent most of his childhood, the locals mangled the pronunciation of Guillet by attempting to Italianise it. But he had never cared that he did not share the sharp consonants and prickly vowel sounds of their names. Nor, though he was teased for his northern accent, would he try to fit in by taking up their dialects. When he was a boy, he would scrutinise an old map on his bedroom wall showing the patchwork of Italian states before unification, and his attention would be drawn to the ancestral possessions of Savoy. His finger would trace the frontier from Savoie itself and then down, over the southern slopes of the Alps to Piedmont, the core of the kingdom with Turin its capital, and the name by which the state was always known in Italy. There was no natural explanation for the line, which ignored the contours of mountain ranges and the course of rivers, as it did the linguistic borders of French and Italian. Every province, every town and village, had been painstakingly acquired as the House of Savoy, Europe's oldest and most tenacious ruling dynasty, rose from being counts to dukes to kings. Every encroachment, whether in France or Italy, had been held by force of will and blood. A fair share of it, Amedeo knew with pride, belonged to his own family.

From his earliest years, he had been aware that to be Piedmontese was to be born into the élite of the Kingdom of Italy. All the best regiments – the Bersaglieri, the Alpini, the cavalry – owed their origins to the old state of Piedmont, or the Kingdom of Sardinia as it was misleadingly named in its last stages. Even in the Thirties, the officer corps and the high civil service were still drawn disproportionately from the region. Italians from elsewhere, who may have thought that their own local achievements cast those of the Alpine region into shade, resented its lingering influence at the top of society. But only Piedmont had not slept during the long torpid centuries after the Renaissance and before the national awakening, when the peninsula languished into a dreamland arcadia amid the ruins of former greatness. In Turin, the seeds of a modern state were sown, nurtured by families such as the Guillets, created barons in the seventeenth century, who lived modestly on their own lands and equated their role with public service. When the movement for national unity began after the Napoleonic wars, only Piedmont could provide the leadership to free Italy from foreign rule; it alone survived while the territories of Venice and Florence, the Papal States and the Kingdom of Naples, and all the other smaller fragments, disappeared from the map forever.

Whenever the Italian tricolour was raised there was a reminder of this truth, for in the centre was the red shield and white cross of Savoy. To Amedeo, it was an emblem that demanded greater loyalty than the three colours themselves.

Neither the causes of the conflict with Ethiopia, nor the Guillets' sense of dynastic loyalty, were uppermost in Amedeo's mind as he lay in his cabin. It had been his decision to go to war; using family connections to fix a transfer to the Spahys di Libya, a regiment of colonial cavalry that was shortly to join the invasion force mustering in Eritrea. But having achieved his aim of serving under arms, he found it gave him little pleasure. Instead, a sense of guilt gnawed at him insistently as the old steamer clunked towards

Tripoli. He had made a choice of a type that the Duce would doubtless describe as 'irrevocable', and there was no going back from it. Three weeks before, his life had seemed so simple and untroubled, as he worked his horses in preparation for the Olympics that were due to take place in Berlin in early 1936. Now, doubts and uncertainties surfaced. And he still could not quite believe that he had given up everything that he had achieved as a competition rider and had quit the national three-day eventing team. When he walked away from the training ground at Turin, he knew that the others in the team felt he had let them down and old friendships had been severed. The life he had been leading for the past five years, ever since he had been commissioned, was at an end. And they had been good years. Very good years.

With the decision made for him that he would have a military career, he had always known which part of the army he wanted to join. His older brother, Giuseppe, had opted for the artillery, but for Amedeo, who had ridden his father's dressage horse from the age of five, it was the cavalry. Few occupations in Italy were then quite as glamorous. Only naval officers, who affected a certain *inglese* hauteur, or the pilots of the new Regia Aeronautica, the air force, came close. And the clothes were wonderful. Cavalry officers sauntered through piazzas wrapped in sky blue cloaks, wearing the dragoon's helmets or the hussar's fur busbies of the previous century. Olive-grey jodhpurs with double stripes in red were worn below a tunic that fastened at the neck, with just a hint of a white stock showing above. Riding boots, silver spurs and immaculate white leather gloves were part of the ensemble for a *bella figura*, even if the officers had only dismounted from a tram. And, of course, wherever they went, and at all times of the day, they held at their side their sabre. Even Amedeo had to concede that it was a little overdone, as he strapped his sword to the handlebars of his bicycle and pedalled off through the streets of Turin and Rome.

While the bright young things elsewhere were discovering jazz, experimental literature and sex, the 'fathers' were still in control in Fascist Italy. And Amedeo was an obedient son. The carnage of the First World War had not dented the army's social allure, nor was there a feeling that a generation had been betrayed and led to senseless slaughter. On the contrary, the wider population, though resistant to Fascism's efforts to make a cult of war, viewed Italy's victory at the side of Britain, France and the United States as a source of pride, and believed that the common sacrifice of 600,000 dead had moulded the nation at last. Under the regime, the role of the army was even more exalted than had been the case in 1915, and at the top society's rituals continued unchanged as though a reprise of the *belle époque*.

Amedeo's outlook on the world perfectly complemented his anachronistic uniform and he fitted seamlessly into the make-believe, hand-kissing Ruritania of Italian society in the early Thirties. These were the last of Mussolini's 'years of consensus', when the country seemed at ease with itself, the violence of the Fascist takeover in 1922 long forgotten and the leap into the abyss yet to come. There were no strikes, no social unrest and apparently no discord. Opponents of the regime either quietly left the country, or, if they openly defied it, were sent into internal exile, *al confino*, in the remote South. But on the whole, Italian Fascism, like the Catholic Church, contented itself with outward conformity, and seldom looked too closely at the real feelings that lay within. As for Amedeo, the strongest reproach he felt towards the regime was resentment that officers in the Fascist *Milizia*, the Duce's private army of Black Shirts, were able to box three competition horses on trains free of charge, while he, a regular cavalry officer, could only box two.

Besides, there was always the king. Diffident and awkward and not quite five foot tall, Vittorio Emanuele III was hardly an inspiring figure for most ordinary Italians, although there were times, as during the First World War, when they loved him. Throughout his forty-six year reign, that spanned meeting Queen Victoria to suffering the snubs of Allied liaison officers at the close of the Second World War, he remained an enigmatic, and often barely visible head of state. But with the Fascists presiding over an ever-changing theatre of varieties, his presence at the top of society reassured many and what he represented was held in respect.

On occasion Amedeo was invited to little receptions at the Villa Savoia in Rome, where the royal family lived in preference to the grander Quirinale. Princess Jolanda, eight years his senior and the oldest daughter, whom he had known since childhood, became a close friend. An intrepid *amazzone* – as modern women riders were called, for they rode astride – she shared Amedeo's passion for horses and his talent, once beating him in a jump-off when they competed against each other. He would join her set when riding out with the Rome Foxhunt, the fashionable winter pastime introduced in 1836 by Lord Chesterfield who, wearying of his wife's convalescence from tuberculosis, had shipped his hounds from England. The hunt would gallop under the arches of aqueducts, and wait at the coverts as the hounds sniffed about the ancient ruins that abounded in the Roman *campagna*.

Amedeo was also friendly with the affable Crown Prince Umberto and his intellectual wife, Maria José of Belgium, whose lack of enthusiasm for Fascism was the subject of widespread gossip. There had been a dinner in a rambling Alpine castle above Pinerolo, after which they all had played a version of hide-and-seek, and the woman who would be the last queen of Italy gave herself away by squealing from behind a tapestry. He was fond, too, of the shy Princess Mafalda, newly married to the German Prince of Hesse, who offered sweet words of consolation whenever *Tenente* Guillet arrived, as was often the case, bruised or with an arm in a sling after a fall. He would bow over her hand and click his heels, little imagining that within a decade no trace would remain of his Ruritania, nor that Mafalda would die half-starved and abandoned in the concentration camp at Buchenwald.

Whenever Amedeo was presented to the king and Queen Elena

they would welcome him warmly, and ask after his family, for the Guillets could always be depended on. With such old Savoyards, the royal family were certain of a devotion that was never guaranteed in wider Italian society. The kings of Italy tried, but never quite succeeded, in gathering up all the strands that had brought the nation together in 1860. By placing themselves at the head of the Risorgimento, the House of Savoy took uninvited charge of a national movement that was both liberal and republican in origin. A minority in parliament, which included ministers, never accepted the monarchy, and even the Fascist Party had a strong, albeit silenced, republican wing. The dynasty – which ruled by grace of God and the 'will of the nation' – had also made enemies among conservatives, especially the Catholic Church, whose territories, and Rome itself, the new kingdom had absorbed. The Lateran Treaty of 1929 had reconciled the Vatican to the Italian state, but no king of Italy ever received the papal blessing of a coronation in church. Nonetheless, the majority of Italians, especially the army, were loyal to a institution that, however imperfectly, had united the country. And none more so than those families from the dynastic heartlands of Piedmont and Savoy.

As a sportsman, Amedeo was not a household name, but nor was his fame confined solely to the army. Newspapers carried his photograph and reported his triumphs at showjumping and eventing competitions in Turin and Rome, Udine and Naples – a city he visited so often that the Gandolfos gave him a room of his own in their apartment. Before the Olympics, his principal ambition had been to enter his big Irish grey, Riario, in the English Grand National but events had always intervened. Instead, he contented himself by twice coming second and once third in the Grande Steeplechase di Roma, the most important in the Italian season, watched by the royal family from their pagoda-like box beside the course at Tor di Quinto. He also came second in 1934 in the Coppa del Duce, which was becoming almost equally prestigious, receiving a hearty handshake for his efforts from Mussolini.

But these achievements did not match being selected for the Olympic team. The regime, fully aware of the popular appeal of sport and its importance in terms of international prestige, expected much of the four riders. Although training was left to the army, Achille Starace, Secretary General of the National Fascist Party, was kept closely informed of their progress. A fanatic to physical fitness as well as for elaborate uniforms, he was a stickler for correct Fascistic speech and 'Roman' salutes and, as a result, the butt of endless jokes. But he ran the Italian Equestrian Federation well, and was himself a competent, albeit flashy rider. On his visits to the team, he would park his Alfa Romeo sportscar in the middle of the sand school and then jump over it on his horse.

Italy was not a country associated with an outstanding equestrian tradition, yet in the early years of the twentieth century it transformed the whole approach to riding. At the cavalry school at Pinerolo, outside Turin, Federico Caprilli evolved his theories of the 'forward seat', training riders to move with the horse, especially over cross-country and jumps. When the Italian cavalry, on modest mounts bought during the annual trawls through Ireland, began setting showjumping records of more than two metres high, the rest of the world took notice. By 1930, when Amedeo spent a year at Pinerolo, the school offered the best training in horsemanship available anywhere at that time. Mixed among the Italian officers in olive-grey were the uniforms of several other European countries, as well as the United States, Mexico and even Japan.

Colonel Francesco Amalfi, the Olympic team's trainer, whittled down a shortlist of riders from the cavalry, the Black Shirts and the horse artillery from ten, to eight, until finally settling on four, among whom was Amedeo. The colonel had been one of Caprilli's star pupils, and on the walls of the vast art nouveau manège at Pinerolo, named after the maestro and of the dimensions of a railway terminus, were the records that Amalfi himself had set as a showjumper before the First World War. From the moment of his selection, Amedeo's regimental duties with the Cavalleggeri di

Monferrato, whose commanding officer was his Uncle Ernesto, were reduced to a minimum.

Instead, his life became a hectic round of competitions up and down the country, as he trained two horses to the standards in showjumping, dressage and cross-country that he was likely to encounter in Berlin. The shelves in his bedroom were weighed down with little silver cups and, as his fame spread, a fashionable claque turned out to watch him, headed by Carlo Colonna of the grand Roman family, whom he had befriended at military academy. Amedeo would cross the winning post cheered on by society women, such as Giuliana Rota, later to marry one of the sons of Marshal Pietro Badoglio, and Clorinda, daughter of Admiral Thaon di Revel, the navy chief, who enjoyed the title of Duca del Mare, the 'Duke of the Sea'. For a while his photograph advanced from the sports pages to the gossip columns as he was linked as a *flirt*, of Elsa Merlini, one of Italy's earliest talkie film stars. There was even more excitement at the course at Tor di Quinto when the Hollywood stars Douglas Fairbanks and Mary Pickford, on holiday in Rome, turned out to watch, the latter chatting to Amedeo in passable French. The swashbuckling actor took photographs of him in his splendid uniform and sky-blue cloak, perhaps wondering whether Amedeo's make-believe world were not even more fantastic than his own.

In spring 1935 Colonel Amalfi sent Amedeo away for three months to the cavalry school at Orkenyi, outside Budapest, where he could perfect his dressage, and pass on what he learned to the rest of the team. The other riders would arrive later so that they could compete with the Hungarian and German teams in a pre-Olympic session. The interval in Budapest was the most idyllic period of Amedeo's career as a showjumping soldier. After long days spent working the horses, he and the Hungarian officers would pile into cars and head towards Budapest. They were amateurs in the true sense of the word, competing for the love of their sport. By contrast, the German team seemed to be joyless representatives of modern athleticism shepherded by a dour general, who would announce in the mess – as though, Amedeo felt, he were declaring the invasion of France – that at half past nine his riders had to retire to bed.

By the time Colonel Amalfi and the others arrived, Amedeo had another interest in his life apart from his horses. He had fallen in love, or believed that he might have done so. Maria was one of beautiful identical twins, the daughters of a minister in the regime of Admiral Horthy, the conservative dictator of Hungary.

'How on earth can you tell them apart?' Amalfi asked, the first time he saw them dancing together.

'With the heart, *colonnello*. With the heart,' Amedeo replied.

Brought up in a society of often stultifying conformity, he found Maria to be uninhibited and modern in a manner he had seldom encountered before. Those women he knew in Italy were either sheltered debutantes he met in society, the sisters of friends and relatives or the demi-mondaine girls found in bordellos in every town of significance to whom Italian males owed their sexual initiation. But Maria occupied a different level. They would converse in French, and Amedeo was smitten by the novelty of a woman who asserted her own point of view and did not hesitate to contradict opinions he offered of the world if she happened to disagree. She kept her thick black hair in a bob, wore a bright red slash of lipstick which stained the cigarettes she smoked with *soigné* elegance, and had high cheekbones and beautiful dark eyes which, to Amedeo, hinted at exotic Magyar ancestors from the steppes. Her parents allowed the two to spend long periods alone together, which would have been quite unthinkable in Italy. One afternoon, they went bathing in the Danube and Maria, in a one-piece black-and-white costume, swam through the icy water to St Margit's Island, in the centre of the river. Amedeo struggled after her, but by the time he finally arrived and pulled himself, exhausted, onto the shore, he looked round to find that she was already swimming back again.

He was in love, he decided, which meant he had to show that he was. After the Italian riders returned to Turin, Amedeo poured out his heart in long letters to Budapest. When Maria told him she was accompanying her mother and sister to Trondheim in Norway to see the midnight sun that summer, he decided to join her. It took four days to travel across Europe to spend less than four hours at her side. Maria was delighted by the *amour fou* of her ardent Italian, and as she waved goodbye to the train taking him back to the south, Amedeo was besotted. He was still feeling love-struck several days after his return. It only dawned on him gradually that one word alone seemed to be on everyone's lips: Abyssinia.

THREE

# *The Spahys di Libya*

No observer of the international scene in the early Thirties would have imagined that the peace of Europe would be threatened by a dispute involving Italy's colonies. They may not have been quite the collection of deserts that Mussolini had memorably described when he was a fiery socialist editor, but they were the plate scrapings of the imperial feast. Besides, colonial adventures were considered quite démodé by this time, the preoccupation among the British, at least, being to quieten the urges for self-government, rather than acquiring new territories. It was all such a pity that the Duce seemed determined to make an issue of a petty dispute with Ethiopia, especially as he had behaved so well in the previous thirteen years of his rule.

Not that the beginning had been at all promising. According to the Fascists' own mythology, they had come to power after a heroic revolutionary struggle against the forces of Bolshevism and anarchy, which culminated with the March on Rome in 1922. In fact, they had done so with the collusion of Italy's upper classes and the army, and Mussolini's first government included such solidly reassuring figures as General Armando Diaz, commander-in-chief during the Great War, and the philosopher Benedetto Croce, who was no friend of Fascism. In spite of these compromises, the iconoclastic, anti-bourgeois self-image of Fascism never entirely died out.

Mussolini had scraped the depths of Fascist *menefreghismo* – I don't-give-a-damn-ism – during his first trip abroad to London in December 1922, barely a month after he came to power. Strutting about with his bodyguard of Fascist streetfighters, the *squadristi*, he cultivated the messianic pose of a man of destiny, which included a slightly imbecile, penetrating stare. His hosts in the Foreign Office were perplexed by his boorishness, and scandalised when a meeting had to be cancelled as he was holed up in Claridges with a prostitute. He followed this debut in 1923 with the bombardment of Corfu after an Italian general was murdered on the island by Greek nationalists, an action that was condemned as both brutal and unnecessary. In the years that followed, however, the regime became more settled, having weathered the storm after Fascist fanatics murdered the Socialist deputy Giacomo Matteotti, and the dictatorship that was proclaimed in 1925.

In his foreign dealings, which involved incessant conferences to mitigate the damage of the Treaty of Versailles, Italy's young leader – Mussolini was thirty-nine when he came to power – was mercurial, unpredictable and, on occasions, constructive, as in 1932 when he urged the French not to insist on the final tranche of war reparations from Germany (the year before the Nazis came to power assisted by just this sort of grievance). The revival that the Fascists had wrought in Italy was widely admired, albeit with a degree of amused condescension. Mussolini was praised by British politicians like David Lloyd George and Winston Churchill, who hailed him as 'The Roman genius . . . the greatest lawgiver among living men' in one of the hack books he wrote to keep himself solvent during the wilderness years. The pacific Sir Austen Chamberlain, the Conservative Foreign Secretary of the Twenties, became an unlikely friend, being a great believer in the League of Nations (which later Mussolini, more than any other man, helped to destroy). In his positive initiatives he was encouraged by his clear-sighted Jewish mistress, Margherita Sarfatti, who had been the art critic when Mussolini edited the daily *Il Popolo d'Italia* after the First World War. Well-travelled, francophile and fluent in several foreign languages, Sarfatti's restraining influence over her lover remained strong until her allure began to fade in the mid-Thirties. But always, and doubtless to Mussolini's great delight, the Foreign Office and the Quai d'Orsay considered him capable of a 'mad dog act'.

Italy's grievances in these years were that she had been promised much to enter the First World War, in particular Italian-speaking territory along the Dalmatian coast, but had received little. Instead, her expected spoils had been handed to the new state of Jugo-Slavia. The age of selfish empire-building was over, Britain and France declared, but then helped themselves to Palestine and Syria, which had been Turkish, and to the German colonies in Africa, dressing up some of these acquisitions as new-fangled 'mandates' of the League of Nations. Versailles had been a 'mutilated peace', declared the poet Gabriele D'Annunzio, who set off with his ultra-nationalist followers to occupy the port of Fiume in 1919 in defiance of the United States, Britain and France, as well as the feeble government in Rome. Amedeo had only been nine at the time, but he recalled a rowing regatta at Bari, with teams taking part from all over the country. As the boats sped towards the finishing line, they stopped and raised their oars to allow the team from Fiume to win. The crowd erupted, cheering over and over again *Viva Fiume italiana!*

With some justification, Mussolini ridiculed his predecessors, who had signed a peace treaty at Versailles 'of which a representative of San Marino would be ashamed'. The revolving-door nature of Italian governments immediately after the war had left Italy's voice unheard. With the Duce in charge, there was little danger of that. By the early Thirties, he was a familiar figure on Europe's political scene; a dictator but not a tyrant, and a leader who, for all his bellicose posturing, seemed to be on the side of those who sought to maintain the peace of Europe.

The Nazis' rise to power had not interested Mussolini, in spite of the warm admiration Hitler felt for the senior dictator. The bloodletting of the Night of the Long Knives seemed to have shocked him, and the mumbo-jumbo of Nazism, its deification of Nordic Aryanism and hatred of the Jews, he thought ridiculous. The first meeting between Mussolini and Hitler at Venice in June 1934 was a disaster. 'A gramophone with one tune,' had been the verdict of the Duce, who also speculated wildly about the German prophet's sexual orientation. Similar feelings were expressed by his son-in-law, Galeazzo Ciano, then the propaganda minister, who for all his many failings – frivolous, cynical, opportunist, philandering, perhaps also a crook – had an intellectual honesty that would never entirely abandon him, and resulted in the extraordinary testament of his diaries. To journalists gathered in the bar of the Hotel Danieli, Ciano declared: 'Hitler has just one aim: war and vengeance. For his people he is a kind of Mohammed, with the plans of Genghis Khan.'

The first of these materialised the following month when the Nazis tried to seize Austria, murdering Chancellor Engelbert Dollfuss, whose wife and family were spending the summer as guests of the Mussolinis at Riccione. An enraged Duce immediately mobilised Italian divisions on the frontier and Hitler backed down. Britain and France applauded from the sidelines, but in the crises that were to follow neither was prepared to act with similar resolution.

With Europe so volatile, Mussolini's foreign admirers were perplexed by their hero's interest in Italy's colonies, which he had previously disdained. The most recent acquisitions had been Libya and the Dodecanese islands, centring on Rhodes, which had been wrested from the Turks in 1912. It had been a short war against a weakened enemy, vigorously opposed by most of the powers and the left in Italy, foremost among whom had been Benito Mussolini, who urged railwaymen to stop the troop trains. Little fighting had been involved, although in Libya the Italians had the distinction of being the first power to use aircraft in war. For the Greeks in Rhodes, the Italian occupation was welcomed as an improvement on the Turkish, but the advantages were less obvious to the tribes of Libya, where the conquest remained incomplete until the late Twenties. The Senussi tribesmen of Cyrenaica rebelled, resulting in a nasty little war in which operations were led by General Rodolfo Graziani. Desert wells were filled with concrete, the Beduin were rounded up, or their encampments were bombed from the air and the Senussi leader Omar al Muktar was hanged out of hand. These were the methods Graziani would later adopt in Ethiopia, and they had already succeeded in making Italy's most celebrated colonial soldier detested by many of his senior officers.

Scarcely less arid was Italian Somaliland, which was acquired when Britain and France divided up the coast of the Horn of Africa in the 1890s. France had taken the smallest but most important bit at Djibuti, with which it hoped to control access to the Red Sea, or at least counter the British at Aden on the opposite shore. The French territory also became the entry point to landlocked Ethiopia after the development of the Djibuti to Addis Ababa railway. A longer stretch of barren mountains and sand was handed to Britain, whose administrative centre was Berbera, and then came the vast tract of Italian Somaliland down to the Kenyan border.

The Somalis were strangers in the main to ordered government, and until Fascism the Italians seemed happy to leave them in this state. But in 1923 one of Mussolini's closest supporters, Cesare De Vecchi, arrived at Mogadishu as governor. A former university professor from Piedmont who had fought bravely in the Great War, De Vecchi was a man of some ability who was to hold a wide ensemble of portfolios during the regime, being governor of Somalia, Minister of Education and, finally, governor of the Dodecanese. Known and respected by the Guillets – his son was a cavalry friend of Amedeo's – De Vecchi was one of those in the Fascist hierarchy who reassured conservatives, and his dedication to the monarchy was unquestioned. He set about introducing an efficient colonial administration in Somaliland, which by 1939, had an Italian population of 8,000 living amid 1,200,000 natives.

But the jewel in the crown was Eritrea, named after the ancient Greek for the Red Sea, through which the Italians had long hoped to control Ethiopia, the only significant part of Africa as yet uncolonised. But here their ambitions had gone disastrously wrong. A Genoese entrepreneur, Michele Rubattino, bought the port of Assab in 1869 from a local potentate so that his ships could penetrate the Indian Ocean without paying to use British harbours. In hesitant steps, the Italians enlarged the boundaries of their possession. General Oreste Barattieri, a veteran of Garibaldi's Thousand, was sent to Eritrea in the 1890s with orders from the combative prime minister Francesco Crispi, a Sicilian who had also been a *Garibaldino*, to enlarge its borders at Ethiopia's expense and create a vast Italian colony. Protectorate status was to be imposed on Ethiopia, in an arrangement similar to that of the British in Egypt.

At first, Barattieri was highly successful, exploiting the power vacuum in the region. The Mahdi rising in the Sudan, which led to the death of General Gordon at Khartoum in 1885, had ended the Egyptian presence on the Eritrean coast and in the southern Sudan. The dervishes then turned their attention to the Christian infidels of Ethiopia. A bloody battle was fought, from which the Ethiopians emerged victorious, but in the mêlée the last Tigrinian emperor, Johannes, was killed. After bitter civil war, the throne passed to the first emperor of the Amharic-speaking Shoan dynasty, Menelik II, named after the son of Solomon and the Queen of Sheba who had founded the empire 2,500 years before.

Barattieri, meanwhile, quietly expanded the borders of Eritrea, finding the Tigrinians who made up the bulk of its population more disposed to submit to Italian rule than to Shoan. He pushed on to the oasis of Kassala in the Sudan and deep into Tigre. But he finally went too far when his incursions approached the holy city of Axum, the religious and cultural heart of the Ethiopian empire, where the Ark of the Covenant was supposedly housed.

Menelik's response was to issue a *chitet*, the imperial summons to war. With his army of 100,000 warriors he annihilated 2,000 Eritrean *ascari* led by Major Toselli at Amba Alagi, deep within Ethiopia. Urged on by Crispi, and in danger of being recalled to Rome with his reputation in tatters, Barattieri recklessly moved forward from his defences in the Eritrean highlands to confront the enemy. With an army of 16,000 men, and fifty-two cannon, the largest European force ever deployed in a colonial war in Africa, the Italian general was confident that victory would be his.

At dawn on 1 March 1896 Menelik attacked the four columns of Barattieri's army, which had become separated in the mountain passes above Adowa, perhaps owing to some confusion with the maps. One column was immediately surrounded and a second, rushing to its aid, was caught on the move and wiped out, its general killed. Soon the entire Italian army was faltering under attacks from waves of warriors brandishing swords and leather shields, led by officers wearing lion manes. Rifle fire rained steadily down on the Italians from the ambas, the table-flat mountain plateaux which typify the Ethiopian landscape. Empress Taitu herself supervised the firing of six modern cannon, comforted by a statue of the Virgin. In an operatic touch, she prevailed upon the emperor to hurl the 25,000-strong Shoan reserve at the stricken Italians.

Three columns were washed away by waves of warriors. Barattieri himself rallied the Alpini and Bersaglieri. But in the midst of the carnage, he explained at his court martial – at which he was acquitted – 'my heart was being torn in two, as I despaired of ever being able to give an order or of getting it carried out'. Although he managed to hack his way back to Eritrea, and rally what remained of his army, two generals were left dead on the field, with 260 officers and almost 4,000 men. A further 1,900 men were captured, including one general, and were led in triumph to Menelik II's capital, Addis Ababa (New Flower). Within a year, the Italian prisoners were released unharmed. But a more severe punishment was meted out to the Tigrinian-speaking *ascari* of

Eritrea who had fought with dogged bravery; each had his right hand and left foot amputated. Even in the Thirties these old veterans were a familiar sight on the streets of Asmara, Eritrea's capital, hobbling in their heavy prostheses in pride of place at the head of parades.

Adowa had been the most humiliating defeat for Italy. A country that had repeatedly demanded an imperial role had been revealed, in the eyes of the world, as inadequate for the task. Feelings ran so high that the Duke of Torino, the king's cousin, fought a duel with one of the princely Orléans family of France who had cast doubt on Italian valour. In the years after the defeat other European powers tactfully acknowledged Italy's special interests in Ethiopia, but there was no question of it imposing its will on Menelik II, or his successors. To some degree, even before Fascism, all Italian governments wanted to avenge Adowa.

When Ras Tafari, then regent of Ethiopia and later to become Emperor Haile Selassie, visited Rome in 1923, a preoccupied Mussolini displayed his habitual lack of interest in far-flung places, accompanying the prince to official receptions with his hands in his pockets. He was in any case up to his neck in the scandal of the Matteotti murder, which very nearly undid him. The prince presented a lion to Rome's zoo, and the Italians, without much thought, backed Ethiopia's entry into the League of Nations, a decision they came later to regret bitterly. Britain opposed the move on the reasonable grounds that Ethiopia was not a nation, but an anarchic empire quite likely to fall apart. It had doubled in size during the scramble for Africa, absorbing Muslim principalities, such as the sultanate of Harar, and truculent tribes like the Galla.

The unasked question at Ras Tafari's coronation in 1930, when he assumed the title of Haile Selassie, meaning the holy trinity, was whether he would be able to hold the empire together. No warrior, he had nonetheless succeeded in outmanoeuvring all his rivals to assume the crown of the Negus Negusti, the king of kings, as he would many of their children and even grandchildren by the time he was finally deposed and murdered by the Communist Dergue in 1975. As ruler, Haile Selassie's position was similar to that of Louis XIII, surrounded by over-mighty, semi-autonomous feudatories, the *ras*. Unlike the French king, however, he had no need of the services of a Richelieu. Thirty-eight-years old at his coronation, the emperor conscientiously set about attempting to modernise his empire. He was often thwarted – by the *ras*, by the conservative Coptic clergy and by his people's modest appetite for central government – but he was a patient man who never lost sight of the main objective. He adopted the parliamentary constitution of Japan, taking its success in avoiding colonial domination as a model for Ethiopia, and he had ambitious plans to build roads, schools and hospitals. With most of the country still in the middle ages or under tribal rule, and Addis Ababa little more than a shanty town, the gulf between the emperor's ambitions and what could be achieved was obvious to all. To hostile observers such as Evelyn Waugh, who reported on Haile Selassie's coronation for *The Times*, Ethiopia and its hapless little emperor, who wanted so much to be Western, were ripe for satire.

At the end of 1934, the Ethiopians and the Italians clashed over the wells at Walwal in the Ogaden desert on the border with Italian Somaliland. In spite of dark suspicions on both sides, the incident does not appear to have been orchestrated by either Rome or Addis Ababa. With 107 Ethiopians and a *fitaurari*, commander of the advance guard, killed, it was serious, but it was not unprecedented; a month earlier the Ethiopians had killed a French officer on the border with Djibuti. But Haile Selassie's decision to complain to the League of Nations turned the dispute into an international crisis. Being a believer in modernity and international law, he may simply have thought that this was the correct and proper course to follow. Or he may have already calculated that a clash with Fascist Italy was unavoidable at some time, and he might as well make the issue Walwal as any other, and milk the sympathy of the other powers as Italy was revealed as the aggressor. Either way, it was a highly dangerous strategy, for a dictator like Mussolini, who after all was 'always right', could never publicly climb down. At risk of being outbid by Hitler in the bellicose posturing that had been his monopoly, Mussolini thought Fascist Italy could manage a little war in Africa. And who was going to stop him? A man with his sharp political antennae knew that the old men who governed Britain, and the succession of emollient conciliators in France, would never intervene on behalf of an African potentate.

The morning coat and wing collar that Mussolini had worn since becoming prime minister were laid aside, and he squeezed himself into the first of his vast wardrobe of military uniforms, which would continue, in bewildering variety, until the end.

As the army lorry pulled out of Tripoli, Amedeo's nerve began to falter. Zuara was only eighty kilometres away on the border with French Tunisia and they would arrive in an hour and a half. He was dreading how he would be received. The name of his new commanding officer, Major Antonio Ajmone Cat, suggested Savoyard origin, but Amedeo doubted whether that fact would make his reception any more cordial. From what he had heard, the major was tough and independent minded, well able to stand his ground before his superiors. He himself had raised the Spahys di Libya, a unit of irregular Arab cavalry, commanding them against the Libyan rebels. How he was going to react to having a general's nephew imposed on him, Amedeo could only guess, but he wasn't expecting a slap on the back and *spumante* served in the mess.

But worse, far worse, was the guilt he felt towards Colonel Amalfi. Three weeks before, he had been waiting in the anteroom of the colonel's office in Turin. On the wall were photographs of Italy's riding legends. Among them were pictures of the colonel, jumping a horse over a single kitchen chair – a great feat of control – and between the seats of an open-topped landau, still hitched to its horses. Amalfi's familiar voice called the lieutenant into his office.

Amedeo announced that while he realised that the timing was extremely inconvenient, with the Berlin Games less than a year away, he had to leave the team. Italy was at war, or very nearly, and he had been called up to serve in Abyssinia. The colonel had said nothing, but gave the young lieutenant a long, scrutinising look. Every young fool in the army, and quite a few old ones as well, was pleading to be sent to join the Italian forces gathering in Africa. Almost all Amedeo's friends were trying to transfer to regiments certain to be sent. It had become a stampede and Italy's summer watering holes began to empty. Vittorio Mussolini, the Duce's son, was going and so was his seventeen-year-old brother, Bruno, straight from school. Ciano had flown out with the Regia Aeronautica's squadron, 'La Disperata', named after a Florentine Fascist squad. The Futurist poet Filippo Marinetti and neo-Nazi ideologue Roberto Farinacci had rushed to join the colours; and the royal dukes of Bergamo and Pistoia, cousins of the king, had been given commands.

It had been one blessing for the colonel that Achille Starace was off his back, having been placed in charge of a motorised column of Black Shirts. But who the hell would be left, he asked himself. Spread in front of him was a magazine feature from *L'Illustrazione Italiana* on the Tevere Black Shirt Division, perhaps the most bizarre unit in any European army, shortly to leave for Somalia. One legion was made up of veterans of Italy's colonial ventures pre-1900 (hardly very encouraging, the colonel may have thought), another incorporated the war wounded, or veterans of D'Annunzio's occupation of Fiume, or of the Fascist struggle before 1922. Italians from abroad, from as far afield as Australia and the United States, had formed another and there was a juvenile legion, *I Goliardi*, of university students. In charge was General

Boscardi, who had lost an eye capturing a trench in the Great War.

But the one thing this circus lacked, in Colonel Amalfi's mind, was one of four riders on whom he had expended months of effort in training and preparation. And Lieutenant Guillet's excuse for not representing Italy in probably the most prestigious equestrian event in two decades was some nonsense about having been 'ordered' to transfer to the Spahys di Libya. It was the hypocrisy that pained Amalfi, the young lieutenant pretending that he had been called up, rather than that he had pulled every string possible to get himself sent to Africa. Floundering in the silence, Amedeo began repeating himself, and while expressing his sincere regret that he was abandoning the team, incautiously added the thought that one had to obey the call to defend the Patria.

'Do you think I'm completely simple-minded?' Amalfi asked, gently. 'No more of these stories to me. I know who you have been talking to.'

The mildness of the colonel's reproaches, coupled with his blessing in the coming war, aggravated Amedeo's sense of guilt as he took his leave. It had not been his father, Baron Guillet, who had swung Amedeo's transfer, for he had retired and was living at the family palazzo in Capua managing, with little enthusiasm, the family estate. Nor had Amedeo approached his bluff, bonhominous Uncle Ernesto, called in the family *Zio Murat*, who had been his commanding officer. He had turned instead to his Uncle Amedeo, the middle of the three Guillet brothers and the one whose career had been the most brilliant.

Fourth or fifth in Italy's military hierarchy, Uncle Amedeo was an exceptional man who, during the Great War, had twice received the Kingdom of Italy's highest military decoration, the Ordine Militare di Savoia. For officers only, it was an acknowledgement of ability to command as well as of outstanding valour. To win one ensured an officer's straight path to the top; to win two was almost unheard of. Good-looking, and a familiar figure in Roman society, Uncle Amedeo had definite presence and whenever the family gathered both Amedeo's father and Uncle Ernesto deferred to him. He was a man of wide culture as well as a full army corps general. Benedetto Croce, the philosopher, was an intimate friend, as was Guglielmo Marconi, the Nobel Prize-winning inventor of radio, while D'Annunzio had dedicated a book to the general as 'the purest embodiment of the Latin genius'.

Before 1914, Uncle Amedeo had once been in love with an American woman, but for reasons no one in the family fully knew it had come to nothing, and he had remained single. As a result, his family feelings concentrated on the children of his older brother, and particularly on the youngest boy, his namesake. In childhood, Amedeo had always felt over-awed in the presence of his distinguished relative, but as he grew older he became closer to his uncle than any other man, and almost all his ambitions were spurred by a desire to win his respect and good notice.

During an evening together in Rome, Amedeo poured out his thoughts. All his life there had been talk of the League of Nations heralding an era of peace. Now there was going to be war: Italy's African colonies were at risk from the Ethiopians. He had to be a part of it. It was the aim of all the training he had received, and what he had joined the army for.

Uncle Amedeo took seriously his nephew's request to transfer to the Spahys. He was not sure about this war which Mussolini had set his heart on. All Italy seemed agreed that it was necessary except a few dissidents on the left, whose opinion could be ignored. But the consequences in Europe were more troubling. Britain and France, firmly against it, were threatening Italy with economic sanctions if the war went ahead. Not that Mussolini seemed to care. Like the popular newspaper editor he, at heart, always remained, the Duce couldn't see further than the next day's headlines, and fighting the 'black hordes of barbarism' was a story with legs. Uncle Amedeo was worried how the regime was beginning to change, its tone increasingly hectoring and bombastic. A report had recently arrived on his desk with a memo from the Duce: 'Victory is ensured by the aggressive spirit of the army.' To which he had added laconically, 'And good artillery.'

The morning after his meeting with his nephew, the general summoned his adjutant into his office and the cogs of Italy's military machine began to turn. A week later a note arrived for Major Antonio Ajmone Cat in Libya from the Ministry of War informing him that he was about to receive a new lieutenant.

The sun was going down and there was a cool breeze blowing across the desert by the time Amedeo arrived at Zuara. A cluster of officers, mostly Spahys, sat talking on the terrace of the neat white bungalow that served as the mess. Major Ajmone Cat, wrapped in the bright blue burnous of the Spahys, was recounting a story that had now become part of the regimental mythology. At the height of the action at Bir Tagrift, the last battle against the rebels in Tripolitania, his horse had been shot from under him, and a mysterious Spahy had given him his own, complete with its high-sided Arabic saddle. But afterwards no one could say who this man was, nor did anyone come forward to reclaim the horse. His men were convinced that the Spahys, and their commander, were watched over by a benign spirit, or *marabut*. Whether true or not, it was their belief, the major concluded, urging the officers never to make light of such superstitions in front of the men.

Amedeo hovered at the edge of the group waiting for the story to end. He took a deep breath, walked forward and made his sharpest Modena salute before the major, then presented himself.

'Ah yes, Lieutenant Guillet,' the major replied coolly, while the other Spahy officers adopted expressions of uninterest. 'I'll be frank with you, Guillet. You are the only officer I have not chosen for this unit. I don't doubt your qualities, but everyone else has earned his right to be here. Try to learn the ropes as soon as you can.'

Amedeo stammered a reply, his cheeks burning. It had been a short and sharp public humiliation, but the major was not the sort to prolong it. To Amedeo's relief at that moment an old friend from Pinerolo, Lieutenant Luigi Cavarzerani, clapped him on the back and breezily welcomed him to the regiment. The other officers had heard of Amedeo's riding successes, and received him without resentment. He had got off lightly, they assured him once the major had left. Two other young officers, for whom strings had been pulled, had been sent straight back to Italy.

FOUR

# *Riding through Clouds*

Amedeo was reminded of Neapolitans piling off a crowded tram, although instead of people pushing and shoving this involved steamships. The whole of Italy's merchant navy seemed to be choked into the harbour of Massaua forming an ill-tempered queue to disembark. On the quayside were scurrying Eritrean dock workers, and in among them, helping unload artillery, lorries and light tanks, were scores of Black Shirts. They had come to fight; but morale was high and they were eager to help. Major Ajmone Cat shouted down to a port official demanding that the Spahys should be given priority owing to the horses. He had not lost one during the ten-day voyage from Libya, and he had no intention of doing so now. When they had refuelled at Port Said, the ship and all its passengers had been covered in coal dust, but the major ordered the men to use the sea for their ablutions: the fresh water was for their mounts. In spite of the major's impatience, the Spahys sweltered at anchor in the roads of Massaua for a day and a half, as temperatures rose to 45 degrees. Nor, alarmingly, was it much cooler at night. One by one the Spahys' mounts were finally winched up from the hold in a canvas sling and lowered ashore into a throng of excited dockers.

The Spahys rode down the quayside of Massaua, then the biggest port in east Africa, and through the narrow labyrinthine Turkish and Arabic streets. They were arcaded to provide some protection against the unremitting sun, a device the Italians had continued in the adjoining European quarter, reminding Amedeo of De Chirico's paintings. On the Yacht Club terraces some Europeans raised their glasses as the Spahys rode down a wide seafront avenue that led to the domed and dazzling palace built for the Turkish-Egyptian pashas, now home to the Italian governor. It was so white in the daytime sun that it strained the eyes and in front of it, defying every horticultural law of survival, was a form of lawn. Above the pedimented portico was a vast red shield with the white cross of Savoy, visible from several kilometres out at sea, which the officers saluted as they rode by.

The desert began on the city's outskirts, stretching monotonously towards the mountains and the Eritrean hinterland. Only five kilometres out of Massaua, the major brought the column to a halt and ordered everyone to dismount and walk. The horsemen had been told not to clog up the asphalt road, along which lorries filled with infantrymen and supplies were speeding up to Asmara. Instead, the horses had to pick their way painstakingly forward across the scrubby, broken desert land, covered with rocks as though sprinkled from a castor. To speed their progress, the Spahys kept as far as possible to the wadis. Lethal torrents for a few brief weeks during the great rains of July and August, when dry they offered a smooth, sandy path.

By nightfall the column had reached the Menabrea Bridge, where the road to Asmara crossed the wadi. On the bridge's concrete girders were incised in Piedmontese dialect the eponymous general's exhortation to his troops: *Ca custa lon ca custa* (Let it cost what it cost). For not far away, on a barren little hillock at Dogali, was a marble column with an eagle bearing an olive branch: the memorial to 500 Italian troops wiped out to a man right at the beginning of Italy's colonial adventures.

When the march resumed the next day, the ground began to rise almost immediately and the desiccated scrubland gave way to greener vegetation. The air became cooler and sweet, and within a dozen kilometres the column was riding – for the major had allowed this concession – through a landscape of woods and cultivated fields. Neat Italian villas were dotted around the hills, which echoed with the tolling bells of the Coptic and Catholic churches. At Dongollo, where a large low building proclaimed itself the source of the colony's *acqua minerale*, the local Italians turned out to greet the cavalrymen, handing them bottles of water. Thereafter the route rose sharply, and kept on rising through the green, wooded mountains. One moment Amedeo and his men were following the precipitous zig-zagging road in the pleasant afternoon sun, the next the air suddenly chilled and it became almost impossible to see the rider in front: the Spahys di Libya were enjoying the unusual experience of riding through clouds. At the mountain monastery of Debre Bizen, one of the holiest Coptic sites, Major Ajmone Cat and his officers looked down over the valleys with their lingering clouds to Massaua and the Red Sea, 80 kilometres away, and beyond to the Dahlak islands, the Buri peninsula and the gulf of Zula. The Abuna Filipos had established his church here in the fourteenth century because, it was said, he preferred the roar of lions to the distraction of women's faces. But the view itself was more splendid to Amedeo than that over the Liri Valley from Bramante's terrace at Monte Cassino, and would summon reverence and awe in the least promising soul.

They camped on the plain beyond Asmara, and the next morning Amedeo caught a lift into the city with a passing lorry. He was astonished by what he saw. Between the Islamic world of the Red Sea, and the Africa that lay beyond, was a model Italian city, perched 2400 metres above sea level. Neat art deco villas were swathed in vivid jacaranda and bougainvillaea. The streets were paved and clean. The governor's palace, with its shady gardens and menagerie, and the army headquarters were buildings which would not have been out of place in Rome. He had an espresso in Bar Vittoria and walked down the Corso Italia, the main thoroughfare, past pavement cafés, cinemas, restaurants and even a Pizzeria Napoli. Set in its own gardens, and behind palm trees, was an opera house, where Caruso himself had sung. A little further, on the opposite side of the tree-lined Corso, was the city's cathedral, built in red brick in mediaeval Lombard style as though it were set in the middle of Milan.

Amedeo had thought little about the wider objectives of this war, seeing it simply in soldier's terms: the Patria had to be defended. But now he began to embrace the imperial enthusiasm of the Duce. A people who could built a city like Asmara could transform Ethiopia from a wilderness into an empire that would echo the glory of ancient Rome. In place of the despotic Negus and feuding *ras*, Italy would offer law, order and progress. Settlers from the south would cultivate the land, rather than ignominiously emigrating to the slums of the United States. And the local population would benefit too from this new Pax Romana, Amedeo reasoned, receiving roads, schools and hospitals in the place of superstition, slavery and poverty. In Eritrea the achievements of Italian rule were apparent everywhere, with an infrastructure that surpassed much of Calabria and Basilicata. Why should not Ethiopia, five times the size, be transformed in the same way?

Amedeo shared the indignation felt by almost every Italian that Britain and France, their allies in the Great War, were siding with the enemy and even threatening to impose economic sanctions. That they were doing so in order to defend international agreements that Italy herself had signed was not a point he chose to dwell on. At this time of heightened emotions, old suspicions resurfaced. In the hierarchy of world powers, Italy seemed condemned to occupy a place near the bottom. For many Englishmen, it would always be the disaster-prone, comic turn of Europe. While the map of the globe was covered with British pink or French blue, Italians seemed condemned to leave their motherland only as desperate, huddled masses.

But times had changed and the demands of the new Italy, Fascist and modern, were not to be brushed aside. Whatever Mussolini's faults, he had given Italians back their self-respect. When the

Spahys' ship had sailed through the Suez Canal, a vast crowd had been waiting on the western bank. The entire Italian community of Alexandria had turned out to cheer them on to victory. At their head was a strikingly attractive young woman, Maria Uva, wrapped in a figure-hugging tricolour, who blew kisses to them as they passed (later receiving the war's campaign medal for her patriotic fervour).

Italy was going to take her proper place among the powers at last. In this, the Duce and the Italian people were agreed. And two nations which had the least right to tell her that she could not make an empire out of Ethiopia were Britain and France, who sat in fading glory over more than a quarter of the world.

The next day, the Spahys rode on past Asmara, through the central massif of Eritrea and down to the Lowlands that led to the borders with Anglo-Egyptian Sudan. They established their camp at Barentu, a one-street town of modest bungalows, beside an Italian infantry battalion and a 'Gruppo Bande' of irregular, locally recruited cavalry. All were part of the 2nd Corps of General Pietro Maravigna, who would command the western flank of the eventual invasion. For six weeks, however, the Spahys were to kick their heels on the sweltering Lowlands, and wait.

The Spahys were less soldiers in a modern army than warriors. For the most part Bedouin, they had been formed into a military unit in the same way as the Cossacks. Each trooper provided his own horse, saddlery and some arms, and was paid ten *lire* a day, the wage of a skilled worker in Italy. All were dressed in a flowing dark blue burnous, waistcoat and a red cummerbund and *takia*, a low fez with the badge of the army star. But the minutiae of military discipline was not insisted upon. When the major had dismissed the parades in Libya, the Spahys' wives and children came on to the parade ground to relieve the men of their rifles and lead the horses away.

Amedeo was grateful for the delay. After little more than a month with the Spahys, he knew the names and faces of all eighty men in his squadron, but could only issue elementary orders in Arabic. To his surprise, he was one of the few Spahy officers who set out to learn the language, rather than rely on an Italian-speaking *shumbashi*, or senior sergeant. The complexity of tenses he learned from a grammar, applying the rules with the help of the regimental barber, whose Italian was excellent. When Major Ajmone Cat saw the two of them sitting in the shade conjugating verbs, he paused for a moment, nodded approvingly, and walked on.

Then there was the matter of his horse. The grey four-year-old Arab stallion had been brought across from French Tunisia just before he joined the Spahys, but had caught Amedeo's eye immediately. He was not pretty in the way that many Arab horses are, but tough and lean, with an intelligent head, excellent conformation and lively paces. At fifteen hands high he was far smaller than the competition horses Amedeo was used to, but now his needs were different. In Ethiopia, he would require a mount that could survive off almost nothing, never go lame and endure routine marches of 60 kms a day. An old *muntaz*, or corporal, had bought the horse but found him too lively, for the animal was barely schooled. He was eager to exchange him. There was a suitable horse going spare from the same herd, which none of the other Spahys wanted for it carried a *berrima*, a spiralling whorl, on its coat. On the front of the horse the mark brought good fortune, the Spahys told Amedeo, but on the hind quarters, as it was, it meant that the animal wanted its rider's death. The *muntaz* barked at the men that they should not repeat such nonsense in front of Italian officers. He handed over the young grey to the lieutenant and led away the marked horse for himself.

The heat on the Eritrean Lowlands was nothing compared with the desert after Massaua, but humid and heavy so soon after the rains, it turned the horses sluggish by midday. With a rifle over

Beatrice Gandolfo.

Khadija, photographed by Amedeo before the Second World War.

The invasion of Ethiopia, October 1935: Amedeo, on Sandor, pauses with the Spahys di Libya. In the background are columns of Italian infantry.

*Left* Uncle Amedeo, hero of the First World War and a full army corps general, was fourth or fifth in the Italian military hierarchy. On his recommendation, Amedeo was transferred to Ethiopia.

*Above* Sotto-Tenente Amedeo Guillet, newly commissioned at the Cavalleggeri di Monferrato, 1931. The regiment was commanded by his Uncle Ernesto.

*Left* Amedeo, in full dress uniform of the Guides cavalry, 1935.

Amedeo mimics a martinet while reviewing some splendidly attired fellow officers, before the regime introduced the modern shirt-and-tie uniform in 1935. It wasn't an improvement, he felt.

Fresh faced cadets at the Military Academy at Modena, 1928. Amedeo is in the centre.

*Above* Amedeo rides down a steep hillside during an exercise at the Cavalry School at Pinerolo, which probably provided the best training in horsemanship in the world during the Twenties and Thirties.

*Left and below* Genoa, 1934: Amedeo during his career as competitive rider.

THE ITALIAN CONQUEST OF ETHIOPIA, 1935–36

*Right* A horseman from the Spahys di Libya.

*Below and right* An extraordinary sequence of photographs showing the Spahys in action in Ethiopia in early 1936.

Ethiopian irregulars, disadvantaged in white, confront their better-armed adversaries. Italian infantry on the mountain lay down a barrage as ten Italian Fiat Ansaldo light tanks advance past Ethiopian positions (left). Realising their position is hopeless, some Ethiopian warriors (right) take flight.

The Spahys di Libya charge over the brow of the hill, and the light tanks push forward, completely surrounding the remaining Ethiopians.

Panicking warriors flee amid the Italian light tanks, which are armed with twin machine guns, and the dead heap up (right).

The Spahys charge on, leaving the stranded enemy to the Italian infantry.

Italian infantry pour down the hillside, while those Ethiopians who can still do so, make a bid to escape.

*Above* Ethiopian warriors parade through the streets of Addis Ababa at the start of the war.

*Left* Marshal Badoglio arrives at the front with his staff.

his back, for there were leopards and lions on the Lowlands, Amedeo rode his young horse across the plains green with vegetation and through woods of acacia and sycamore. Every two or three hundred metres he would have to cross a wadi, for these streams of dry sand streaked down from the mountains and spread across the Lowland landscape like blood vessels in a slab of meat. Often accompanied by Cavarzerani, he would make for a wadi, shaded by a huge and majestic baobab tree. The sandy river bed provided a serviceable manège to school the horses, and with the corners marked out by large stones, Amedeo carried out the training exercises he had learned at Pinerolo. As the horse trotted and cantered around him on a lunge rein, the wadi echoed with his onomatopoeic endearments: *piccolone*, *poppolone*, *coccolone*, *bello bello . . .*

Amedeo would have chosen to name his new horse after Maria, his Hungarian amour, whose photograph he carried in his wallet. But as the horse was a stallion, like all the Spahys' four hundred mounts, he lamely decided to name him after her father Sandor, the diminutive of Alexander.

By mid-September Major Ajmone Cat despaired that the war would ever start. He kept the Spahys occupied, sending out regular patrols to the border with the Anglo-Egyptian Sudan. But before even a shot had been fired they were rapidly deteriorating. Most of the officers, including Amedeo, had already gone down with malaria, but far worse in the major's view was the loss of eighty horses to mandef, a form of pneumonia picked up when they grazed. He had had to remount an entire squadron on Ethiopian horses, the Dongolai, which were virtually ponies.

The major was not alone in his frustration. Among officers in the invasion force muttered criticisms began to be directed towards the commander-in-chief, General Emilio De Bono. White-bearded and already sixty-nine years old, the general was an engaging character who worked a masterful charm on the ordinary soldiers, his *figlioli*. A distinguished general in the Great War – and the author of popular humorous books – he had been a Fascist from the beginning. Providing the movement with precious respectability, reassuring the king and the army, De Bono was one of the four quadrumvirs of the National Fascist Party, a long-standing confidant of Mussolini who was owed much. But as a conquering commander, he was never wholly convincing. And with the awful memory of Adowa always at the back of his mind, he wasn't going to budge until the Duce had sent enough men to cover all possible contingencies. On occasion, Amedeo visited De Bono, a great friend of his Uncle Amedeo, at his headquarters in Asmara, and found the old general quite immune to the impatience of his subordinates and his political master in Rome.

Haile Selassie had cause to be grateful to his dilatory adversary as the diplomatic temperature rose alarmingly in Europe. Italian aggression would be met by force, Sir Samuel Hoare, the British Foreign Secretary, declared forthrightly in Geneva on 11 September. A few days later the British Home fleet was mobilised and sent to the Mediterranean; and the Italian fleet returned from the Dodecanese to La Spezia.

Feverish preparations for war continued in Addis Ababa. The emperor's Swedish senior military advisor, General Virgin, had had to retire owing to altitude sickness – a common difficulty – but the army cadets' training continued under Captain Viking Tramm. Belgian officers, meanwhile, introduced the imperial guard to the rudiments of modern warfare. In addition, scores of adventurers and assorted misfits eager to fight the Italians poured into Addis Ababa. Among them were a sixty-two-year-old English master of foxhounds, Major Gerald Burgoyne (later killed driving an ambulance) and Colonel Hubert Fauntleroy Julian, 'the Black Eagle of Harlaam', who on arrival proceeded to crash one of the emperor's half dozen aircraft.

More valuable, perhaps, was a growing bivouac of foreign journalists and newsreelmen, who had arrived to report the war from the Ethiopian viewpoint. Though Evelyn Waugh, now accredited to the *Daily Mail*, was of the view that the sooner the Italians marched into Addis Ababa the better – 'I hope the organmen gas them to buggery,' he wrote to Diana Cooper – the sympathy of the world was with the dignified little emperor. Nowhere more so than in Britain. Sylvia Pankhurst, having previously espoused the cause of women's suffrage, revolutionary socialism and unmarried mothers – she was one herself – rallied to the emperor. Loathing Italian Fascism – her lover was a leftwing dissident and journalist Silvio Coria – she soon demonstrated that Haile Selassie could not have wished for a more energetic propagandist. Although she had never met the emperor and knew nothing of Ethiopia, the justice of his struggle against a totalitarian enemy stirred within her a righteous wrath. In the years that were to follow, she would ensure, more than anyone else, that the plight of Ethiopia was never far from the public mind.

In Rome, meanwhile, a chapter closed on the career of another remarkable woman, as Margherita Sarfatti gave her former editor and lover her parting advice: 'You have enough to colonise in Apulia, Sicily and Calabria . . . If you go into Ethiopia you will fall into the hands of the Germans and you will be lost. If we have to pay for the empire with the ruin of Europe, we will pay too high a price.'

At 9pm on 2 October 1935 the cathedral bells in Asmara began to toll. Catholic and Coptic churches across the colony followed suit, their peals echoing down to the small parish at Barentu. Major Ajmone Cat summoned his officers and told them to prepare to cross the frontier at dawn.

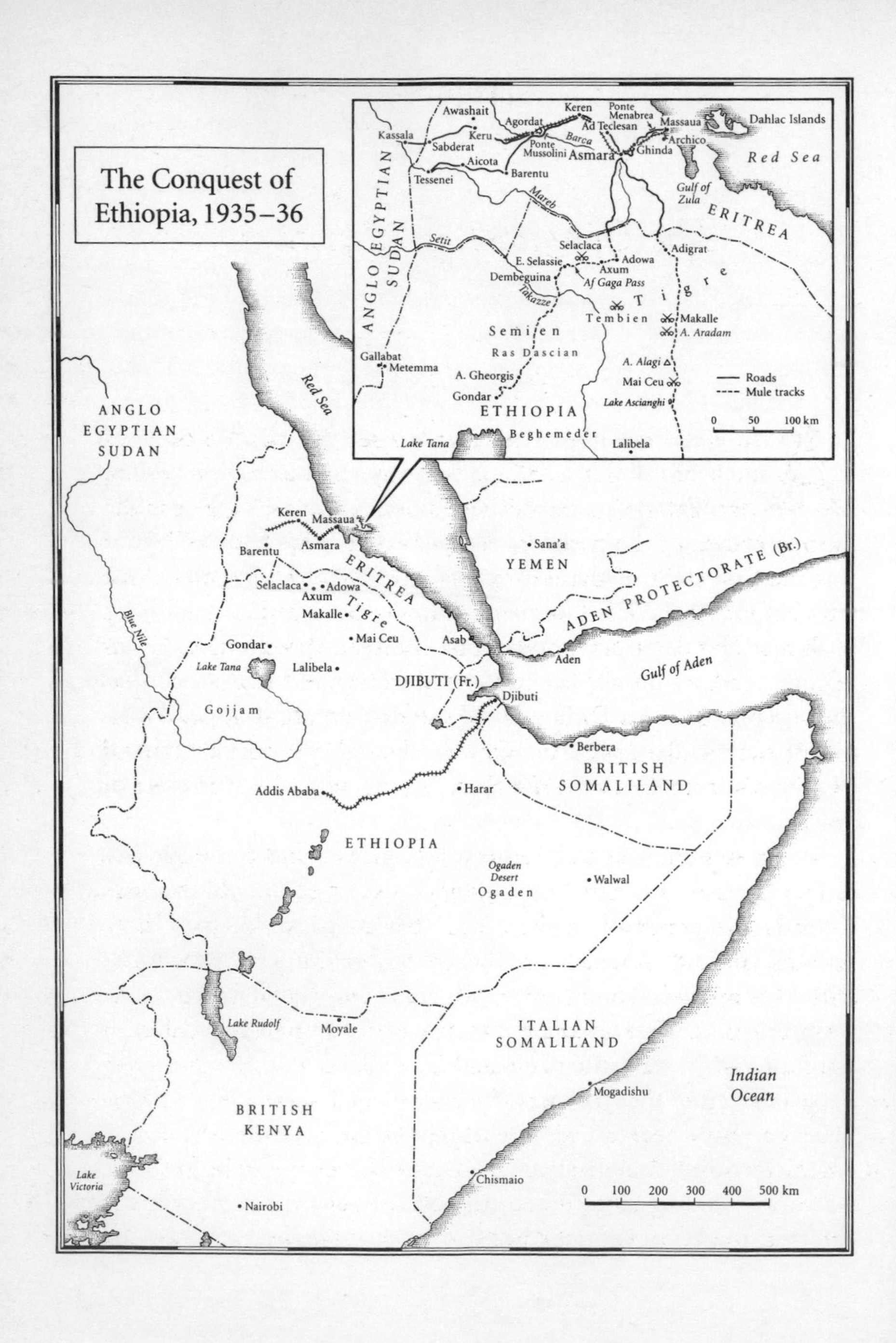
The Conquest of Ethiopia, 1935–36
Awashait
Keren
Ponte Menabrea
Massaua
Dahlac Islands
Agordat
Ad Teclesan
Kassala
Keru
Barca
Archico
Sabderat
Ponte Mussolini
Asmara
Ghinda
Red Sea
Aicota
Tessenei
Barentu
Gulf of Zula
Mareb
ERITREA
ANGLO EGYPTIAN SUDAN
Setit
Adigrat
Selaclaca
Adowa
E. Selassie
Axum
Dembeguina
Af Gaga Pass
Takazze
Tigre
Tembien
Makalle
A. Aradam
Semien
Ras Dascian
A. Alagi
Gallabat
Metemma
A. Gheorgis
Mai Ceu
Roads
Mule tracks
Gondar
ETHIOPIA
Lake Ascianghi
0 50 100 km
Lake Tana
Beghemeder
Lalibela
Red Sea
ANGLO EGYPTIAN SUDAN
Keren
Massaua
Asmara
Barentu
ERITREA
Sana'a
YEMEN
ADEN PROTECTORATE (Br.)
Selaclaca
Adowa
Axum
Tigre
Makalle
Blue Nile
Gondar
Mai Ceu
Asab
Aden
Lake Tana
Lalibela
Gulf of Aden
DJIBUTI (Fr.)
Djibuti
Gojjam
Berbera
BRITISH SOMALILAND
Addis Ababa
Harar
ETHIOPIA
Ogaden Desert
Walwal
Ogaden
Lake Rudolf
Moyale
ITALIAN SOMALILAND
Indian Ocean
Mogadishu
BRITISH KENYA
Lake Victoria
Chismaio
0 100 200 300 400 500 km
Nairobi

FIVE

# *The Conquest of Abyssinia*

Amedeo did not need binoculars to see the men on top of a small hill about a kilometre away. In their white robes, the Ethiopian skirmishers stood out clearly against the burned brown of the rocky landscape. For the Spahys di Libya it was the first sight of the enemy since crossing the frontier three days before. At the front of the invasion force, Amedeo had looked back that first day from a high amba and seen three long columns of men, 100,000 in all, fording the Mareb river. And above flew the aeroplanes of La Disperata, whose first bomb, dropped on an unsuspecting village near Adowa, was released by a journalist friend of Ciano's from *Corriere della Sera*. Mussolini had got his war at last.

Major Ajmone Cat lowered his field glasses and turned in the saddle towards his officers, singling out Amedeo. His feelings towards the general's nephew had thawed over the past three months. Indeed, Amedeo had become something of a favourite with the irascible commander, who was impressed by his conscientiousness. He had wanted to leave the lieutenant behind at Barentu, as he was still weakened by malaria, but Amedeo had persuaded him that he was fit enough to serve. The young man may have been a little too eager. At dusk on the first day in enemy territory, Amedeo had strode up to his commanding officer, who was standing alone some way off, to report that the camels carrying the tents and supplies had been unloaded and that the encampment was secure for the night. The major had grunted in acknowledgement and turned his back; Amedeo had continued, '*Comandante* . . .' Again the major turned away. For a third time, '*Com* . . .' The major exploded: 'Damn it man! Can't you leave me to piss in peace!' Amedeo's excess of zeal had been a source of great amusement. But now, faced with the first appearance of the enemy, there was no trace of levity when the major held the lieutenant's eyes for a moment, and said: 'Guillet, clear that hill, if you please.'

So that was how it was done, Amedeo thought. Only a few short words, casually spoken as though he were being asked to round up a loose horse. But what they meant was vast. This was how it must have been for his father when he was ordered into action on the Carso for the first time. He could feel the eyes of the other officers on him, and he looked away towards the hill for a moment. Without a word, he calmly eased Sandor into a turn, taking care not to yank the bit in his excitement, and cantered down the column to his men. Although it was a hot afternoon and the Spahys had been marching all day, the major's words had shaken off Amedeo's torpor, and he felt as clear and focused as he had to be during the final jump-off in the show-jumping ring.

'Shumbashi Sarduk, have the squadron draw up in line behind me,' Amedeo told his senior sergeant.

He watched his eighty horsemen detach themselves from the rest, sending up puffs of dust as they sorted themselves out and formed a long line, each rider three or four metres apart. Amedeo turned to face the hill, and began trotting towards it over the uneven rock and sand. He closed his eyes for a second and thought of his mother, before whom he had knelt to be blessed with the sign of the cross before he had left for war. The black sword of his father was strapped to the saddle behind his leg. In his dreams, war was still something out of a painting by Baron Gros, serried ranks of cuirassiers crying *Vive l'empereur!* Now was the moment of his awakening. He took his Glisenti revolver out of its holster, unravelled the cord attached to its grip and placed it like a noose around his neck.

The white figures on the hill were moving about excitedly, some taking cover behind rocks. But Amedeo was less anxious about those he could see. There could not have been more than a couple of dozen, probably poorly armed tribesmen. It was what they would encounter on the far side of the hill that concerned him.

'Canter march!' He ordered, putting a slight pressure on Sandor to ease him up a gait.

The enemy began firing and Amedeo could hear the shots whistling over his head. Four hundred metres away from the enemy, he turned in the saddle and shouted: '*Caricat!* Charge!'

At last he gave Sandor his head, letting him surge forward into a furious gallop straight towards the hill. The horse was plunging up the slope towards the enemy when Amedeo turned again behind him and felt his heart miss a beat. Only Sarduk and two others were still with him. Of the rest there was no sign.

The shumbashi caught his appalled expression. 'Keep going, *Comandante*. Don't stop!'

It was too late for that anyway. Amedeo cursed and invoked divine protection at the same time, digging in his spurs to keep Sandor bounding in cat-leaps up the hill. It was only when nearly at the top that he saw that his Spahys had fanned out, and were charging up at the enemy from all directions.

'*Comandante*! Watch out to your left!' cried the shumbashi again.

Amedeo turned to see a crouching figure level his rifle at him. He quickly aimed and fired his revolver, and a small dark circle instantaneously appeared on the man's forehead and he jerked back against a rock. Other Spahys had reached the crest, firing their rifles with one hand at a gallop, reloading and firing again. Complete panic set in among the enemy, who stumbled and ran down the far side of the hill.

Almost as soon as it had begun, the charge was over. Amedeo's heart was pounding. He had survived without a scratch, and felt elated and proud. He had not hesitated, even when he thought that he had been abandoned. And at the price of one wounded Spahy, five or six of the enemy had been killed, and several captured. The rest had fled into the dense woodland.

'An interesting manoeuvre, Guillet,' said Major Ajmone Cat, when he rode up. But he was pleased. The Spahys' first engagement of the war had been a triumph, and the officers celebrated that evening with bottles of the major's chianti.

A few days later, the Libyan cavalry were the first to arrive at Axum. Three huge granite columns, venerating the southern Arabian deities of the sun and the moon, rose above the juniper trees, and beside them many others were lying broken on the ground. These were all that remained of the ancient city of the Queen of Sheba, where she returned after her seduction by Solomon, according to the Ethiopian version of the biblical story. From the church of Mariam priests emerged carrying gold Coptic crosses of beautiful intricacy. The Spahy officers dismounted and kissed them: the first Christian invaders to seize the land of the mythical Prester John. Adowa was taken at the same time and Amedeo made a point of riding over the plain where Barattieri's army had been destroyed forty years before. Little fields rippled down the contours of the hills, newly ploughed or filled with ripe crops. But of the populace there was hardly a trace. Only slowly and hesitantly did the inhabitants of Adowa emerge from their huts, the older ones remembering the last time the Italians had come south across the Mareb.

Later, column after column of Italian infantry and Eritrean *ascari*, wearing high red fezes, marched into Adowa and Axum, led by officers mounted on horses or mules, the flags and pennants of the unit behind them. The whole of Tigre seemed there for the taking, but instead of pressing on, General De Bono halted the advance. He had not been surprised by the lack of resistance. During the months of waiting, considerable efforts, and funds, had been expended to turn the Tigrean nobles against the emperor.

The biggest catch was Haile Selassie Gugsa, the twenty-seven-year-old lord of Makalle, who had been married to the emperor's favourite daughter until her early death. A notoriously debauched young man, he declared for Italy, but instead of bringing over an army of 30,000 warriors, as he had promised, only 1200 followed him in his treachery. The spark De Bono had hoped would set the empire ablaze fizzled out. Tigre might be his, but he was going to have to fight his way to Addis Ababa, and for that he had little appetite. For nearly a month the army stood idle, while its commander pleaded with Rome for yet more men.

But time was working against Mussolini. In the British general election in mid-November, the Labour Party pledged to close the Suez Canal to Italian shipping: virtually an act of war. Marshal Pietro Badoglio, chief of the general staff, and Alessandro Lessona, the colonies minister, were sent to Africa to assess the situation. The army was eager to fight, morale was high and the condition of the crack Italian regiments and the Eritrean *ascari* was excellent, Badoglio reported (though noting the poor state of 2nd Corps mules and horses after the *mandef* epidemic). The chief problem was De Bono, 'a tired, almost totally exhausted man'. After much prodding, De Bono hesitantly resumed the advance, seizing Makalle without a fight, but then again halted. Mussolini's patience finally snapped. He bumped his old friend up to marshal and reluctantly handed the command of the regular army over to Badoglio.

In the British elections, the National government of Stanley Baldwin was returned, but though less bellicose than Labour, it pledged 'all sanctions short of war'. These were imposed on Italy by the League of Nations on 18 November 1935. A 'Black Day' of mourning was declared by the Duce and the wives of Italy, wearing widows' weeds, followed Queen Elena in donating their gold wedding rings to the Patria. Amedeo's mother became the first woman to do so in Capua, receiving an iron one in return.

For Nazi Germany, the breakdown of the old First World War

alliance was an opportunity. German coal and steel were freighted into Italy from the north, ensuring that the League's sanctions were ineffective. If an oil embargo, which remained to be discussed in mid-December, were imposed, Mussolini's war machine would grind to a halt and he would have to begin negotiations. He need not have worried. The resolve of the democracies was already cracking. Both Sir Samuel Hoare and Pierre Laval, the French prime minister, were appalled that Italy was being thrown into the arms of Hitler on account of Ethiopia. The only solution, which at any rate was preferable to full conquest, was a secret pact whereby a large chunk of Ethiopia – all Tigre, some of the Ogaden – was handed over to the Duce.

It was the first of many acts of appeasement in the coming years, but when details of the ignominious deal leaked out, it caused outrage. Coinciding with the news of the Italian bombing of Dessie, during which the emperor was photographed gallantly firing an anti-aircraft gun, the public indignation was uncontrollable, particularly in Britain where Hoare had been praised for his previously tough stand. Both he and Laval were swept from office. But in the resulting furore the issue of oil sanctions on Italy was quietly dropped. The Duce's war went on.

It was not long, however, before he was complaining about Marshal Badoglio's interminable delays. A cautious man, the chief-of-staff was a Piedmontese of the higher peasantry, devoted to the king, who had raised him to *marchese* after the Great War. Having witnessed at first hand the disaster of Caporetto, he knew that it was best to leave nothing to chance with his troops. Like the legions of Rome, the invaders advanced with painstaking attention to their lines of communication. Behind the army, a labour corps of many thousand began building a network of roads and bridges of a quality Tigre had never seen before. Only when these were complete would the army nudge forward again.

But now the initiative passed to the Ethiopians. While the main armies faced each other thirty miles apart, a daring Ethiopian attack was launched against the exposed 2nd Corps of General Maravigna at Axum. Ras Imru was one of the emperor's most devoted followers, and his best general. Before the war, he had been entrusted with the governorship of Gojjam, a rich and semi-autonomous province separated from the rest of the country by the Blue Nile. From here he had marched north, over four hundred kilometres, with 25,000 men. In early December, he had been bombed from the air for the first time and his force had been halved, with the Gojjam levies heading for home. He had made good his losses with the forces of Dejaz Ayeluw Birru of Gondar, a princeling – he was a 'commander of the threshold' – who seemed to be hedging his bets in the fighting with the Italians, although not risking open treachery.

By fast night marches through the mountain massif of Semien, Ras Imru arrived unspotted by Italian air reconnaissance at the river Takazze, which divided western Tigre, held by the Italians, and the Ethiopian province of Beghemeder. Again under darkness, his men crossed the river, overwhelming the Italian guard posts. Army command in Axum sent forward to recoinnoitre a *gruppo bande* of 250 Eritrean infantry, supported by a squadron of ten two-man Fiat Ansaldo tanks. These were commanded by Captain Ettore Crippa, who had been the motorised cavalry instructor during Amedeo's time at Pinerolo. At the pass of Dembeguina, the tanks encountered Ras Imru's vanguard, which fled when the Italians opened up with their machine-guns. Taking advantage of their flight, Crippa's unit then drew to a halt in a clearing amid acacia trees and attempted to refuel. Unaccountably separated from their infantry support, it was a further misfortune that the reserve supplies were stored on the roofs of the vehicles.

All of a sudden, the Italians were ambushed by hundreds of screaming warriors, who charged forward firing their rifles and hacking down the crewmen with swords and spears. Within seconds the clearing was a scene of carnage. Running warriors hurled burning brushwood onto the miniature tanks, which burst into flames. According to colourful accounts, Balambaras Uvene Tashemma, a 'commander of a fort', displaying the cool head and cunning that Amedeo would later appreciate, sneaked up behind a machine and began hammering on the turret. The stupefied crew opened the hatch, and with sweeping sword Tashemma beheaded them both.

Some kilometres away, the Eritreans were also surrounded and outnumbered by Ras Imru's advance guard. Cunningly, they drove out their baggage train of mules in the hope that the Ethiopians would be distracted by loot. But when this ruse failed they broke out of their encirclement, charging with the bayonet. Having lost a fifth of their force, the Eritreans were chased back to Ende Selassie, which was hastily abandoned. Ras Imru had come within eighteen kilometres of Axum.

Two days after the disaster a dishevelled, bloody figure appeared at the Spahys' camp. He was Sergeant Bruno of the tank squadron, and the only survivor of Crippa's unit to make it back to Italian lines. The ambush had been so sudden that the crewmen had been unable to do anything, he said. And he cursed the Fiat Ansaldo tanks, which were supposed to be one of the Italian army's few modern weapons. During the rare periods when they did not cast off their tracks, they deafened their occupants and the twin machine guns had only a 15-degree traverse. In the confusion of the Ethiopian attack, the sergeant fled to safety down a crevice. He had wandered the countryside before stumbling across the Spahys, followed by a family of baboons.

Two weeks passed before the Italians could return to the scene of the massacre. Ajmone Cat ordered Amedeo to have his squadron bury the dead at Dembeguina and look for other survivors. There were none. In the clearing were the burned-out hulks of the tanks, and the rest of the debris of the massacre. The vehicles were neatly parked side by side, caught completely by surprise by Ras Imru's warriors. The hatches had been flung wide open and beside the hulks were the stripped corpses of the crews, which had been partially eaten by hyenas. Amedeo only recognised Crippa's by the strands of his grey hair. A jovial, heavy man, the captain had been so proud of his machines at Pinerolo, telling the young cavalry officers that the age of the horse in war was over. Perhaps, but not quite yet, Amedeo reflected, as he watched his Spahys bury Crippa's body. He rode away from the clearing grateful that he had gone to war on Sandor's back, rather than in a metal box.

The speed and success of the Ethiopian advance appalled the Italian command. Ras Imru was in a position to outflank Maravigna's 2nd Corps and attack the Italian supply lines that stretched back deep into Eritrea. To stop him, General Appiotti's division of 12,000 Black Shirts was ordered forward from Axum; the Spahys di Libya sent ahead to provide reconaissance.

Cautiously, the Spahys pushed deeper into enemy territory towards Ende Selassie, along narrow rocky gorges which were ideal for ambush. They were wary, too, of having to rely on Black Shirts for support. Of varying quality, they could be among the most excitable units in the army, but at least Appiotti's division seemed to be made up of middle-aged veterans of the Great War, and all the officers, including the general himself, were seconded from the regular army. Like most of his friends, Amedeo had little regard for the pretensions of the full-time Milizia officers. Many had transferred from the army to the Black Shirt legions because their careers had stalled, and their evocative ancient Roman ranks – *console*, *centurione*, *capo manipolo* – were regarded with irreverence. In spite of the official favour of the Duce, the extravagant black uniforms, the bloodcurdling songs and the dramatic oaths declared over unsheathed daggers, among the public at large there was no social comparison between a Milizia officer and one in an elite regiment of the regular army.

Towards Ende Selassie the landscape became more dramatic.

As the morning mist cleared, the serried levels of the mountain ambas slowly emerged. Often several kilometres wide, the plateaux were perfectly flat, until the level ground suddenly fell away in steep, precipitous ravines. Before dusk each evening, the Spahys rode up narrow goat tracks to set up camp on the ambas, which were safest from surprise attack.

The officers celebrated Christmas Eve 1935 with the last of their bottles of chianti. At first light the next morning, they were awoken by excited pickets and the sound of shots. Large numbers of Ethiopians were emerging from the gorge below onto the amba of Selaclaca. Several hundred were advancing at a run, spreading out into the cover of the woods and rocks. There was every sign that there were many more to follow.

Amedeo ordered his men to saddle up as fast as possible, seeing to Sandor himself. Captain Fausto Pittarelli and his squadron moved off first to scatter the Ethiopians as they climbed up from the ravine below. But nearly 350 of them were working their way around through the woods to the far side of the Spahys. If they succeeded, the horsemen would be caught in crossfire. Ajmone Cat recognised the danger, and ordered Amedeo to stop them immediately, while he himself held back with two hundred men until the scale and direction of the enemy attack became clear.

With his shumbashi behind him, Amedeo galloped towards the skirmishers in the woods, hearing the reassuring shouts of 140 Spahys behind him: *Uled! Uled! Uled!* On boys! On! On! But this time, the Ethiopians did not break and run. The fighting became a chaotic free-for-all, the horsemen lashing out at scurrying figures, bludgeoning them with their rifles and slashing with their swords. Amedeo had been taught that a horse was a cavalryman's main weapon and that few men on foot would keep a steady aim if you galloped straight towards them. Sandor pounded forward, scattering all the men in his path, while Amedeo fired into the mêlée with his revolver. He wheeled around sharply and charged again, spreading terror and confusion. But a chilling feeling ran down his spine. The impetus of the initial charge had gone, milling figures surrounded the horsemen and casualties were rising.

Amedeo cursed to see the number of riderless horses galloping in and out of the trees, adding to the mayhem, when suddenly an enemy warrior grabbed his waist and began pulling him out of the saddle. His revolver, hanging uselessly from the cord, its six shots fired, was somewhere underneath his attacker. With his left hand Amedeo stretched down to reach for the black sword. He eased it partially out of the scabbard, but could not pull it clear with his attacker pinioning his right arm. If he fell, Amedeo knew that he would be dead, his body castrated by his victor according to Ethiopian custom. He pulled Sandor out of a panic-stricken, spinning circle, and spurred him into a canter, the three of them plunging awkwardly forward as Amedeo hammered the hilt of his sword on to the Ethiopian's head.

At last, the attacker's hold broke and he fell sprawling. Amedeo pulled the sword clear, shifted his weight in the stirrups to straighten the saddle, and then galloped back through the throng. He made sharp whipping cuts at a couple of scurrying figures, and hearing one scream in pain behind him, wheeled and prepared to charge again. But something was wrong. He could sense a rifle being aimed at him a split second before he heard the shot. There was a sudden pain in his left hand and at the same time Sandor leapt sharply sideways, nearly throwing him from the saddle. Amedeo looked down at his left hand holding the reins; it was covered in blood, the thumb dangling awkwardly. A dum-dum bullet had hit the pommel of his saddle, sending fragments into his hand and Sandor's withers. He had been lucky; had it hit a fraction higher, the bullet would have torn his intestines to shreds. In the excitement of the moment, the pain was bearable and his grip still strong enough to hold his horse once he had wiped the blood off his reins. The Ethiopians at last had had enough, he saw with relief, running in panic back towards the edge of the ravine pursued through the wispy acacia trees by ululating Spahys.

But now, instead of a few hundred, there were more than a thousand enemy warriors spread across the amba. Amid them, hopelessly outnumbered, were Pittarelli's men, supported by the squadrons of Cavarzerani and Second Lieutenant Francesco Azzi. As they plunged into the horde, Azzi was in the act of drawing his sword when he was shot through the spine and mortally wounded. 'Avenge me!' he shouted as he fell from his horse. To Amedeo's astonishment, Cavarzerani was making his horse do perfect *haute école* dressage movements, as though he were one of Eugene of Savoy's cavaliers at Blenheim. The horse leapt forward, kicking behind in a capriole, while Cavarzerani fired his pistol elegantly over its shoulder. Then he too was hit, falling back slumped in his saddle. Shot through the neck, he was pulled from the fray by two Spahys, who held him upright in the saddle until they rejoined the main force.

Ajmone Cat had been watching the events fixedly, holding back his men until the moment he knew for sure that he only had the enemy in front of him to deal with. Suddenly, the major took off his red cummerbund, stood in his stirrups and waved it over his head, shouting: 'Spahys of the Bir Tagrift! *Caricate!* Charge!' As the Spahys galloped past his flank, Amedeo had his squadron fall in with the charge. Faced with 350 galloping horsemen, their flowing burnous adding to their diabolic appearance – 'like a stampeding herd of centaurs', according to the regimental account – the Ethiopian warriors ran to the safety of the valley below.

That night the Spahys sheltered behind makeshift walls of stone on the edge of the amba, and kept their horses saddled. With darkness the resolve of the enemy returned and isolated attacks began to be made on their positions. During one of these a delirious Cavarzerani staggered out of his tent, blood spurting from his neck wound, and shouted, 'Where's my squadron? Where's my squadron?' and fired his pistol wildly in the air. Amedeo had to throw him to the ground, holding him down with his knee, while he returned the enemy fire. Three times the Spahys issued forth beyond their wall, pushing the attackers back down the ravine, where they could be showered with grenades. With more than thirty-five horsemen killed that night, and an equal number of wounded, only the uncoordinated nature of the enemy attacks saved the Spahys from annihilation.

The next morning Amedeo rode over the amba, which was strewn with corpses. Lying in the dust, he saw the old Spahy who had given him Sandor. The *berrima*, the evil eye on his horse's coat, had claimed its victim after all.

Among Ethiopians it hardened into historical certainty that Ras Imru's brilliant offensive was broken up and destroyed by the Italians deploying poisonous gas. Badoglio was sufficiently concerned by the threat to sanction the use of his most infamous weapon. But the cited example of a gas attack at this time took place in the Tekazze valley on the morning of 23 December – two days before the fighting at Selaclaca. The Ethiopians had grown used to aerial bombing, taking cover whenever aircraft flew overhead. But this time instead of bombs the planes dropped cylinders, which broke open on impact releasing a colourless liquid. Exposed hands, feet and faces were instantly burned, and some warriors were blinded. The Italian tanks may have been useless, but the effect of mustard gas was immediate. Panic set in among Ras Imru's warriors, who scattered, even though the gas, old First World War materiel, dropped on an enemy not hemmed in by trenches, who could usually flee to higher ground, was seldom fatal. 'It was a terrifying sight,' Ras Imru later said. 'I myself fled as though death was on my heels.'

To Amedeo and the Spahy officers – including Ajmone Cat, whose brother was the commander of the Regia Aeronautica in Ethiopia – it was a shameful act. The Ethiopians may have been fighting dirtily, killing prisoners and castrating the dead – neither of which had been a feature of the Adowa campaign in 1896 – but that did not justify the use of gas. The Spahys had fought the enemy hand to hand *all'arma bianca*, 'white weapons' of swords and bayonets, and had won. To bomb them with gas, a weapon Italy had declared in 1926 that it would never use, tainted the Spahys' victory. Some weeks later, as the horsemen rode down the valleys towards Hamle, they came across villagers with burns on their hands and faces. The doctors of Appiotti's division treated the blistering wounds as best they could. The use of gas proclaimed the Ethiopians' victimhood in this vicious war, for although the Italian army tried to keep the bombings secret, and great efforts were made by diplomats to obfuscate the issue, the news leaked out.

Many times Mussolini had spoken of his hatred of mandolin-playing Italians, given to gaiety and laughter; he loathed too, as Ciano sniggeringly recalled in his diary, museums filled with Raphaels and Leonardos, instead of enemy flags. Italians should aspire to be feared rather than liked, the Duce declared. As his pilots bombed and gassed tribesmen from the impunity of the air, the latter part of his wish was fulfilled.

With Ras Imru's offensive checked, Badoglio resumed his meticulous preparations for attack. Facing a fluctuating horde of up to 100,000 Ethiopians, who were picking the country clean without any prospect of re-supply, he had no intention of rushing matters. Meanwhile, the Regia Aeronautica bombed and strafed anything that moved on the narrow mule tracks between the front and the emperor's headquarters at Dessie, 270 miles south. Like a good First World War general, Badoglio concentrated a mass of artillery in front of the enemy stronghold at Amba Aradam, and set about pounding it for weeks, again using gas.

With no movement on the front, the Spahys, badly mauled at Selaclaca, were relegated to policing duties far behind Italian lines. Thousands of labourers and Black Shirt volunteers were building a network of roads in northern Tigre that stretched all the way back to Eritrea. But this conquered territory was still far from secure. Late one afternoon, near Axum, the Spahys came across an encampment of two hundred Italian workmen with the Gondrand construction enterprise. Huge bulldozers were parked behind a barbed wire enclosure, where neat rows of tents had been erected. A powered water pump operated a washroom with showers, and from the kitchen wafted the aroma of *pasta al forno*. The men were building a road and among those supervising them was Count Enrico di Colloredo Mels, an engineer whom Amedeo had befriended at Udine, when he was serving with his Uncle Ernesto's regiment. The Spahys stopped and watered their horses, while Colloredo invited the officers to have a glass of marsala and something to eat. As they sat and chatted, Amedeo was surprised when an attractive Italian woman joined them. She was the wife of the project manager, Signor Rocca, who had decided to join her husband, believing that Tigre was safely in Italian hands.

Colloredo himself seemed less convinced, asking Amedeo quietly whether he could spare some bullets for his revolver. He handed over a box of fifty and the Spahys rode on. A couple of hours later, darkness had fallen and they were beginning to unsaddle and make camp when they heard gunfire down the valley. Ajmone Cat ordered the Spahys to mount again.

'Whenever you hear shooting, it means that a friend is in danger,' he said, leading the column into a fast canter, their path lit by a full moon.

The whole encampment seemed to be on fire. Flames were licking around a bulldozer, several tents were burned out and the camp, so orderly that afternoon, had been plundered. Broken boxes of supplies, upturned beds and clothing lay scattered between the tents. And amid the destruction lay the bodies of the dead and dying labourers, all of whom had been castrated. A dozen of the straggling looters were still behind the barbed wire, running in terror from one end of the camp to another as the Spahys cantered into the enclosure. A few succeeded in scrambling over the wire into the darkness, while the rest were shot.

Only one workman had survived the massacre, having thrown himself over the barbed wire perimeter and climbed a tree. Amedeo found Colloredo's body lying in the doorway of the Rocca's hut, where he had made a stand. Beside him were two dead Ethiopians. Inside lay the body of Signora Rocca, who had been stripped naked and had had one breast cut off. Her husband lay dead and castrated beside her. Only Colloredo had not been mutilated, perhaps in tribute to his valour.

Ajmone Cat turned to Amedeo. He was to gather up his squadron and pursue the enemy through the night in the direction of Adi Ghilte. These were Ras Imru's men, and at some point they would make for the Tekazze valley and the bulk of his forces.

Grey mist swathed the village as Amedeo and his men approached at first light the next day. A brushwood wall surrounded the tukuls, the faint shapes of their thatch roofs discernible in the half light. In the centre stood two high juniper trees in front of the stone church. Amedeo rode through the open gate, told his men to spread out and search all of the houses, and then approached the church with eight or so horsemen. A priest emerged, in a faded red cape and a tall hat, covered in intricate braid. Amedeo kissed the cross which the priest held up to him and dismounted.

Speaking through the Tigrinian interpreter who accompanied the Spahys, the priest said he had seen no sign of the men the *comandante* was pursuing. Ignoring his protests, Amedeo entered the small stone church followed by his Muslim troops. A solitary figure was kneeling before the altar, over a wooden hatch in the floor. He was a leper, the priest explained, who came to pray before the rest of the village was awake. Amedeo scrutinised the priest's face for an instant and decided he was lying. He drew his revolver and shouted at the kneeling figure to move aside. Guns at the ready, the Spahys opened the wooden door and went down into the crypt below. They emerged carrying some Italian rifles and a metal hatch from one of Captain Crippa's tanks destroyed at Dembeguina a month before, which was now being kept as a trophy in the church.

At that moment, they heard gunfire from the edge of the village. Amedeo ran outside to find that his look-outs were being shot at by a band of a hundred Ethiopians. On foot and on horseback, the Spahys charged, driving the enemy back. They retreated to a large cave in a rockface that overshadowed the village. After a fierce exchange of fire, the Spahys began to close in on their adversaries. Back in Italy, incensed by the Gondrand massacre, the scene was later made famous by Beltrami, whose *Boys' Own* style illustrations appeared on the cover of *Domenica del Corriere* magazine. The Spahys, wrongly depicted wearing fezes, were being led by an unrecognisable Amedeo, in a pith helmet and khaki. The perpetrators of the Gondrand massacre were 'exemplarily punished', readers were assured.

But before the Spahys could finish off the men in the cave, the sound of more shooting came from the far side of the village. Hundreds of figures, each carrying a rifle, were running towards them. Amedeo ordered his squadron to mount up and they rode off as fast as they could. When he got to higher ground, Amedeo looked back towards the village with his field glasses. There were about a thousand armed men below, far too many for his Spahys to deal with.

Time and again Haile Selassie had told his *ras* to avoid pitched battles with the better-armed enemy, and fight instead as guerrillas. But throughout its history the empire had always saved itself by staging a large, decisive battle. In this manner they had defeated the mahdi, and many other Muslim aggressors, as well as the Italians at Adowa. But against Badoglio's powerful, and comparatively well-armed forces, such tactics were disastrous. By the time the Italians stormed Amba Aradam, there were eight thousand corpses strewn over the mountain as a result of aerial and artillery bombardment, which Ethiopians claimed included the use of gas. Ethiopian morale had crumbled before the Italians advanced up the slopes. Black Shirts were given the honour of raising the flag on the mountain peak and their war cry '*Eia! Eia! Alalà!*' resounded over the ambas.

The retreat that followed turned into a rout as the shattered Ethiopians were harried from the air, and then the Raya Galla turned on their detested Shoan overlords. Among those killed by the wrathful tribesmen was Ras Mulugueta, Haile Selassie's minister of war, and the commander of his now non-existent 'army of the centre'.

Badoglio then turned his attention to Tembien, a seemingly impregnable mountain stronghold which fell after a daring night climb by the Alpini. Finally, it was the turn of Ras Imru, whose army of 25,000 was still facing off the 2nd Corps of General Maravigna. The battlefield was again Selaclaca, and again the Spahys were in action. Ras Imru's guard and the levies of Ayelew Birru fought with great courage but, outgunned and outnumbered, were finally worn down. The Ethiopian general extricated his exhausted men under cover of night, but the Italians caught up with them the next day. As they tried to cross the Tekazze, aeroplanes dropped incendiary bombs which set light to the woods on the edge of the river, 'rendering utterly tragic the plight of the fleeing enemy', Badoglio wrote.

With the Spahys at the forefront, General Maravigna set off in pursuit of the remnants of Ras Imru's army, which had fled over the highlands of the Semien. With a landscape like a parched Switzerland, its tallest peak Ras Dascian 15,000 feet high, the Amhara heartland of the Semien should have been impregnable. But Ayelew Birru, lord of Gondar, had had enough and no efforts were made to resist the advancing Italians. When Amedeo rode into mountain villages, the local priest would emerge carrying the community's cross. Then the women would be sent out to dance in supplication to the newcomers. Finally, the men would appear.

It was a walkover, and Amedeo would bless the smiling multitude with the sign of the cross feeling like a visiting cardinal.

Poised to enter Gondar, once Ethiopia's capital, the Spahys were suddenly ordered to halt. This prize, the most impressive city in Ethiopia with its stone palaces and forts, was to be taken by Achille Starace and his tardy motorised column of Black Shirts. When Ajmone Cat protested, General Maravigna signalled back: 'We cannot always say no to Rome.' The Spahys waited for several days until they saw Starace's dust trails in the desert to the west, pounding his path towards Gondar. Remembering him well from his days when training for the Olympics, Amedeo could imagine the secretary-general of the National Fascist Party enjoying his moment of glory to the full, encouraging his 3400 men with eccentric exhortations. 'We are a poor nation,' Starace told them. 'That is good, for it keeps our muscles firm and our shapes trim.' Not like the portly *inglesi*, whose digestions had been ruined by centuries of wealth and, as a result, 'their brains were addled'.

Great resentment was felt throughout the regular armed forces at the regime's efforts to make the war a Fascist victory. Ciano, who liked to compare the excitement of war with the sexual act, received a Silver Medal for making a forced landing in a field. He deserved the Gold Medal for having the gall to accept it, said the journalists accompanying the invasion force. Nonetheless, a second Silver Medal followed after Ciano pointlessly touched down at Addis Ababa airfield, flying off quickly when the machine guns opened up. Even less deserving was Roberto Farinacci, the influential anti-conservative Fascist. He was widely ridiculed throughout the army after he too received a Silver Medal for bravery when wounded – whereas he had, in fact, blown his hand off with a grenade trying to catch fish in Lake Tana.

By mid March 1936, Haile Selassie had lost the northern half of his empire, while Graziani was pushing forward to the ancient

Muslim city of Harar through the Ogaden desert to the south. The defeats of Amba Aradam, Tembien and Selaclaca had been crushing. In despair, the emperor wrote a message to Ras Imru, that never arrived for it was intercepted by the Italians:

> If you think that with your troops and with such of the local inhabitants as you can collect together you can do anything where you are, do it. If, on the other hand, you are convinced of the impossibility of fighting, having lost all hope in your front, and if you think it better to come here and die with us, let us know of your decision ... From the League [of Nations] we have so far derived no hope or benefit.

Ignoring his own advice about guerrilla warfare, the emperor resolved on one last desperate battle on the shores of Lake Ashangi. He rallied his forces at Mai Ceu, surrounded by the greatest names of the empire, princes whose fathers, like Haile Selassie's own, had defeated the Italians at Adowa forty years before or, as in the case of Ras Kassa, had actually fought there themselves. Haile Selassie's presence revived the Ethiopians' flagging morale and even the day chosen for the attack, 31 March, was deemed auspicious; according to the Coptic calender, it was St George's Day, the patron saint of the empire. The emperor himself distributed money and gifts to the horsemen of the Azebo Galla, in whose lands the battle would be fought, in an effort to retain their dubious loyalty.

Knowing even the day of the attack, Badoglio summoned his best troops: elite regiments from Piedmont, the excellent Eritreans and the best of the Black Shirts, who took up position fortified behind barricades of thorn *zeriba* hedges. After their light artillery barrage with all the guns and mortars available, the Ethiopians hurled themselves against the Italian lines with desperate courage. Twice the Italians scythed them down.

In the third and final attack, the emperor threw in his Imperial Guard, which broke the 2nd Eritreans, forcing the Italians to counterattack with the bayonet. As his men faltered, Haile Selassie saw through the heavy rain the horsemen of the Azebo Galla prepare to intervene at last. But instead of descending on the Italians, they charged the rear of his own beleaguered warriors. Pursued by the Galla and bombed from the air, the Ethiopian retreat became a rout.

Gondar had fallen, Ras Imru was virtually a fugitive in rebel-infested Gojjam, and Beghemeder and Semien were refusing to fight at all. Many of the emperor's closest friends and allies were dead, others had betrayed him. He faced not only the destruction of Menelik II's enlarged empire, but the end of 2500 years of Ethiopian independence. For three days, a despairing Haile Selassie disappeared, retiring to the ancient carved rock churches of Lalibela, where he prayed. By the time he emerged, Badoglio's re-named vanguard, the *colonna di ferrea volontà* – the column of iron will – was driving towards the capital.

The emperor contemplated his options. Some advised him to retreat to Gojjam, behind the Blue Nile, which the Italians could not cross until the end of the rains: or he could kill himself, as Emperor Theodore had done at Magdala when Lord Napier had called for his surrender; or he could appeal to the powers in Europe and shame them with his presence for abandoning him. To a hard-headed realist like Haile Selassie only the third course offered any practical assistance to his beleaguered country. On 2 May 1936 he and his family took the train down to Djibuti, where he sailed to England and five long years of exile.

All semblance of order in Addis Ababa went with him. Embittered and confused warriors crowded into the city, which they pillaged and burned. The European population barricaded themselves into their diplomatic compounds. The British minister, Sir Sidney Barton, a veteran of the Boxer siege of Peking, had taken no chances: his highly fortified residency was defended by a company of Sikhs.

After three days of looting, Badoglio finally arrived, riding a beautiful chestnut horse through the smouldering ruins of the city. As advance units of the Italian army paraded through the streets, the Europeans turned out to wave handkerchiefs and applaud them, as though greeting their saviours. But when the Black Shirts marched past Barton's residency, above which flew the Union Jack, they began hooting and whistling. The British went inside.

On the evening of 5 May 1936, Mussolini strode out on to his balcony at the Palazzo Venezia in Rome and looked down on the vast crowd of upturned faces. Two searchlights had been placed in his office behind him, casting his huge, menacing shadow over the piazza. Flaming urns illuminated the white marble columns of the Altar of the Patria, and many in the heaving throng that stretched all the way down the Corso held lighted torches. A master showman was playing to the fullest house of his career, and his performance, punctuated by the crowd's deafening roars, was faultless:

> Blackshirts of the revolution, Italians and friends of Italy beyond the frontiers and beyond the sea: Listen! Today, on May 5 at 16.00 hours, Marshal Badoglio telegrammed: 'At the head of victorious Italian troops, I have entered Addis Ababa.' [Pause] I announce to the Italian people that the war is over! [Pause] I announce to the Italian people that peace is re-established! [Pause] It is not without a certain emotion and a certain pride that after seven months of bitter hostility, I pronounce these words. But it is necessary that it be understood that this is a Roman peace. One that expresses itself in this simple, irrevocable and definitive proposition: *L'ETIOPIA È ITALIANA!*

Four days later, Vittorio Emanuele III, Duke of Savoy and king of Italy like his father and grandfather before him, was proclaimed emperor of Ethiopia. For the first time in 1500 years, the streets of Rome echoed to the cries of '*Imperatore!*'

SIX

# *The Sword of Islam*

Italo Balbo, air marshal of Italy and governor of Libya, stood on a platform in the main square of Tripoli, the Italian tricolour draped over the balustrade in front of him. It was July 1936; the Libyan veterans of Ethiopia had come home and the whole city turned out to honour them. European luminaries sat in the shade, the most important behind the governor, but Tripoli's Arab and Jewish population were also packing the streets to hail the conquering heroes. The tricolour was flying from every rooftop and shopfront, and military bands were playing patriotic tunes. The Zaptie colonial police headed the parade, some on camels, followed by Zuave infantry and, finally, the Spahys, who had had to be remounted after leaving their own horses behind in Eritrea.

Amedeo stood to attention in his crisp, white colonial uniform, his sword by his side, and his face almost invisible in the shade of his pith helmet. Beside him were Major Ajmone Cat and a Libyan colonel, all three waiting to receive medals from the governor. They approached the raised dais. Balbo decorated the senior officers first and then pinned a Bronze Medal to Amedeo's chest, in recognition of his valour at Selaclaca. To the others' surprise, Balbo embraced him: 'Bravo, Amedeo.' As Ajmone Cat marched back to the Spahys, he cast an inquisitive look at the lieutenant. Given the circumstances of his arrival the year before, Amedeo had felt it more tactful not to mention that Italo Balbo, the second most influential figure in the Fascist regime, was a close family friend.

When Amedeo received his commission as a second lieutenant in 1931 he had been posted to Udine, a provincial city in north-eastern Italy with a strong Austrian flavour. Yet it was there, while serving in Uncle Ernesto's Cavalleggeri di Monferrato, that he had met and befriended two of the era's most extraordinary personalities. One was Amedeo, Duke of Aosta, a cousin of the king and future viceroy of Ethiopia; the other was Italo Balbo then at the height of his fame. Literally so, for as Italy's most celebrated aviator Balbo had led a mass formation of twenty-four aircraft to the Soviet Union and to South America, and then trumped both these achievements by flying over the north Atlantic to the United States. Chicago honoured his extraordinary feat with a ticker-tape reception, and immortalised his name in Balbo Avenue, which exists to this day. Balbo's wife was the socially elevated Countess Florio, whose family came from Udine and had long been friends with Uncle Ernesto. Through this connection, Amedeo was accepted into the intimate circle of the great aviator.

A virile figure with a sharp black beard, Italo Balbo was hugely popular in Italy, which contributed to a growing chill between him and the Duce. For he was far more than a sporting hero. Balbo was also the country's youthful air minister who had established the Regia Aeronautica. As one of Mussolini's most pugnacious followers during Fascism's rise to power, Balbo had set up the *squadristi* street gangs, purging with brutal vigour his native Ferrara, and later the whole of Emilia Romagna, of communists, anarchists, socialists and army deserters. No other Fascist *ras* was so disposed to resort to the *sacro manganello* – the 'holy cudgel' – as this son of a schoolmaster who had been a highly decorated officer in the Alpini during the Great War. It was he who introduced that peculiarly Italian touch to the *squadristi* brawling: the forced administration of castor oil, which gave its victims a humiliating bout of diarrhoea. When Mussolini planned the March on Rome, which imposed the Fascist regime in 1922, Balbo marshalled the Black Shirts.

Over years in government, Balbo's thuggery had been forgotten and his early Fascist fervour, which included republicanism, became more moderate. A natural leader, he was widely regarded as one of the most able and independently minded ministers in the regime. But his success and showmanship, which rivalled his leader's, both angered and worried Mussolini, always sensitive to the momentum of power. He removed Balbo from the command of the air force he had created, packing him off to Libya as governor in January 1934. But this was not the end of the career of a man who had captured the world's imagination with his flights across the Atlantic.

In the twenty years since the Italian conquest, little had been done to improve Libya; the eastern province of Cyrenaica was still reeling from Graziani's ministrations. 'All the Arabs here are in concentration camps,' Balbo complained on arrival, and one of his first acts as governor was to release the prisoners and unburden himself of the general, whose methods he deplored.

In the next few years, Balbo transformed the colony. Under the Turks, Tripoli had been the least impressive city along the north African coast, being little more than a village clustered around the ancient Roman arch of Marcus Aurelius. Under Balbo, wide, tree-lined avenues and piazzas were laid out, leading to imposing, starkly geometric white buildings, unadorned save for an exhortation or two of the Duce's. The streets were spotlessly clean; public gardens were planted with flower beds laid out in the shape of the *fasces*, or spelling 'DUX'. Tripoli was the 'Cannes of North Africa', said admiring European visitors; while Americans compared Libya to Florida or California. 'Tripoli was a jewel personally carved by Italo Balbo,' wrote George Steer of *The Times* in 1938, who, as a devoted supporter of Haile Selassie, was no friend to Fascist Italy. 'He had built nearly everything in it and built well.'

And it was exciting, too. Balbo filled the calendar of his pristine, filmset capital with glamorous sporting and social events, such as the celebrated ten-day Sahara Air Rally, when aeroplanes from across the world flew over the deserts and mountains of Libya to the remote oases of Ghadames, Brak and Kufra. The track of the Libyan Grand Prix ran through the streets of Tripoli, attracting so many visitors that Italian residents were instructed to take in lodgers while the army established a tent village for the overflow. More high minded tourists visited the ruins of Leptis Magna, which Balbo had excavated from the desert sands, or came for the annual festival at the Roman theatre at Sabratha.

In Rome, Balbo's place as the darling of society had been taken by the altogether less appetising Galeazzo Ciano, but in Tripoli he and Countess Florio had established a summertime rival. Some society figures moved permanently to the colony, such as Princess Jolanda, whose husband, Count Calvi di Bergolo, commanded the Libyan cavalry. Glittering receptions were held in the governor's castle above the city. Dances were set in the gardens, where the immaculate white uniforms of the army officers and the fashionable clothes of the women were illuminated by coloured lights set amid the trees. Nothing quite like Balbo's Tripoli existed in Italy: the circle of the king and queen was notoriously dowdy, while the Duce and Donna Rachele never entertained at all.

Stationed in Tripoli, Amedeo was flattered and captivated by Balbo's friendship, his energy and enthusiasm. Barely in his forties, the governor felt genuine affection for the younger man and fellow sportsman, who shared his sense of fun and risk. He was fed up with sedentary, middle-aged army officers playing bridge all day, he once declared, adding that it would be better for them to have an affair rather than get excited over an old woman's card game. Balbo even banned officers from playing bridge, at least while in public and in uniform. More red-blooded excitements were to his taste. Amedeo often accompanied the governor as he flew up and down the colony. Partly as a dare, and partly to show that it could be done, Balbo enjoyed terrifying his companion by landing in the desert without lowering the aeroplane's wheels, and they would slew to a halt in a spray of sand.

Balbo spoke to Amedeo of his ambitions for the colony. Some were realised, as in 1938 when, with great fanfare, he welcomed the 'Ventimila', 20,000 skilled Italian peasants who would work the thin coastal strip that was Libya's only farmable land. Others were not. A project to involve American surveyors in the search for oil was overruled by the Duce, and the Italians never discovered Libya's most valuable asset.

Amedeo fully shared Balbo's flattering self-image that they were benevolent colonial civilisers, transforming the north African desert into the granary and, perhaps, the playground of the new Rome. This was where his future lay, he decided. With reluctance, he tore himself away from the distractions of Tripoli to visit his parents in Italy in the autumn of 1936.

Almost the whole of Capua turned out to greet him, and waiting on the steps of his parents' palazzo was the town's *podestà*, wearing a tricolour sash. He hailed 'the return of the local hero' from the war in Abyssinia, and the assembled townsfolk applauded.

Only the old *barone*, Amedeo's father, failed to share the general enthusiasm. There was a new mood in the country in these proud months after the founding of Africa Orientale Italiana, but one tinged with bellicosity and rancour. The war had seen *Italia contra mundum*, and yet she had won. A dangerous view was taking hold that there was no need of old friends any more. The barone was proud of the success of the army, the settling of accounts with the Ethiopians over Adowa and the foundation of the Italian empire. But of all the Guillets he was the least enamoured with the regime. The monarchy had united the conservative and liberal strands in Italy's national movement, but its purpose was to defend the rule of law and parliament, not to collude in the dictatorship of a mercurial man who, for the moment, seemed to have the country in the palm of his hand.

Amedeo could appreciate that Mussolini was not likely to appeal to a man of quiet dignity like his father. He would never speak of his achievements, or of the Great War, from which he, like his more celebrated brothers, he had returned highly decorated. Amedeo remembered as a child the afternoon when a soldier limped across the garden to greet his father who was resting in a wicker chair. The soldier stooped to kiss the *barone*'s hand. They talked for a while, then the man took his leave. When Amedeo questioned his father, he had brushed the matter aside and resumed his *siesta*. So the small boy ran after the soldier, catching up with him in the street. The man had picked him up and embraced him, and told how, badly wounded, he had been left for a day and a night in no-man's-land on the wire of the enemy trenches until Amedeo's father had come out alone to bring him back.

Amedeo loved his father deeply, and listened indulgently to the older man's old-fashioned views on politics. But to lament the end of parliamentary government seemed as pointless in the Italy of 1936 as that gesture, now almost obsolete, of Rome's noble families who kept closed the front gates of their *palazzi* in mourning at the end of the Pope's secular rule in 1870. The world had moved on, and Fascism was Italy's future now.

News of Amedeo's return soon spread and bundles of invitations and letters arrived at Capua. Many were from friends in Hungary, and among them were a couple from Maria. Amedeo took an extra three weeks' leave and set off for Budapest. His riding friends there had been trounced in the Olympics, as had the Italians, by the German team which, contrary to the rules, seemed to know every stride of the cross-country course. But in their eyes the Games were insignificant in comparison with taking part in a cavalry charge in war, and the junior subalterns treated Amedeo with awe. He was invited everywhere, stag hunting on country estates by day and carousing through the night in Budapest with his friends. One evening he was made an honorary Hadek hussar and carried on the shoulders of his friends around the ballroom, everyone so drunk that when he fell to the ground nobody noticed, and he slept where he lay.

However, he was cold sober at a ball when he casually remarked to an attractive Englishwoman with whom he was dancing that he had lately returned from the war in Ethiopia. The woman's face froze, she turned on her heels and left him alone on the dance floor. Amedeo was perplexed and indignant. From what moral peak did the British disapprove of Italy's new empire? Were they not up to their elbows in blood after conquering their own vast territories? And what of the Boers kept in concentration camps, or the Sikhs gunned down at Amritsar? His Hungarian friends, and Maria, could not have been less interested, but Amedeo, neither obtuse nor a cynic, was rankled by this snub.

He was conscious of a mutual disappointment in Maria's company; their former attraction had somehow ebbed away. She was still flirtatious and amusing, but when Amedeo talked of his ambitions of making a career in Africa, he noticed a distance open up between them. Even before he returned to Italy the relationship was fizzling out. A year later, Maria married a banker from Switzerland.

With the conquest of Ethiopia, Italy's colonies assumed a far greater importance in the Duce's calculations. In the spring of 1937 he decided to visit Balbo's Libya. Partly the aim was to reassure the great powers that Italy was satisfied and simply intended to develop its empire; yet the visit also had the contradictory purpose of demonstrating to the Arab world, where the Italian victory in Ethiopia had made a strong impression, that Britain and France were no longer the only players in the Middle East.

Mussolini had briefly visited Libya eleven years before, when he had been an untried prime minister of whom little was known and much expected. Amedeo had rowed out with his father into the harbour of Messina to catch a glimpse of Italy's self-proclaimed saviour, whose cruiser called in at the Sicilian port. Through binoculars, he saw Mussolini strike a Napoleonic pose on the warship's prow, the effect somewhat weakened by a large white bandage over his nose. The day before, the Honourable Violet Gibson had shot at him with a pistol, the bullet only inflicting a graze. Her motives were unfathomable, although Mussolini was held to have a disturbing sexual effect on young women. He gallantly ordered that she simply be deported from Italy. Much had changed since those early years, and on the eve of his second visit to Libya, the Duce was unsettling more than susceptible flappers. From the moment of his arrival, this was to be the triumphal procession of an imperial conqueror.

With his well-merited reputation as an organiser, Balbo was to make this occasion exceed all others in dramatic spectacle. The visit would begin in Tobruk, where the Duce would celebrate the completion of the Via Balbia, the 2000-kilometre coastal road, control of which was to be so important in the Desert War. He would then slowly make his way to Tripoli, his every move reported by 150 Italian and foreign journalists. The climax would come when, in a brilliantly orchestrated ceremony, he would proclaim himself the protector of the world's Muslims – who had not invited him to do so – and receive 'the Sword of Islam'.

Horses should play an important part in the proceedings, Balbo decided, with the Duce and the leading luminaries of the regime riding through Tripoli before the main ceremony. And who better to organise this than Amedeo, the most distinguished horseman in the colony? Amedeo was touched by the confidence of his friend and mentor, but recognised the potential for disaster. Mussolini, whose father had been a blacksmith, was proud of his horsemanship and reasonably secure in the saddle, but some of the other *gerarchi* could barely sit on a horse.

The first task was to find some suitable mounts, for purebred Arabs were prone to over-excitement, as well as being too small for the weightier ministers. With a vet, Amedeo set off to scour Europe for twenty-odd large and tranquil horses, which would not be fazed by the cheering crowds. After passing the word around in Italy, Amedeo visited Germany. He saw a lot of Trakehners, the

Prussian 'thoroughbreds', but felt they were too flighty. Instead, he went for heavier warmbloods, buying seven Hanoverians, including a big chestnut for the Duce. A couple more horses came from Burgundy, and the rest were Italian. From Pariani in Milan, the finest saddler in the world, Amedeo ordered two dozen saddles with appropriate saddle clothes. That of the Duce was black, with silver edging, decorated with the motif of the *fasces*.

When the horses arrived in Tripoli, Amedeo was given *carta bianca* to prepare them. A cavalry barracks was emptied and placed at his disposal. To get the animals used to loud and unexpected noises, he had a machine gun set up outside the stable doors. After firing off a series of blanks, the horses were immediately fed. In time, whenever they heard gunfire they looked over the stable doors, instead of cowering inside. In the middle of the parade ground, a mound was erected to resemble the sand dune where the Duce was to unsheathe the Sword of Islam and accept the acclamation of the multitude. During the first trial run, Amedeo, mounted on Mussolini's chestnut, looked down at the other horses lined up neatly below him, jutted out his jaw in imitation of the Duce and raised his right arm portentously. But at that moment, a squadron of camel corps came onto the parade ground, making the European horses balk and rear, for they had never seen creatures like them. Amedeo put them back in their stables, and had a camel ridden back and forth outside, until the horses realised they had nothing to fear.

Meanwhile, an irrepressible Balbo added extra flourishes to the arrangements. He had the inspired idea that the procession into Tripoli take place in the cool of the evening, when the sun had gone down. So as well as the noise and the crowds, it would be dark, except for the lighted torches – and a few fireworks. Amedeo groaned inwardly, and continued with the task.

The visit was to last ten days, beginning with the Duce's inauguration of the vast Arae Philenorum, a triumphal arch built over the Via Balbia on the border of Cyrenaica and Tripolitania in the middle of the Sirte desert, 320 miles from Benghazi. The ceremony took place at night. Searchlights played over the arch of travertine marble, each piece of which had been brought from quarries outside Rome and meticulously assembled. Dinner was served in the desert, with dishes of fresh produce and vegetables grown by the Italian colonists.

Days passed with the Duce opening schools, visiting Italian farms and receiving the homage of various Bedouin chiefs. Nomads lined the roadside, crying as his motorcade sped past: 'Allah, protect the Duce.' All along the coast, he was rapturously received, by Italians and Libyans alike. Where the crowds formed, Mussolini kept his orations short:

> Comrades of the colonies! I am truly delighted to meet you and to greet you on this tip of African land, which is Italian land as here flies and will always fly the tricolour of the Patria. Comrades of the colonies! You live and work tranquil and secure: you, your womenfolk and your children. Imperial and Fascist Rome watches over you, loves you, protects you and will protect you, come what may. *Viva l'Italia!*

As the Duce and his entourage bore down towards Tripoli like a grisly theatrical troupe, Amedeo was feeling confident. The horses were fully trained now, and there was nothing more he could do with them. But the night before the dignitaries were expected, a colonel arrived at the stables with a couple of women he was trying to impress. He ordered the groom to bring out Mussolini's horse so that they could see it. When the Libyan explained that Lieutenant Guillet had given strict orders that the horses were to remain in their stables, he was brusquely cut short. In the semi-darkness, the big chestnut slipped and fell heavily on the concrete. At that moment Amedeo arrived, and the colonel and his friends quickly evaporated into the night. Although the horse was not lame, a big swelling was rising on its hind quarters.

Two vets were summoned, who felt that nothing could be done. Amedeo stayed up all night with the horse, rubbing warm linseed oil on to the bruise until, at about six in the morning, it became soft. With a scalpel he cut a cross. Syrupy blood oozed out and the swelling went down. Leaving the wound open, Amedeo applied on top some fine sand that he had had sterilised by heating over a griddle.

When Mussolini arrived that evening from Benghazi, he got out of his open-top Alfa Romeo three miles outside Tripoli, where the horses were waiting, immaculately groomed and with polished tack. 'Which is my horse?' the Duce asked Balbo, who pointed out the big German chestnut. 'What's he called?' the Duce demanded. Balbo turned to a colonel and asked him. He did not know. Amedeo was summoned. 'What's the name of my horse, lieutenant?' the Duce asked him. After buying the animals, he had renamed each after the dignitary who was going to ride them: 'Starace', 'Lessona', and so forth. The big chestnut was 'Benito'. 'Er . . . He's called Spahy, *Eccellenza*,' Amedeo said quickly. 'Spahy? An Arab name isn't it?' Mussolini said. 'Yes, *Eccellenza*. He is becoming an Arab,' Amedeo replied, plucking at thin air. The Duce gave him a quizzical look, mounted the block and heaved himself on to the horse.

The Duce and the others safely in the saddle, the cavalcade was ready to move off, preceded by a military band and followed by 2500 camel corps and colonial cavalry. Amedeo rode a little distance behind, keeping his fingers crossed. Yet in spite of the cheering and the accompanying *Zaptie* on camels bearing torches – and even the Fascist hymn *Giovinezza* sung in Arabic – the horses remained calm. Only the mount of Achille Starace played up, rearing a couple of times. That evening, after Mussolini had gone to bed well satisfied with the day's events, Starace stormed up angrily to Amedeo. 'What have I ever done to you that you give me such a vile horse?' Amedeo replied that as the mount was the most tricky of the lot he felt that only the head of the Italian

Equestrian Federation could handle him. This struck the right note with a man of Starace's overweening vanity, and he marched off to bed, declining Amedeo's offer to exchange the horse. Before turning in, Amedeo checked the stables. On the big chestnut's door a piece of paper was pinned: 'Ariosto'. The horse had been renamed after the renaissance poet.

The next day the cavalcade began again, and Amedeo rode behind the Duce to a space outside the city. Once clear of the streets, Mussolini could not resist digging in his spurs and Ariosto surged forward into a gallop. The other horses followed, one ridden by a terrified *gerarca* clinging on to the mane. Several thousand Libyan soldiers were lined up in front of a sand dunc, where the Duce, alone, would be seen by the huge crowd that had gathered. Amedeo showed him the way up, and when Mussolini appeared on the top of the dune there was loud cheering. A Berber chief, Colonel Yusuf Cherbisc, who had served Italy for twenty years, then handed the Duce the Sword of Islam, saying:

> In the name of the soldiers and Muslims of Libya, proud to feel themselves to be sons of Fascist Italy, I have the honour of offering to you, O victorious Duce, this well-tempered Islamic blade. The hearts of all the Muslims on the shores of the Mediterranean quiver with ours at this moment, in which, full of admiration and hope, they see in you the great Man of State who guides, with a firm hand, our destiny.

The Duce then drew the sword – which, in fact, had been made in Florence – and raised it above his head. The crowd roared with approval and a brilliantly choreographed series of photographs spread across the world. Balbo had excelled himself. The 'Sword of Islam' was one of the greatest spectacles Fascism ever staged. What it all meant was less obvious and, for the Duce and Balbo, rather less important. Both had got the headlines they wanted.

## SEVEN

# *Black Flames*

ZARAGOZA, SPAIN, MARCH 1938

In the fading dusk they seemed like the only survivors after the city had experienced a horrific visitation. An Italian officer, aide-de-camp's braid threaded through his epaulette, was walking through the empty streets with a young whore at his side, who, with one hand, was swinging the little doll that he had bought her. Rubble and splintered timber spilled onto the pavements, apartment blocks were burned-out shells, shutters hung off their hinges and the few remaining shops were boarded up. No one else was lingering in Zaragoza with the fighting on the Ebro so close at hand. From the cathedral came a luminous glow, its altars covered in candles, and in the nave the devout were kneeling, huddled in their overcoats, oblivious in their prayer to anyone else. The baroque cupola was open to the sky, and the three bombs which had broken through it, but miraculously had not exploded, were stacked in a side chapel as though objects of veneration. It did not surprise or even alarm the Italian officer that their fuses were still intact. A bout of malaria had required Amedeo to be pulled out of the trenches, and he felt weak and curiously detached from the desolation all around him. He was glad of the respite from the front to the south at Teruel, the scene of the most horrific battles of the war. Food would arrive by mule at the lines almost frozen in the cold, and in the dugouts rats would scurry over the men's blankets as they slept. The soldiers on both sides would launch attacks as much to keep warm as for any tactical rationale.

While the girl beside him bowed her head and recited her rosary, Amedeo asked himself, not for the first time, what on earth had brought him to Spain to fight in its poisonous civil war. Of course, he remembered with a bitter smile. It had been love.

Beatrice Gandolfo. Of all the women he had known or was likely to meet, he never imagined that he would fall in love with his young cousin. Until the year before he had barely thought of her as an adult – he had barely thought of her at all. Nor, of all things, could he have guessed that it would be his wound at Selaclaca that would bring the two together.

Like his recurrent malaria, the pain from the wound never entirely went away. For months, Amedeo tried to ignore it, convincing himself that the persistent ache would disappear in time. The wound had been cleaned and dressed at the field station after the battle. But tiny metal fragments from the explosive bullet were still embedded in the delicate bones of his hand and fingers, which caused excruciating pain. When his hand began closing in on itself, like a petal in the frost, it had to be operated on. An eminent surgeon in Bologna broke open the bones and picked out the metal shards one by one. As his parents were abroad, Amedeo asked the Gandolfos whether he could convalesce with them. He arrived in Naples with a soaring temperature and his jaw frozen in a permanent clench so that he could hardly speak. The pain from his re-setting wound was so great that Uncle Rodolfo slept with him in his room, administering through the night little shots of morphine into the veins of his wrist. Gradually, Amedeo's agony eased and an orthopaedic leather gauntlet was fitted to prevent his hand from becoming a useless claw.

He had been at the Gandolfos' for a fortnight before Beatrice returned from Florence where she had been staying with her older sister, Margherita. Bice was eighteen, although her assured manner made her seem much older. The features were firmer than he remembered, showing her character and intelligence, and he would catch himself guiltily casting an eye over her slender waist and the curves of her athlete's body. Amedeo was taken aback by how attractive he found her.

Over the weeks that followed, Bice spent hours in his company, gently rubbing camphor oil into his twisted hand. He talked to her about the war in Ethiopia, the beauty of the country and of his ambitions to return there. He found himself telling her the brutal details of the fighting and of his own secret fears, which he never mentioned to others. Bice, too, discussed her hopes for a life more rewarding than a *buona famiglia* marriage in provincial Naples. He was fortunate to be a man, she told him, with seemingly limitless opportunities in his life.

Amedeo found himself becoming increasingly dependent on her friendship, missing her when she was not around. Bice was so natural and unaffected, especially compared with the socialites at Balbo's court in Tripoli. Though witty, she was never cruel, and when she gave an undertaking to meet a friend or visit a relative, she was steadfast, despite all his efforts to dissuade her.

In the heat of July 1936, the Gandolfos retreated to their summer-house, the Torre Crestarella, an old Angevin watchtower beside its private beach at Vietri. Amedeo and Bice were left to themselves for days at a time. They would sail into Salerno in a little boat to go shopping, or head up the coast towards Amalfi, where they would swim in the deep, cool water. They read to each other *Gone With The Wind*, which had just been translated into Italian, marvelling at 'Rossella O'Hara'; the sort of extraordinary woman who Amedeo believed would be at home in Italy's new African empire.

Donna Rosa, Bice's grandmother, was the first to notice the changed feelings between the two cousins. One afternoon, she asked Amedeo to stay with her for a moment as she was confused by a newspaper report and wanted to know exactly where Chile was. Amedeo came back with an atlas and as he began looking through the pages, she said: 'You are in love with Bice, aren't you?' He could not deny it, though he knew that as first cousins the Gandolfos would resist their marriage. The last thing he wanted was to cause hurt and divisions in a family of whom he was so fond, and owed much. Once he returned to Tripoli, he told the old woman, both he and Bice would discover how enduring their feelings for each other were.

Donna Rosa studied him intently. 'The compassion of God is endless,' she said.

Amedeo looked up in astonishment. He had made his first ally. He decided that he would declare his love, for now a life without Bice seemed empty and purposeless. By the time they returned to Naples, Amedeo had again gone down with malaria, which crept up on him whenever he was overwrought. Once the fever had broken, he felt exhilarated – and emboldened. Bice came into his room, with his usual cure-all of lemon juice made from boiled-up pith and skin. She sipped it, grimacing, and wondered how he could bear to drink the concoction. After she had placed the glass on the bedside table, Amedeo gently took her hand and told her that he was in love with her. He wanted to marry her, but would she accept him?

Bice was silent for a long while, and looked away. She could not marry him, she said at last, and he knew why. They were cousins, even more closely related than first cousins, for as well as Uncle Rodolfo being brother to Amedeo's mother, their paternal grandmothers were the daughters of that citizen of Capua who had been so proud of becoming an Italian. How could she forgive herself if they had children who were handicapped? But Amedeo pressed on. No one on either side of the family had been handicapped or mad for generations, unless – reasonably enough – she counted him. From the breeding of horses he knew that consanguinity in good stock improved rather than weakened the offspring. When Bice threw him a curious look, he realised that this line was not going very far. He changed rein. All Amedeo wanted to know was whether she loved him? If she didn't, he would return to Libya and the subject would never be mentioned again.

But Bice could not say that. She had loved Amedeo from childhood, when he had only had time for Rosa and Margherita. Whenever Amedeo visited excitement would fill the house, and the two older girls made him take them into Naples or up the coast to Sorrento. While Bice, the youngest, was always left behind. She admitted that she loved him but, no, they could not marry. And then she ran from the room. The next morning she left the house early, taking the train to Florence.

Amedeo no longer felt discouraged, regarding their close kinship almost as an annoyance. He had never intended to fall in love with a cousin, but he was prepared to take the risks that marriage to Bice would involve. If she really loved him, then so should she. But it was to be some months before he could renew his suit, as he had to return to Libya. Agonised protestations of love flew back and forth between Naples and Tripoli. Before Christmas in 1936, Bice was again in Florence with her sister and Amedeo, on leave, decided to follow her. He trudged through the streets of the city in the snow, wrapped in his blue burnous, and for four days they went over the same discussions that they had in different forms many times before. Finally, Bice agreed to marry him, crying out that if it all ended badly then it was not her fault. She had done everything she could to dissuade him.

The blessing of Bice's parents was more hesitant. But both were sure that she loved Amedeo, and in time that overcame their fears. The Guillets warmly welcomed the union. Uncle Ernesto congratulated his nephew, sharing the insight that while the best marriages were *paradiso* and the worst *inferno*, most were *purgatorio*. 'But if you marry Bice I am sure that your journey will end in fulfilment, as it did for the divine Dante.' A dispensation for the cousins to marry was obtained from the Archbishop of Naples, and in early 1937 Amedeo and Beatrice were officially engaged.

Amedeo had wanted to marry Bice as soon as possible, but his enthusiasm to do so cooled four months after their engagement when Mussolini passed the Matrimonial Law. Under its regulations, only married civil servants and army officers were considered eligible for promotion. Bachelors, irrespective of their abilities, except those displayed on the field, were to remain in their existing rank. Their responsibilities could increase, but their salaries remained the same. The law was a hamfisted attempt to increase Italy's population and a typical *cazzata* – cock-up – of the Duce's, declared Balbo, which thwarted young talent and smacked of the fecundity medals the Nazis were handing out to German mothers. To Amedeo, the regulations were humiliating. He knew army officers well into their forties who had rounded up a country cousin and married her simply to win promotion. That anyone might think that he had done the same with Bice was intolerable. Besides, he was determined to win his promotion, not have it given to him as though a wedding present. At twenty-eight he felt he was getting old, for at that age Uncle Amedeo had already made major. His best prospects for promotion on merit were likely to be in Africa Orientale Italiana, and he set his mind to organising a transfer, though without upsetting Balbo, his friend and benefactor. It had not occurred to him that there might be other possibilities rather closer to home in the Duce's latest military adventure, the Italian intervention in the Spanish Civil War.

In June 1937, Amedeo was in Rome, taking part in the military review to celebrate the first anniversary of the empire. After his success with the Sword of Islam ceremony, he had been entrusted with ensuring a suitably choreographed display of the Spahys. Furiously charging Libyans galloped past the crowds standing in their stirrups, while others formed a circle and fired over their prostrate horses. They were one of the highlights of the tattoo. A solemn ceremony followed at the Altar of the Patria, where the king honoured regimental standards. The officers taking part were received by the Duce at the Palazzo Venezia across the square, once the Venetian embassy to the Papacy, where the dictator had his tennis court-sized office. Mussolini spoke informally and with some insight into the army's role in Abyssinia, avoiding the mannered artifice of his public performances to the small assembly. Among those present was General Luigi Frusci; he and Amedeo discovered that they were both invited to lunch with the Colonnas in Trastevere afterwards. The two men struck up a rapport and talked about the war, Frusci having fought on the southern front, commanding Somali troops under Graziani.

Back in Libya, two months later, Amedeo received a letter from the general inviting him to become his aide-de-camp. Frusci had been given the command of the *Fiamme Nere* (Black Flames) division fighting in Spain supporting General Franco. Much to Mussolini's fury, the division had been among the Italian units humiliatingly routed on the Guadalajara by the International Brigades, and Frusci had been appointed with orders to bring in new blood. Amedeo was flattered by the offer, especially as he did not know the general, and had not been recommended by one of his uncles. Even more attractive, however, was that the post carried the temporary rank of captain with the certainty, Frusci informed him, that it would become permanent once the *Fiamme Nere* returned home. In his heart, he recognised that the war was best left to the Spanish themselves, to resolve one way or another. But his sympathies were wholly with the conservative Franco and, like millions of Italians, he was revolted by the atrocities carried out by communists and anarchists at the beginning of the war.

Italy's involvement in Spain was never a formal act of war. The fiction was maintained that units of the regular Italian army joined Franco as 'volunteers' – even though they eventually amounted to 70,000 men, taking with them artillery, tanks and hundreds of aircraft. Bearing false papers under the name of 'Alonzo Gracioso', Amedeo was flown to Cadiz, where he was fitted out in a strange uniform of a corduroy jacket and breeches, thick socks and hiking boots. He was then transferred to divisional headquarters in northern Spain.

With the fighting stalled around Santander, Amedeo soon discovered that he was surplus to requirements. His duties as an ADC involved making the luncheon arrangements for visiting dignitaries, including Generalissimo Franco himself. Though impressive in a quietly determined way, Spain's self-proclaimed saviour was hardly an engaging, still less a convivial guest. His Italian hosts were well aware that their rout at Guadalajara had given him sour satisfaction, after Mussolini's boasting that he would win his war for him. The more thoughtful officers, like Frusci himself, realised that it suited Franco's interests that the Duce was now determined to redress this unfortunate slight to Fascist prestige, pouring more men and weapons into a war which involved no serious Italian interest.

The hatreds underlying the Spanish civil war had been festering for more than a century, and appalling atrocities characterised both sides from the beginning. The suffering was made worse by it becoming a duel between the mutually loathing ideologies of the Thirties. Leftwing idealists poured into Spain, determined to make Madrid the 'tomb of Fascism' or the 'Verdun of democracy'. (The *Madrileños* quipped, 'Why not somewhere else?') Italy provided the bulk of the Nationalists' foreign levies, while the Germans used the war to experiment with their modern weapons and tactics, as at Guernica, which the Luftwaffe obliterated in April 1937 in the first example of a 'Blitz'. Stalin sent in tanks and aircraft to the beleaguered Republicans – in exchange for Spain's gold reserves – as well as some of his most murderous Comintern henchmen, who seemed more keen to settle accounts with Trotskyists, anarchists, liberals and socialists, than win the war against the Fascists.

Amedeo had seen the conflict as an opportunity that would advance his career, but soon discovered what war in Spain really involved. Frusci had given his frustrated ADC a unit of 300 *arditi* commandos in the coming battle for Santander. Amedeo was not expecting a tough fight. From civilians who crossed the lines he knew that the Republicans' morale had fractured. Having executed 3000 Nationalist supporters when they took over the city, they expected no quarter and now panic had set in. Some Republican officers even attempted a midnight flit in the port's fishing boats, but were dragged back by their soldiers.

In August 1937 the Italians launched a surprise attack at San Pedro de Romeral. Meeting only half-hearted resistance, the men broke through the trenches. At the head, Amedeo had passed three lines of defences when he came across a squadron of armoured Russian lorries, as yet unaware that the forward positions had been overwhelmed. The crewmen were having lunch inside one of these vehicles, when Amedeo ran up and hurled in a grenade. Deafened and smoking, the Russian survivors emerged and were led away as prisoners. The road into Santander was wide open.

The Italians were struck by the locals' relief that they had captured their city; far better the *Fiamme Nere* than Franco's Nationalists troops or, worst of all, his dreaded Moroccan foreign legion. It was the same story wherever the Italian army went in Spain. The Republican prisoners were desperate. They crowded around the Italian officers, tugging at their sleeves, pleading not to be handed over to the Nationalists. But nothing could spare them from what awaited further down the line, and Amedeo prayed that he never saw Italy descend into civil war.

By the time Amedeo, feverish and weak, was invalided from the fighting at Teruel in March 1938, he was heartily sick of the war in Spain. The Republicans were faltering, and as far as he was concerned, Franco could finish them off alone. He had done enough, transferring from Santander to the Aragon front, where the *Fiamme Nere* fought across the wooded hills and orchards of the Codoñera for several months. Amedeo's *arditi* distinguished themselves again, capturing three mined bridges from Barcelona's

Communist militia. His battle-hardened men, many of whom were veterans of the Ethiopian war, gathered up the identity papers from the corpses, covered in appropriately revolutionary slogans: '*Sin dios, sin amos*' (No God, No bosses). Barely any of the enemy dead were older than eighteen.

After washing off the grime of the trenches at a hotel in Zaragoza, which miraculously had hot water, Amedeo set out through the darkened city to find something to eat. Only one place was open, a brothel, whose bar was packed. The corpulent madam beamed to see an *italianito* and he joined a crowd of Spanish officers for a few glasses of brandy. Sitting at another table were six or seven Luftwaffe officers from the Condor Legion. A pretty, dark girl in her late teens brought their drinks, one arm in a sling. When one of the Germans grabbed her and roughly forced her to sit on his knee, she cried out in pain. The bar fell silent, as the girl struggled and begged to be set free.

'Leave her alone,' said Amedeo in German, for the Spanish would not risk offending their allies.

'What are you, her fiancé?' said the German, threateningly. 'I get the feeling you don't like Germans.'

'Beethoven and Goethe please me, but a pig like you leaves me cold,' Amedeo replied.

With an outraged bellow, the German pushed the girl away and rose from his seat. Amedeo hurled himself on the bigger man, who lifted him bodily from the floor, then overbalanced and they crashed onto a gilded sofa, which collapsed under their weight. When the other Germans began to join in, pummelling the Italian officer, the Spanish finally intervened, seizing them and bundling them out of the door.

Another bottle of brandy was ordered, and the Spanish officers dusted Amedeo off and slapped his back. The Nationalists felt little warmth towards their Nazi allies, who treated them with a barely veiled disdain. Then the girl with the bad arm came up. Somehow managing to invest the words with great dignity, she apologised for being in no condition to carry out her work, but asked whether she could make him a coffee in her room. Breathless and almost faint from the brawl, which he had been certain to lose, Amedeo was touched by this invitation and accepted. As the two went up the stairs, everyone below laughed and began to sing the wedding march.

They spent the next day together, Amedeo grateful of the girl's company, after nine months of living with men. After visiting Zaragoza's cathedral, the young prostitute even invited him to meet her parents and share a meagre lunch, with Amedeo providing a few ration tins and Italian cigarettes. The girl was called Carmen Arias y Arias, and when Amedeo asked why it was that the name was repeated, she replied, '*Casualidad*.'

It was an answer that seemed to him to sum up the whole tragic experience of Spain. In July the now desperate Republicans launched an offensive on the Ebro, during which Amedeo was lightly wounded in the leg by an artillery burst. These injuries, coupled with another bout of malaria, had him invalided back to Libya.

# EIGHT

# *The Viceroy*

In February 1937, Crown Prince Umberto had a son, the Prince of Naples, whose birth ensured the succession of the House of Savoy for another generation. It was an event that was celebrated throughout Italy and its colonies, but nowhere more so than in Naples itself. A grand pageant was staged, in which the leading families of the city dressed up in mediaeval costumes which evoked the times of Count Amedeo VI of Savoy, the so-called 'Green Count', who had been an intrepid crusader. Beatrice Gandolfo, newly engaged, was among the young men and women who rode in procession through the streets on caparisoned horses. At the park of Capodimonte, formerly the residence of the Bourbon kings of Naples, now the home of the Aosta branch of the Savoy family, mock jousts were staged, bands played and as darkness fell there was a medieval banquet in the palace itself. The day ended with fireworks and echoing cries of '*Viva il Principe!*'

The little prince's birth was also celebrated in the capital of Italy's African empire, Addis Ababa. Badoglio had been appointed the first, temporary viceroy of Africa Orientale Italiana, but had handed over to the newly promoted Marshal Rodolfo Graziani. The idol of every Italian schoolboy, Graziani looked the part, his chiselled features and martial jawline likened by a sycophantic press to those of the great Renaissance *condottieri*. Among his fellow officers in the army, especially those who had served under him in Libya, his reputation was less exalted. Vain, arrogant and brutal, he was a disastrous choice to administer Italy's new empire.

Most of the country was still in Ethiopian hands at the time when its conquest was proclaimed. Barraged by almost daily instructions from Mussolini and Lessona, minister of colonies, who could not resist tinkering with their new possession, Graziani immediately set about imposing Italian rule on the far-flung provinces. Large-scale operations involving thousands of troops and local levies, the *bande*, were mounted to hunt down the *ras*, who refused to bow to Italian rule. Graziani's first instincts were repression and summary execution, but there were acts of clemency, notably in regard to Ras Imru, who on Mussolini's orders was exiled to the island of Ponza (ironically the ex-Duce was to be confined to the same villa seven years later). At Addis Ababa airport, waiting to be flown to Italy, the bemused *ras* was berated by Graziani for being 'a liar, an assassin of Italians and a braggart', but the marshal had been instructed not to kill him. Two sons of Ras Kassa were less fortunate. Surrendering on the promise that their lives would be spared, they were shot out of hand.

By February 1937, the country had been brought under a form of control, and most of it was peaceful. Ethiopian dignitaries who had submitted to Italian rule, either from hatred of Haile Selassie or simple opportunism, would be summoned before the viceroy, where, uncomprehendingly, they would raise their arm in Fascist salutes and hum along to *Giovinezza*. Graziani did little to ingratiate himself with them. 'Your principal defect is your habit of lying,' he would tell them. 'Deceit is the base of your every thought . . .'

To celebrate the birth of the Prince of Naples, leading figures of Africa Orientale Italiana and local notables gathered at the Little Ghebbi, which Haile Selassie had built on the model of a Norfolk country house he had visited in 1924, and was now the viceroy's residence. Silver thalers were to be distributed to the poor before lunch. On the steps, Graziani stood impatiently with his hands on his hips, telling the Zaptie colonial police to 'hurry up or we will still be here tonight'. Moments later the scene was interrupted by shattering explosions and terrified screams. Two grenades were hurled at the dignitaries, but went wide, while another exploded directly behind Graziani. He fell down the steps screaming in agony. As more grenades followed, Italian officers and Ethiopians were also injured including the Abuna Cyrillos, the head of the Coptic church, whose umbrella-bearer was killed.

As the viceroy was sped to hospital, his body peppered with more than 300 grenade fragments, chaos broke out. It was an assumption of colonialism that natives ran amok, but now panic set in among the Italian overlords. They gunned down any Ethiopians they could see, notables and mendicants together. In the excitable atmosphere of the Bar Fiammetta, Guido Cortese, the Fascist Federal Secretary, took matters into his own hands, urging the local Italian population to exact reprisals. Feeling vulnerable in the middle of a country still far from secure, ordinary Italians – clerks, lorry drivers, builders and assorted carpetbaggers – unleashed a terrible, indiscriminate fury. Screaming *Duce! Duce!* and *Civiltà italiana!* they gunned down or bludgeoned to death any Ethiopian – man, woman or child – they came across. Tukuls were set alight with petrol and hand grenades were hurled down randomly from the upper parts of the city into the Ethiopians below, who were trying to flee. No army units took part, nor the regulars of the Diamante Black Shirt Division, and the *Carabinieri* sought to bring matters under control.

The journalist Ciro Poggiali, on to whom the heavy form of the wounded Abuna Cyrillos had fallen at the Little Ghebbi, wrote in his diary:

> All the civilians in Addis Ababa have assumed the duty of a vendetta, resorting as quick as lightning to the most authentic methods of Fascist *squadrismo*. They are going around armed with cudgels or metal bars, beating to death any native they see . . . I saw one driver who, after having floored an old negro with a club, then rammed a bayonet

> again and again through his head. Needless to say, the slaughter has fallen on the unknowing and the innocent.

Three days of mayhem resulted in the worst massacre carried out under the Fascist regime, with most estimates placing the dead at 3000. When Graziani roused himself from his sickbed he halted the lawless bloodletting, but then spread terror more methodically throughout the countryside. Almost unhinged by his injuries, the marshal turned his hospital into a fortified bunker, his paranoia inflamed by an absurd official investigation which concluded that the assassination attempt was part of a vast plot, aided by the British secret service. In fact, it had been carried out by two Eritrean sympathisers of Haile Selassie.

Graziani ordered his governors to make examples of any Ethiopians suspected of rebellion or involvement in the assassination plot, 'according to the directions of the Duce repeated 1000 times yet little observed by many'. Nearly two hundred nobles were immediately exiled to Italy, including Ayelew Birru of Gondar; considerably more were sent to camps in Eritrea, where conditions were far worse. Almost all Graziani's governors complied to some degree. The notable exception was General Guglielmo Nasi at Harar, a principled and highly respected officer (renowned for having repatriated peculating officials and carpet-baggers). Graziani demanded that he change his 'political outlook' and carry out exemplary reprisals, telegraphing him on 3 March: 'Shoot all, I say all, rebels, notables, chiefs, followers either captured in action or giving themselves up or isolated fugitives or intriguing elements . . . and any suspected of bad faith or of being guilty of helping the rebels or only intending to and any who hide arms.' Fortune tellers and witch doctors were also to be dispatched. Nasi simply ignored the orders.

Graziani then disastrously turned his wrath on the Coptic clergy, killing the four hundred monks and deacons at the monastery of Debra Libanos in Gojjam. The atrocity backfired badly. Gojjam, which had fallen to the Italians without a shot, flared into rebellion, followed by the formerly peaceful territories of Beghemeder and Semien. Anxious reports gathered in Rome from colonial officials and army officers, complaining of Graziani's methods. Lessona repeatedly urged the Duce to dismiss him, which he finally did in November 1937. Annoyed at having to sack a man of firm loyalty whose excesses he had encouraged, Mussolini decided to part with his colonies minister as well. Lessona's career was finished and, unlike Graziani's, it never recovered.

The new viceroy was Amedeo, Duke of Aosta, the thirty-nine-year-old cousin of the king. It was a surprising choice, as the duke, who was an air force general, had negligible political weight and was only moderately well known in Italy. Mussolini's motives are unclear. He may have genuinely admired the handsome, extremely tall prince, who was the most glamorous figure in the royal family. When approached by officials asking 'Your Highness?', he was wont to reply, 'One metre ninety-eight centimetres' – it was thirty-five centimetres more than the national average. Perhaps, too, the Duce was motivated by gratitude towards Aosta's parents, who had been sympathetic during his rise to power, particularly his father, the only Italian army commander to emerge from the Caporetto disaster with his reputation enhanced. Or Mussolini may have wanted to snub the king, by again raising the profile of the Aosta family, who had been perceived as rivals to the throne.

For the previous five years, the Duke of Aosta had been living quietly in the accursed Habsburg Palazzo di Miramare in Trieste, the former home of the luckless Emperor Maximillian of Mexico, where his widow went mad. When based in nearby Udine, Amedeo had often visited the duke, who had served as an artillery officer under Uncle Amedeo in the Great War. Like so many of his contemporaries, he succumbed to the prince's charm, although appreciating that he was far more than simply the glamorous socialite he was believed to be. In the Twenties, the duke had gone to live with his uncle, the Duke of Abruzzi, a celebrated polar explorer and maverick in the royal family, who had settled in Italian Somaliland, where he ran a vast model estate, comforted by his native mistress. Afterwards Aosta had worked incognito for a couple of years as a clerk for Lord Lever in the Belgian Congo, under the name of Della Cisterna, one of his many titles. Broadly educated – including a detested spell at a British prep school – by his clever and ambitious mother, Hélène de France, a princess of the Orléans dynasty, the duke was also the only prince in the Savoy family with tattoos on his arm. It is unlikely that he ever had many illusions about Fascism, or its chief.

In place of Graziani's new Fascist order, the Duke of Aosta saw the British in India as the model for Italy's empire. As soon as he arrived in Abyssinia, he set about introducing a more humane and rational administration. The less savoury opportunists were ejected. 'Supposing you had shoved all the scum of London's East End into Ethiopia and let them run wild,' the duke reportedly told his British friends in Cairo. 'You can imagine the sort of thing that would have happened. That's just what we did, and I have to clean it up somehow.' He sacked almost all Graziani's appointments, and when the marshal attempted to remain in command of the army until the Ethiopian rebellion was crushed, Aosta cut him short: '*Eccellenza*, I'll make my own mistakes myself.'

The execution of suspects on flimsy evidence was ended, serfdom abolished and reforms in land ownership introduced. Four of Africa Orientale Italiana's five governors were dismissed, the sole exception being General Nasi at Harar. Among the new talent introduced by Aosta in 1938 was Amedeo's old commander General Frusci, who was made the governor of Amhara at Gondar, one of the hotspots of the continuing Ethiopian resistance.

As Amedeo recovered from his malaria, these developments came as cheering news, for his involvement in Spain had failed in its principal aim: he had not been promoted to captain. Frusci had repeatedly promised that he would be confirmed in the rank, but to the general's mortification the war ministry announced that as the army's role in Spain had been semi-clandestine, no promotions in the field were to be validated. Amedeo received one Silver Medal for his heroism in Santander, and another for capturing the three bridges in the Codoñera, but he remained a lieutenant. As soon as Frusci was confirmed in his appointment at Gondar he offered Amedeo a senior command. Under the Duke of Aosta as viceroy, Frusci was sure he would be able to make amends by securing his protégé's promotion.

But Amedeo could not leave for Ethiopia immediately. He was still weakened by malaria, and the old wound to his hand was causing trouble again. Every morning he went to the hospital in Tripoli for a couple of hours of electro-therapy, which loosened the muscles and tendons and eased his pain. A Libyan Jewish nurse, Mariam Banin, attended him and while he held his hand in the machine, they would talk together. One morning, he noticed that she had been crying. When he asked why she explained that her sister, who was in her final year at school, had hoped to study medicine. But as Mussolini's Race Laws had come into force, depriving Jews of all public positions and their rights to an education in Italian schools, she would have to leave before her final exams, and all the family's hopes for their daughter would come to nothing.

Like hundreds of thousands of young Italians, Amedeo had spent the bulk of his life barely giving a thought to the politics of Italy. The Duce now seemed as if he had always been there, guiding the nation's destiny, supported by the upper classes, applauded by the masses and praised by a tightly controlled media. The Church approved of the Fascist government, and was unhindered by it, and the monarchy, although snubbed by the cult of the Duce, was still a vital part of national life. Amedeo's conversations with Balbo, and his own experiences in Spain, had made him begin to question the dictatorship and its slogan: 'Mussolini is always right'. But it took the injustice of an unknown Jewish girl being forced to leave school to shake Amedeo out of his complacency.

There had been a time when the Italian newspapers, even the overtly Fascist ones, mocked the Nazis for their obsession with Jews and racial purity. But now in the late thirties the Italians were imitating them. Coincidentally, Amedeo had lunch with Balbo that day and the governor noticed at once that his friend was out of sorts. When he told him about the sister of his nurse, Balbo commiserated. Italy had changed during the time Amedeo had been in Spain, and not for the better. The pernicious alliance with Nazi Germany was to blame, Balbo explained. The governor had hinted at his feelings a few weeks earlier, when Hermann Goering had flown to Tripoli. Amedeo had stood to attention beside Balbo on the runway as he received his exact opposite number: the heroic Italian aviator greeting the Nazi air ace. Dressed in an extravagant uniform and carrying his marshal's baton, Goering's huge bulk loomed towards them. Balbo leaned towards Amedeo, and said dryly: 'He's not looking at us; he's just wondering how many bombs it would take to flatten the Castello.'

Like the majority of Italians, Balbo, a Mazzinian romantic in his youth, felt no anti-semitism. Italian Jews were not more assimilated than elsewhere in Europe, in fact, considerably less so in the impoverished Roman ghetto than in pre-1933 Berlin. But a visceral hatred of Jews was simply absent in Italy. Nor had Italian Fascism had any anti-semitic origins, unlike all the other extreme nationalist movements in Europe (including Sir Oswald Mosley's). On the contrary, exalting the secular government and nation – rather than the Catholic Church – was attractive to Italy's 50,000 Jews, who had been strong supporters of the Risorgimento. It was a source of pride to the community that Garibaldi's Thousand had included Jewish patriots. In Balbo's fiefdom of Ferrara, where his *squadristi* had swept communists and socialists off the streets in the early Twenties, barely an adult Jew was not a member of the PNF, the Partito Nazionale Fascista (or, as they and other Italians used to term it irreverently, the *Per Necessità Familiare*).

As governor of Libya, Balbo's duty was to enforce all Italy's laws, even those he knew to be ludicrous. But he had gone out on a limb over the Race Laws, speaking out against them courageously at the Grand Council of Fascism, backed by only a handful of others, including Marshal De Bono. He had repeatedly reminded the Duce that many Italian Jews were members of the Fascist Party and had fought in the Great War. Those who had the *Croce di Guerra* should at least be exempt from losing their government jobs, he argued. When Mussolini said that that was impossible as the award was too common, Balbo spat back: 'Then if you were Jewish, you would not be exempt.'

While Jewish army officers, teachers and officials employed directly by Rome lost their jobs in 1938, those employed by the colonial authorities were exempt. As a result, many Italian Jews began to move to Libya. There had been a stir in Rome when Balbo appointed Colonel Levi in charge of tourism for the colony after he had been removed from his army post in the Carabinieri. Balbo had become an 'honorary Jew', sneered the neo-Nazi Roberto Farinacci.

He offered to help Mariam Banin's sister, although the question of a Jewish girl in an Italian state school in Libya did not come within his authority. He gave Amedeo a letter to take to Rome to his friend Cesare de Vecchi, who had, until recently, been the Minister of Education and was one of the three surviving Quadrumvirs of the Fascist Party, along with Balbo and De Bono.

Amedeo was well known to De Vecchi, as his son had been a friend at Military Academy. After arriving in Rome, he was invited to dinner by the minister's wife. The Quadrumvir looked pained when Amedeo raised the matter of his visit. 'These damn laws are a disaster, spreading ill-feeling and causing chaos all through our schools,' he said. He made no overt criticism of the Duce, but his opinion was plain. It was not his task, he thanked God, to establish Jewish schools up and down the country. But he agreed to do what he could for the girl.

Amedeo left the De Vecchis' house that evening feeling deeply troubled. A man whom he had known for years, and who had always been talked about in his family with respect, had done little to hide his view that the government was presiding over a disaster. The regime was undergoing a disturbing change. In the past, those from Fascism's early days could restrain the Duce. But De Vecchi had been shunted to Rhodes as governor of the Dodecanese; Lessona was gone; Dino Grandi, the too pacific foreign minister, was in London as ambassador; and Balbo, the only one who still met the Duce's eye and called him by the informal *tu*, was marginalised as governor of Libya. And, of course, there was the king. His public role had lessened markedly over the preceding years, but he was still there and the regime, for all its increasingly Nazi trappings, still had to accommodate this awkward fact. When Hitler visited Rome in 1939, his irritation was barely disguised that the king stood at his side as head of state, while the Duce loomed awkwardly over their shoulders.

Amedeo stayed the night with his Uncle Amedeo, who was more preoccupied than ever before. Like Balbo and De Vecchi, the general felt deep unease with Italy's course, as Germany repeatedly raised the European temperature. The Anschluss of Austria and Germany, which Mussolini had prevented in 1934, had been carried through in 1938, this time with his acquiescence. It was one of the fruits of the German alliance that was so deeply unpopular with the army. 'They've given us the *passo romano* [the goose-step],' Uncle Amedeo told his nephew bitterly, 'While we've given them the *Passo del Brennero* [the Brenner Pass].' If it came to war in Europe, both general and lieutenant agreed, the state of the Italian army was woeful, its equipment and training almost unchanged since 1915. The Duce had been warned of this many times, Uncle Amedeo said, but as ever was obsessed by spin, rather than substance. With the African empire devouring Italy's national budget, there was hardly any money to spend on the army in any case.

De Vecchi proved as good as his word, and Mariam's sister was allowed to take her exams in the Italian school. She was not, however, exempted from the ban on Jews from attending classes, so she laboured over her revision in the hospital, while her sister ministered to Amedeo's hand. She passed the exams and took a place at the university in Tunis, over the border in French North Africa.

For Amedeo, even Balbo's Tripoli had lost its former gaiety. With a sense of relief, he set out for Abyssinia, far away from Europe and all its complications.

NINE

# *City of Facilidas*

When Amedeo had ridden through the Semien mountains to Gondar with the Spahys di Libya in 1936, it had taken three weeks. Two and a half years later, a lorry could drive to the Amhara capital from Asmara along an asphalt road in eight hours. This engineering marvel was 'the empire's grandest project', according to his Italia Touring Club guide book. The road crossed the baked brown landscape of Tigre, where small clusters of acacia trees amid pampas grass provided the only greenery, and then began climbing. For ten miles, it zig-zagged in a series of vertiginous hair-pin turns up 8000 feet to the pass of Ras Dascian. There the scenery became Alpine, a land of dark volcanic rock, where the air was thin and cool and splashing streams echoed across meadows covered in convolvulus and wild flowers. Wherever springs crossed the road, the engineers had built drinking fountains, carved with allegorical figures representing Italy and Africa. Near the highest point was a memorial arch to those who had been killed carving the road from the rockface, with the inscription: 'We have not died in vain.' Amedeo looked down over spectacular valleys, where villages and cultivated fields clung to the serried terraces, towards Gondar, beyond which, shimmering in the distance, was the vast inland sea of Lake Tana, the source of the Blue Nile.

Ever since his arrival at Massaua, he had been struck by the transformation of Italy's empire. Asmara, before a quaint provincial town, had become a city, with a European population of 50,000. The timber houses Amedeo remembered had been replaced with neat suburbs of villas and apartment blocks. There were shops and restaurants, cinemas, traffic, wide roads and roundabouts. On one intersection stood the massive, gull-winged Tagliero Fiat garage, regarded as the last word in art deco design. But most impressive of all was the *Teleferica*, a cable car network that now carried goods from the coast at Massaua over the mountain peaks and gorges to Asmara, a distance of seventy-one kilometres.

The *vecchi coloniali* – old colonists – called those who had arrived since 1936 the *agame*, the Tigrinian for peasants, and mocked their social pretensions. Rosetta, the Sicilian cleaner, would become Donna Rosa after passing through the Suez Canal; a builder would be transformed into an *ingegnere*, a clerk into an *avvocato*. But worst of all were the swindlers and crooks who had crawled in under Graziani's coat-tails; the houses in Asmara had to be locked these days, Amedeo was warned. But this was just talk, he felt. For the remarkable feature of the expatriate Italian population in the empire was its harmony, the provincial rivalries of the motherland left behind.

After sleeping at one of the military encampments along the road, Amedeo drove down towards Gondar in the early morning. Large regular fields of maize and wheat, with irrigation towers and concrete outhouses, heralded the approach of the town. There was a final curve in the road and then Gondar, where four thousand Italians had made their home, unravelled before him. Wisps of morning mist lingered above the high trees, amid whose greenery the Italians had built their town. There were neat villas and gardens, and a central piazza had been laid out. Overlooking the town were the solid fortress palaces of Facilidas, the Ethiopian emperor who had made Gondar his capital. To Amedeo that morning, it seemed strikingly beautiful.

Frusci and his wife were established in an elegant, single-storey residence on a hill, set apart from Gondar's monuments, which the general was restoring. He welcomed his protégé warmly, holding a lunch to introduce him to the other officers of his command. Among the guests was the local princeling Dejaz Ayeluw Birru, newly returned from Italy where he had been exiled by Graziani. Famed equally for his charm and unreliability, for the moment Ayeluw Birru served the interests of the Italians. But it had been his warriors the Spahys had charged at Selaclaca, and when Amedeo held out his leather-clad hand, that would be his permanent souvenir from that encounter, the *dejaz* took it in his and stroked the wound, offering prayers for its recovery.

Eager to make amends, Frusci had found a good post for Amedeo. He was to have the acting command of the locally recruited 14th Gruppo Squadrone dell'Amhara, based at Amba Gheorgis, 100 kilometres away. It was one of several fortified positions guarding the vital road to Asmara as it passed through the Semien, which had become a focus for the Ethiopian rebellion. Enclosed behind a high barbed-wire fence, Amba Gheorgis stood slightly above the road serving as a refuelling depot and transport café – and safe refuge – for the convoys of lorries between Asmara and Gondar. No one would voluntarily travel on the road at night through territory controlled by the *shifta*, or brigands. The fort had commanding views over the valleys, and Amedeo was comforted by the sight of four ancient Austro–Hungarian cannons, well positioned on the earthworks, as well as embrasures for Schwartzloser machine guns, of similar vintage but still serviceable. Within the perimeter were half a dozen functional wooden huts with corrugated iron roofs, and in the midst of the parade ground, under shade, were tethered the horses of the 360 colonial cavalrymen. He had eight Italian officers under his command, including Lanfranco Colonna, a cousin of his great friend Carlo, supported by an irregular infantry *banda* commanded by the village chief. Provided it was not attacked by an army with artillery, Amedeo decided, Amba Gheorgis ought to be secure enough.

But the writ of the viceroy's rule did not extend very far beyond the walls of the Beau Geste fort. Armed bands, whether loyalists of the emperor or merely bandits, or perhaps both, roamed the countryside, sacking villages, stealing cattle, holding up convoys, settling old scores and killing any Italians they could find. To bring order to the vast territory that had been entrusted to him, Amedeo set out on a series of mounted patrols, often taking two or three days to reach the far-flung villages. Attacks of some sort by *shifta* were virtually daily events, and when the fort was alerted the garrison rode out to the rescue. And, as in the movies, sometimes the cavalry arrived in time, at others they were too late. Early in his posting, Amedeo galloped at night along the Gondar road to Ras Dascian, a favourite ambush spot as the lorries slowed to a crawl, heaving themselves up the pass. Three had been shot up and looted, disgorging a cargo of broken boxes, clothes and, incongruously, a piano. All the Italians were dead except one, a southern builder who had been castrated and left dying on the road. '*Viva Graziani!*' he whispered to Amedeo, before expiring.

The sun had only been up for an hour when the horsemen of the 14th Gruppo Squadrone rode into the village. Three days from the fort, it was at the very limit of Amedeo's territory, and he had no wish to linger before the long ride back. He would greet the chief, listen to his grievances and make sure the populace noted his force of 140 well-armed troopers. This time there would be no cross to kiss nor beakers of alcoholic *tej*, he realised almost with relief, as from the arrangement and orderliness of the village he could tell that it was Muslim. Usually by this time in the morning only a few women and domestic animals would be up and about, but clustered around the largest tukul an agitated crowd was listening to their expostulating chief. As soon as he noticed the horsemen, Sheik Youssef ran over to Amedeo, and began talking excitedly.

That night all the village cattle had been rounded up and stolen by an armed band of *shifta*, the chief explained. Stock that had taken years to raise, and on which the village's entire future depended, had been lost. Amedeo learned that about eighty brigands were driving the livestock through the valleys to the south. The *shifta* would have to cross a wide river, the sheik explained, and there was only one ford for miles around where they could do so. Amedeo was reluctant to venture even deeper into unknown country, but when the sheik said a score of villagers, including his son Asfao, would show the way, he ordered the troops to march. The Duke of Aosta had said many times that Abyssinia's indigenous population would only accept Italian rule when they saw some tangible benefits to it. Policing operations of this kind were exactly what he had in mind.

Within two hours the cavalrymen had reached the ford. Amedeo could see through his binoculars that most of the *shifta* had already gone ahead, leaving only a couple of dozen behind to push the 150 cattle across. The sight of the horsemen and the sound of their gunshots were enough to make the bandits scatter, leaving their loot behind. Later that afternoon the cavalrymen returned to the village, driving the cattle in front of them.

On these occasions it was customary for the army to have a tenth of all that was recovered, but Amedeo suggested to Sheik Youssef that the soldiers hold a *gebir* or feast, instead, in celebration of the happy outcome. The chief agreed, inviting the Italian officer to rest in his tukul, indicating that he should sit in the place of honour on a broken wicker armchair. No wife of his could attend to him unfortunately, Sheik Youssef explained, for though he had been married twice, first to a Copt and then to a Muslim, both women were dead. Instead it would be his daughter to honour their guest, bringing him refreshments and washing his feet.

The girl who appeared at the door, holding a copper basin and pitcher, was beautiful. Dressed in a white cotton shift down to her ankles, her long neck was covered in henna tattoos and her features were open and proud. Although she could not have been older than sixteen, she was not in the least cowed by the Italian officer, but returned his admiring and not entirely polite stare. Without saying a word, she knelt to pour the water over his feet and began rubbing away the grime. As she bent towards him, her firm, supple back strained against the thin gown and as she dried his feet she rested them unselfconsciously on the warmth of her thigh.

Amedeo had grown used to the tall, slender Ethiopian women around Amba Gheorgis, who invested the simplest task, even milking a goat, with natural grace. But the chief's daughter was the most beautiful woman he had seen, and he began to flirt with her. From her headdress, he guessed that she was the daughter of the chief's Muslim wife, and so he asked her name in Arabic. Khadija, she replied, after the wife of the Prophet. And was she likewise married, Amedeo inquired.

'No? And why not, Khadija? Can you find no one to marry you?'

'Many men want to marry me,' she replied, looking up at him sharply, trying to keep the irritation out of her voice. 'It is I who will not marry them. I shall marry a chief.'

Amedeo smiled and allowed the undiscovered princess to continue drying his feet. That evening his soldiers killed three of the cattle, quartered them and hung the hunks on a tree. They and the villagers then lined up to hack off a slice of the meat which they ate raw, with salt and chilli. Only Amedeo and the other Italian, Sergeant Saggiomo, a southerner from Salerno, preferred their meat grilled by being held at the end of a bayonet over the fire. Dancing and singing went on well into the night and though Amedeo soon tired of the endless carousing and circular storytelling he indulged it.

Khadija, too, kept apart from the feasting, wrapped in a white shammah, which emphasised her dark skin. Amedeo caught her furtive glances and, in spite of himself, he was pleased by them – and amused that his men were drunkenly boasting of the bravery of their *comandante*, the Muslims among them extravagantly calling him the *comundar-as-shaitan*, the 'devil commander'.

When Khadija approached him, offering a cow's horn that was filled with milk sweetened with a little honey, Amedeo asked: 'Has your eye found any among my men who could be your chief?'

'Perhaps,' she replied.

'And who is the lucky man?' he asked, wondering which man had made a conquest.

'It is you,' Khadija said.

'No, no. That cannot be,' he laughed. 'But I thank you for honouring me.'

He did feel flattered that such a beautiful girl had offered herself so frankly to him. He could not deny that he had toyed with her a little, but it would go no further. He had quite enough to occupy him in Semien without the complications of a mistress. Besides *madamismo*, as it was termed, was prohibited under the new Race Laws, the Fascist authorities declaring it 'miscegenation'. As in so much else, there was a wide gulf between the letter of the law under the regime and its application, and it seemed to Amedeo as though half the *vecchi coloniali* in the empire had a native mistress. In the past, no disgrace had been attached to these liaisons – and any offspring had to be provided for.

The next morning Khadija showed Amedeo around the village, hoping that he would be impressed by her knowledge of its wealth, the number of cattle and where they could be sold, the crops that were planted, the yields of milk and the production of honey. She was her father's bookkeeper, he was told, and her organisational skills were widely appreciated.

Amedeo allowed his men a second night of revelry, during which he explained to Sheik Youssef that he could do with an extra dozen or so men, if there were any in the village who could be spared. The sheik offered his son Asfao, saying he felt deep shame that, after marrying a Coptic woman, he had then allowed her to bring up their son as a Christian, and not a Muslim. But he had loved the woman, he explained, as though seeking sympathy from the Arabic-speaking Italian, and had acceded to her wishes. If the *comundar* could teach him the profession of arms, that at least would be something he had given to the boy.

The next day, Amedeo gathered up his satiated soldiers and set off at the head of his column through the narrow gorges of Semien towards Amba Gheorgis. Behind him would be Salem ben Amor Kaskas, one of his Spahys who had fought in the conquest of Abyssinia. Balbo had only allowed Amedeo to take him after being waylaid by his wife and his mother-in-law, who were worried that their young friend would be leaving for Abyssinia with no familiar face from Tripoli to accompany him. Then came his two subordinates, Sergeant Saggiomo, a large, powerful man, who impressed the *ascari* with his deliberate defiance of the Evil Eye, riding a horse with an unmistakable *berrima* on its coat, and at his side was Shumbashi Musa, one of his best Eritrean sergeants. Behind the men came the mules carrying heavy machine guns, tents and supplies, and after these, on foot, the women, children and dependants of the newly recruited soldiers from the village, some shading themselves from the sun under umbrellas.

Only when the column was approaching the fort did Amedeo discover that Khadija was among them. When he demanded to know why she was there, she said that she was following her half-brother. He was even more annoyed that the *ascari* had known that she was with them, but had assumed that this had been his wish. Amedeo told her that she would have to return to her father, and that a couple of the new recruits would escort her. But she refused. She was not his, she told him, and she had a right to cook and care for her brother.

Once settled at the fort, Khadija made no attempt to conceal her intentions. Sometimes, Amedeo would emerge from his large command tent to find her sitting outside. He was aware that the *ascari* were exchanging knowing glances when he or Khadija went past. The lovesick girl and the *comundar*, who did not want her, or maybe was not interested in women, provided them with hours of entertainment.

Conscious of being a chief's daughter, and of the social standing her courtship gave her, Khadija haughtily ordered around the other women in the *campo famiglia* beside Amba Gheorgis. They, in turn, kept a close eye on how she fared. Tired at making no headway, Khadija one day walked boldly into Amedeo's tent carrying a battered box. When he brusquely demanded to know what she wanted, she sat down on the floor, opened the lid and spread out the contents: a photograph of a fair European woman, torn from an Italian magazine, an embroidered gauze shammah, a small mirror and silver tweezers to extract jiggers, bloodsucking parasites which were picked up in the mud around wells. Khadija proudly looked up at the Italian. They were her trousseau, Amedeo understood, and he was moved to see her wealth laid out for him to admire. But he was also amused. He politely thanked her for letting him see her treasures and then, indicating the door, invited her to leave. For Khadija, this was a humiliating dismissal. She gathered up her possessions and, without raising her eyes, went out of the tent.

A few days later she was back. Her status among the other women was faltering, her hauteur was gone and she felt confused by his rejection. She bluntly told Amedeo, as though he were having difficulty in understanding, that she wanted to be his woman. Amedeo decided it was time to bring this to an end. In a tone that brooked no contradiction, he told her to get out and go back to her brother – or, better yet, return to the village.

The colonial authorities in Addis Ababa pretended that Uvene Tashemma was just another *shifta*, exploiting the disorder in Semien and Beghemeder. But he was far more than that. During the Italian invasion of Ethiopia, as a *barambaras*, 'commander of a fort', he had fought with distinction. It had been he who had so strikingly decapitated the crew of one of the tanks at the pass of Dembeguina. Promoted to *fitaurari*, 'commander of the advance guard', Tashemma had become one of the most effective of Haile Selassie's guerrilla leaders fighting the Italian occupation. Like other diehard loyalists, he had sworn that until Ras Tafari, the Negus Negusti, had returned to his rightful throne he would neither shave nor cut his hair (adopting the coiffure taken up by subsequent 'rastafarians'). Marshalling a force that at times could number 1000 men, Tashemma created mayhem for the Italians, in certain areas of Beghemeder his authority prevailed over the viceroy's.

Amedeo recognised that this guerrilla band, whose modern machine guns – which the Italians suspected the British had provided – were far superior to his own, was the only rebel force he was likely to encounter that could match his own garrison. As a result, he was constantly seeking additional recruits. The local chieftain, Araia Gheremedin, could provide one hundred foot soldiers, but the numbers were still weighted against him. Only an officer, however, with no regard at all for the Fascist civil authorities in empire – then attempting to impose vexatious laws such as the segregation of Italians and Eritreans on the buses and in the bars of Asmara – would have decided to enlist and train a force of Falashas.

For centuries, Ethiopia's Jews had been condemned to menial trades that brought ill fortune, such as working with fire and metal. They were descendants, it was believed, of the Jews who had accompanied the Queen of Sheba on her return from her tryst with Solomon. Yet, when the other tribes of Ethiopia became Christians in the fourth century AD, albeit with a more Judaic flavour than elsewhere in the Christian world, the Falashas remained unwaveringly Hebrew. After their Empress Yudit (Judith) ferociously set about slaying the Christians in the tenth century, the Falashas had become increasingly marginalised and persecuted, and by the time of the Italian conquest they were only to be found in isolated villages to the north of Lake Tana.

Amedeo enjoyed talking to their local leader Tessalem, hearing the stories of Saul and David which had been kept alive in the Falasha's oral tradition. Tessalem had tentatively suggested that the *comandante* teach the men to bear arms and fight, and put them on the garrison payroll. With some foreboding, Amedeo had taken along a few Falasha foot soldiers on an encounter with *shifta* who were raiding a village. After a couple of shots had whistled overhead, the new recruits fled in terror and declined to return. Tessalem alone in his broad-rimmed straw hat, was still standing, waving his sword at the enemy, like an angry parish priest shaking his umbrella at a departing bus. 'Place a couple of your Eritrean sergeants behind them with rifles and you will see how they learn,' said the old man grumpily. In time, the Falashas became serviceable auxiliaries, and it amused Amedeo that he had been responsible for recruiting the most incongruous unit in the whole of the Duce's army.

Uvene Tashemma had twice made raids in the district of Amba Gheorgis, both punishing villages too friendly to the occupiers and attacking large convoys on the road to Gondar. Unusually, the Italians' network of informers had failed to warn them of his incursions. Amedeo had set off with his column to the area where Tashemma was reported to be, only to discover that the rebel leader had surfaced somewhere else entirely. When rumours began to circulate that the rebel fitaurari was expected to launch a third raid through Italian farming areas thirty kilometres to the south, Amedeo headed out with a column of 140 horsemen as before. This time, however, he doubled back at dusk towards Amba Gheorgis, where he discovered the rebels leisurely looting villages only ten kilometres from the fort. Gathering up the men of Araia Gheremedin and the Falashas, he set off towards the village of Dongur Dubba.

Wisps of morning mist were still hanging over the *tukuls*, as the 14th Gruppo Squadrone took up position shortly after dawn. In the still, cold mountain air the sound of bleating goats and the clanging of cooking pots carried across the valley. Amedeo sent forward the men of Araia Gheremedin and the Falashas, watching them climb up the terraces of maize fields, approaching the village from below. All of a sudden a machine gun opened up from woods behind the village – its quick-fire beat far faster than his sclerotic Schwartzlosers. His foot soldiers took cover behind low stone walls, returned the fire and then began pressing forward again.

Amedeo divided his horsemen, sending two squadrons around the woods to attack the enemy from behind. He formed a third and, following the valley's edge, set off straight for the village and the woods beyond. As soon as the horsemen were among the tukuls and the ground level, the column went into a canter. By now the rebels had roused themselves, their fire becoming more concentrated, turning from the crouching infantry below to the horsemen pounding towards them. Amedeo could hear the sibilant bullets above his head as he drove his horse on towards the light cover of the woods. If he could get the bulk of his men in there, Tashemma's men would break up in confusion. But beneath him, he suddenly felt the movement of his horse fade away, its chest raked with machine-gun fire. As it sank to its knees, almost balletically, he had time to jump clear unharmed before it slewed to a halt in the dust. For a few seconds, the momentum of the charge faltered as the cavalrymen saw that their *comandante* was down. But Salem Kaskas galloped to his side, jumped down and offered his own horse. After scrambling into the saddle, Amedeo pulled the Libyan up behind him and together they galloped forward again.

They were barely into the woods when the second horse was killed outright, sending its two riders sprawling. Badly bruised, they struggled to their feet and Amedeo ran on, firing his Naval Mauser pistol at the figures in front of him. From the shots and shouting he could tell that the other cavalry squadrons had broken through to the rear. Tashemma's men panicked, and fled through the woods in disorder. The only chance of escape was to scramble down the almost sheer hillside, offering themselves as an excellent target as they did so.

In the confusion, Uvene Tashemma escaped, breaking his leg as he jumped to safety. But he left behind twenty-five dead, and forty prisoners, some of whom were also wounded. Among those killed was a senior officer, whose papers contained details of his allies and supply depots. It was a disaster for Tashemma and his prestige in Semien never recovered. Two years passed before he took up arms against the Italians again. Appropriately, it would be Uvene Tashemma, supported by British allies, who in November 1941 invited General Nasi to surrender at Gondar. In a curious message, the *fitaurari* acknowledged the achievement of his adversaries for 'having transformed the mountains, overcome the valleys and dammed the rivers . . . such things would make the son of his son's son remember their works for a thousand years.'

The garrison of Amba Gheorgis had lost only six men, but they included Armedeo's most trusted subordinates, Sergeant Saggiomo as well as Musa, the Eritrean NCO. Tired and aching, Amedeo set off back to the fort at the head of the column on a borrowed horse, Khadija's brother Asfao having retrieved his Pariani saddle from the body of his first mount. It was nearly dark when they approached the fort. The women ran out to greet their menfolk wearing their best clothes, as they always did whenever there had been fighting, and the military order of the column gently dissolved. Seeing Musa's wife in the crowd, Amedeo nudged his horse towards her and she at once understood why she had been singled out. She began to wail, tearing at her clothes and hair and throwing handfuls of dust over her head. Amedeo dismounted and embraced her. The other women removed their white shammahs and made a screen around them. When she had composed herself, Musa's widow took from him her husband's blood-stained tunic and put it on. By wearing it for the next few days she would show that the dead were still among them, as was the custom among the women whose men had died.

Amedeo ensured the wounded and prisoners were provided for and had a subordinate radio a report to Gondar. Then he took himself off to the far corner of the fort where he had his tent, covered in thick thatch to ward off the night cold. He threw himself onto his bed, exhausted. The adrenalin of the battle had long gone, as had any sense of triumph. Sadness overwhelmed him at the thought of Saggiomo, his best NCO. Just like the old Spahy, he had paid the price for defying the Evil Eye of the *berrima* on a horse's coat and was dead with a bullet through his head. And he had lost Musa, another good man who ever since he had arrived at Amba Gheorgis had accompanied him on all his patrols.

Suddenly, he sensed that he was not alone and he opened his eyes to find Khadija standing at the foot of his bed. She had been crying, he could see, for she too had been close to Musa and his wife. Without speaking, she pulled off his riding boots, poured out some water and wiped the grime from his face. She drew some blankets over him, then began preparing her own bed on the cold ground beside him. A few moments passed before Amedeo pulled back the covers. When Khadija climbed in, she was shivering.

At first, Amedeo worried that he would regret complicating his life at the fort, and perhaps somehow compromising his authority. But most of the other officers kept a woman in the *campo famiglia*. Khadija was unusual only in that she shared the *comandante*'s tent within the fort itself, but neither the officers, still less the *ascari*, ever passed comment. In the officers' mess, where Amedeo ate at midday, she was never mentioned, her presence in the fort simply an accepted fact.

Amedeo never treated her as just a woman he slept with. As the months went by he grew deeply fond of Khadija, enjoying her company and often walking with her in the woods behind Amba Gheorgis. Together they would sit in the evening beside a large, dramatic cactus, a euphorbia candelabra, looking down on the little command post, the snaking road and the valleys of Semien beyond. He was frank with her, telling her that he was engaged to, indeed, in love with, a woman in Italy and that one day they would have to part. His world involved more than simply commanding Amba Gheorgis. But to Khadija, Italy seemed a long way away; and the established order of Semien had been turned on its head by the Italian conquest and the subsequent uprisings. *Shifta* and insurgents roamed the countryside and the fighting was constant. Life seemed very fleeting beyond the fort's perimeter. Amedeo had come to Abyssinia to win promotion and marry Bice, but it was just as likely that he would be shot one day, and become just another casualty in a war about which people at home were told nothing.

In time, Amedeo allowed Khadija to accompany him on his patrols, for she rode and shot as well as any of the men. In the skirmishes, she fought at his side, firing her Austro–Hungarian Mannlicher carbine. When a couple of lorries were held up on the Gondar road by *shiftas*, Khadija galloped up to one of them and pulled herself out of the saddle onto the vehicle's roof. From this vantage point she fired down on the brigands as they fled into the woods.

The day after his encounter with Tashemma, Amedeo faced an immediate decision concerning the forty prisoners. His orders were clear. He had them assembled and they lined up passively as they waited to hear their fate. Using an Amharic interpreter, Amedeo began by deriding their leader who had fled to save his own skin, leaving them behind. The new Italian empire was stronger, and if it could defeat the armies of the Negus, in time it would deal with the minor irritants like Tashemma. They should understand that they could all be shot, or sent to Gondar, which would be the same thing. Instead, Amedeo invited them to enlist in the garrison at Amba Gheorgis, where they would be fed, given a uniform and paid. But if any of them betrayed his trust, he told them, he would hunt them down with the same energy as he had Uvene Tashemma. They proudly replied that they would have to give the matter due consideration, and Amedeo allowed them one day to think it over. Six hours later, after intense debate, the captured men announced that they would join the garrison. For several weeks, Amedeo had the new recruits carefully watched. One night he even had them guard his tent, inside which he remained sleepless, his Mauser in hand and with Salem Kaskas for company. To the surprise of his officers, they remained loyal and none of them ever deserted.

Amedeo's victory over Tashemma made a strong impression on his superiors. He was described by Major Giulio de Sivo, in Gondar, as '*un idealista della vita militare*, who has given further proof, as always, of daring, contempt for danger and intelligent aggression'. The Duke of Aosta was delighted and invited Amedeo to Addis Ababa. They had already met since Amedeo's arrival in Abyssinia, at a small lunch given by the Fruscis at Gondar. The duke had asked particularly that *Tenente* Guillet be invited, entertaining Frusci and the other officers with the story of how he had intervened to spare Amedeo from being sent away in disgrace from a fox hunt at Udine after the lieutenant had committed the cardinal sin of overtaking the master.

At the viceroy's palace the duke received him like an old friend, congratulating Amedeo on his exploits. He would be recommending him for yet another Silver Medal and – perhaps catching a momentary look of disappointment, for this was Amedeo's third – promotion to captain. It was long overdue, the viceroy told him, leading him into the drawing room where the duchess, Anna de Guise, was seated with a few friends. Aosta then paused and asked gently whether the rumours were true that he had been recruiting former rebels into his unit.

'You have been ill informed, *Altezza Reale*,' Amedeo replied.

'So, it is not true?'

'I think we both agree that one can lie to defend a woman's reputation, or to save life.'

The duke considered this for a moment. 'Just leave this sort of thing to me, my clement Saladino,' he said seriously. 'If word of it got back to Rome, I wouldn't be able to help you.'

Then he smiled, and the two walked over to join the women.

A few weeks later the viceroy and Frusci went on a tour of inspection of the army posts in the province of Amhara. Amba Gheorgis was transformed for the occasion, every part of the fort swept, cleaned or whitewashed. Alfio Beretta, a correspondent with the *Corriere della Sera*, was on hand to witness the duke's visit. In the prose so typical of Italian journalism under Fascism, Beretta described the duke's departure after the inspection:

> 'A superb squadron of light indigenous cavalry led by Lieutenant Guillet carried out perfect manoeuvres, scimitars up high, and as soon as the viceregal car began to move, a whirling and primitive carousel began in which the strength of the race exulted and the warrior instinct freed itself in a strong and cadenzaed cheering.'

Far from being at ease with his men's exultations, Amedeo was sure they were going to ruin a successful afternoon as they charged pell mell after the duke's car, stumbling and falling on the broken ground. His luck held out, however, and none of his brave *ascari* had to be carried back to the fort with a broken head.

TEN

# *Northern Chessboard*

Amedeo had never felt more fulfilled. The last twelve months had flashed by. The year before he had been shivering in the trenches of Teruel, a soldier of the Duce trapped in the most ideologically charged conflict of the day. Now, in the remote seclusion of Amba Gheorgis, he had his own command where he could cast himself in the role of a heroic empire builder. Policing the Semien and dispensing a form of justice, he fully shared the dreams of the young viceroy and knew that his future lay in Africa. Among Italians, the false start under Graziani had been hurriedly forgotten and the Duke of Aosta had instilled a sense of optimism and purpose. Roads were being built, farms and factories for leather-work established. Addis Ababa was beginning to take shape as a capital. Every time Amedeo drove into Gondar to meet Frusci he passed newly planted fields and there would be another family arrived from Italy. Anything seemed possible in this vast territory, whose wealth and fertility had, as yet, barely been touched.

By 1939 the rebel activity was petering out. There were still a few roads where lorries travelled in convoy, but the bulk of the country had submitted to the new rulers. Amedeo wrote long lyrical letters to Bice, describing the magnificent landscape, the soldiers in the fort at Amba Gheorgis and his dealings with the various chieftains in the Semien. He did not minimise the dangers involved but wanted to settle there, in some pretty spot like Gondar or Keren, and for her to join him.

But even in Amba Gheorgis, Amedeo could not entirely overlook the black turn events had taken in Europe. Mussolini had again been the hero of the hour when he defused the Munich crisis in September 1938, persuading the British and French to accept the dismemberment of Czech-Slovakia. But in the months that followed, the storm clouds gathered again. In a last effort to detach Italy from her fatal embrace with Nazi Germany, Neville Chamberlain, the British Prime Minister, and Lord Halifax, Foreign Secretary, visited Rome in January 1939. The two old men, dressed in wing collars and musty morning coats, failed to impress. 'These men are no longer of the same stuff as Francis Drake and those other magnificent adventurers who created their empire,' Mussolini confided to Ciano. 'By now they are the tired sons of a long series of rich generations. And they will lose their empire.'

In Africa, however, relations between the British and Italians could not have been better. Cairo society was impressed by the handsome Duke of Aosta when he passed through on his way back from Rome in spring 1939. The British proconsul, Sir Miles Lampson, who was married to an Italian, found him polite and affable, with 'never a fault in his sense of humour'. Aosta was introducing just the sort of administration of which his British hosts most approved. Apart from sporadic banditry, most of the country was now at peace, and the duke had restored large areas to their former rulers, or had elevated new ones, who in semi-autonomy governed in Italy's interests. There was little grieving among the British in Egypt for the end of Ethiopia's ancient empire; they were frankly relieved that there were no more alarming-looking *ras* turning up in Cairo and Khartoum, nor wearying ceremonies to be endured in Addis Ababa. Indeed, a visit to Italy's imperial capital had become quite fashionable among the British, to the extent that the Colonial Office administrators in Kenya felt put out that their more brilliant colleagues, the Arabists of the Sudanese Civil Service, seemed more popular with the viceroy and his court. On the fate of Europe, the duke was hopeful. 'Thank

God, that idiotic Spanish venture is over,' Lampson reported him as saying. 'I don't see perpetual peace in the offing yet. But don't take too literally all that Mr Brown (i.e. Mussolini) says.' When he flew down to Khartoum the welcome was similarly cordial, and the duke played polo with the governor-general.

The British had very little appetite to go to war against such congenial neighbours. When junior officers came up with a proposal to foment revolt in Ethiopia on behalf of Haile Selassie in the event of a war with Italy, the governor-general in Khartoum was horrified. 'Utterly fantastic!' he wrote disgustedly in the margin, forwarding the idea to the Foreign Office. All along the common frontiers relations between the British and Italians were cordial. Convivial, even. Twice Amedeo crossed the border into the Sudan with other officers to visit Kassala, driving over the flat desert sands until the striking egg-shaped rock formations and palm trees of the oasis appeared on the horizon. The British commissioner was delighted to have a little company, especially since the Italians would bring along chianti and fruit from the cultivated fields of Eritrea. He was a *poveretto*, they decided afterwards, going out of his mind with boredom amid the nomads and mud huts. Invitations to visit the bright lights of Asmara were eagerly sought by the British officials scattered amid the remote villages of the Sudan.

When Britain and France declared war against Germany in September 1939, the vulnerability of the British position in east Africa suddenly became all too clear. There were barely a thousand Anglo–Egyptian Sudanese soldiers between Khartoum and the frontiers of Africa Orientale Italiana, within which, spread thinly throughout the vast territory, was a European army of 92,000, supported by 250,000 indigenous troops. In addition, the Italians had nearly 200 armoured vehicles, 323 aeroplanes and a fleet at Massaua of six light destroyers and eight submarines which, on paper at least, posed a lethal threat to shipping using the Suez Canal. Against this the British and French, who had a force of

5000 at Djibuti, could muster 40,000 native troops and a hundred aircraft across the whole of east Africa. Any action against the Italians, Khartoum complacently informed London, would have to come from the French at Djibuti, as the small Sudanese Defence Force could not be expanded at this stage. 'It is too late,' minuted a depressed Sir Robert Vansittart, the permanent under-secretary at the Foreign Office, 'our favourite and, if I may say so, unfailing failing.'

On both sides of the border, there was a collective sigh of relief when Mussolini announced, and the journalist within him was particularly proud of the phrase, that his policy was one of 'armed neutrality'. For the moment, at any rate, Italy was staying out of the war. No one was more delighted to hear this than the Duke of Aosta. For all the empire's apparent numerical strength, he was well aware how precarious his position was. If Italy joined the war, its African empire would be completely cut off from the motherland and surrounded by enemies. There would be no reinforcements, or additional supplies of petrol, tyres or spare parts for machinery. When the duke went to Rome to urge Mussolini to stay out of the war, it was said the Duce declared Hitler would have to pull him in by his hair, and then pointed to his bald pate.

At Amba Gheorgis, Amedeo followed the events in Europe as best he could, lulled as everyone was by the false hopes of the Phoney War: no one, it seemed, could face going through the blood-letting of the Great War all over again. In early 1940, Amedeo was more disturbed by family news from Italy: his Uncle Amedeo had died suddenly. There was to be a public funeral, attended by representatives of the king and the Duce, and his coffin was to be carried through the streets of Rome on a gun carriage. Amedeo was given permission to attend, and he set out on the two-day journey, flying from Asmara to Khartoum, and then on to Benghazi and Tripoli. When he landed at the Libyan capital he was passed a message from Balbo, saying that he was too late, as the funeral had taken place earlier that day. Instead of pressing on pointlessly,

Amedeo was invited to stay the night at the governor's residence.

Balbo was standing in his office beside a window overlooking the port when Amedeo was admitted. He walked quickly over and embraced his young friend. He was deeply affected by the death of the general, who had been his commanding officer during the Great War. He felt another bond as well. As a very young minister at the beginning of the Fascist regime, Balbo's task had been to turn the *Milizia* of Black Shirts into a regular armed force, and later establish the air force. These were formidable demands for a man still in his twenties, and many in the armed forces felt they should not be entrusted to someone whose military experience had been limited to being a volunteer junior officer. Balbo had turned for help to his much admired former general. Uncle Amedeo's view was that if the *Milizia* was to be set up it should be done so properly, and be subject to full military discipline. They could not just be uniformed layabouts, like the *squadristi* of Fascism's early years. His guidance had been crucial, and Balbo never forgot it.

There were only a few close friends at dinner at the Castello that night; the atmosphere was subdued and a sad contrast to former times. After dinner, when they were alone, the governor was less guarded than ever before in his criticisms of Mussolini. He referred to him as the 'madman in Rome' who supported entering the war with Germany. Many in Italy had made Balbo the focal point for the peace party, and the more level headed of the Fascist *gerarchi* – De Bono and Ciano among them – had backed his efforts to persuade Mussolini to stay out of the war. But they had failed, Balbo told Amedeo. The Duce seemed determined to link Italy's fate to the whims of Germany's mystical lunatic.

Twice before the end, Balbo went to see Mussolini, once accompanied by Badoglio, who warned the Duce of the parlous state of the armed forces. But to no avail. Mussolini was ready for another turn at the roulette wheel, and this time the stakes were going to be everything. Balbo had come a long way in the twenty years since he and Mussolini had marched on Rome. He had abandoned much of his former Fascist ideology, such as it was, as well as his youthful republicanism. A conservative pragmatist, he saw in the monarchy and parliament the only means by which Italy could save itself from the regime he had helped to establish. But like so many others, when war finally came, he saw no honourable alternative than to fight it. At times, his mood descended into gallows humour. Literally. He would die a soldier's death, he told his colleagues in Rome, 'As for the rest of you, there won't be enough lamp-posts in Piazza Venezia to hang you all!'

Paralysis seized the leading figures of the regime. Ciano, who over the years had done nothing to restrain the Duce, baulked at fighting beside Nazi Germany as 'a crime and an idiocy'. He vented his frustration in reckless frivolity, loudly scorning his father-in-law's Nazi friends ('only Goebbels does not have the stupid frankness of his colleagues'). 'Between German hegemony and English hegemony, the latter is better,' Ciano announced, after the two countries were at war. 'It is the hegemony of golf, whisky and comfort.'

Such quips were eagerly reported to Berlin and in March 1940 he visited the king.

'I am in the German black book,' Vittorio Emanuele III announced.

'Yes, Maestà,' Ciano replied. 'In first place. And if you will permit me to be so bold, I figure there immediately after you.'

'I think so too,' the king replied. 'But that honours both of us so far as Italy is concerned.'

The Hungarian ambassador agreed: calling on Italy's foreign minister, he asked whether he played bridge. When Ciano enquired why, the ambassador replied, 'For the day when we will be together in Dachau concentration camp.'

Bice was waiting for Amedeo at the quayside, when he arrived at Lago Patria just outside Naples on the flying boat from Tripoli.

They embraced and as Uncle Rodolfo drove them into the city, they all sat on the wide front seat, the betrothed holding hands. They spent Amedeo's five days of leave together, in Naples and at his parents' house at Capua. Uncle Amedeo had made him his sole heir, so he was now a wealthy man, with ample means to marry. While the rest of the country was wracked with anxiety, waiting for the real fighting between Britain, France and Germany, the young couple planned their future. They would marry that spring, when Amedeo handed over his command at Amba Gheorgis. By that time, the slow-moving bureaucratic machine in Rome should have processed his promotion. Amedeo would return from Africa in a couple of months, and they would emerge from the mediaeval gloom of the cathedral at Naples man and wife, at last.

It was bitterly cold as Amedeo and Bice waited for the flying boat on the lake to be readied for the flight back to Tripoli. Bice had been knitting a scarf for her fiancé, and had hoped to finish it before his leave was over. But it was still only half done. Amedeo told her to put it away. It might bring bad luck, he said, for Penelope had worked at her tapestry for ten years waiting for Ulysses to return from Troy. They embraced, pulling apart only reluctantly, and he walked down the quay to the aircraft.

Amedeo had been back at Amba Gheorgis for a fortnight when he was ordered to report to Frusci. His old benefactor was moving fast, Amedeo thought, for he had told the general that he wanted to return to Italy as soon as possible. Several boxes of his belongings had already been sent up to Asmara. He had not said anything to Khadija yet, but she had caught the evasive look in his eye. Certain little intimacies that she came to take for granted he now avoided, and their relationship had cooled. She had never believed that Amedeo would really leave, and was unsettled by his recent sudden return to his homeland and his future wife.

As he walked into headquarters at Gondar, Amedeo hoped that General Frusci had not had him permanently transferred to Italy.

After his marriage and honeymoon, a few months leave would be agreeable, but perhaps by the end of the summer he wanted to return to Africa with his bride. The general's brusque greeting made it immediately clear that he had more pressing matters on his mind than Amedeo's post-nuptial happiness. As reluctantly as the British, Africa Orientale Italiana had woken up to the possibility that it might soon be at war with its neighbours. Frusci had been promoted to governor of Eritrea and given the command of the *Scacchiere Nord*, the 'northern chessboard', facing the British in the Sudan, the most likely direction of an enemy attack. Passing on the viceroy's direct order, he gave Amedeo the task of raising a large force of native cavalry, one he was to recruit, arm and train as quickly as possible.

The force was to be a special unit, Frusci explained, used for deep reconnaissance. It was to be autonomous, responsible not to divisional headquarters but directly to Frusci himself. Normal bureaucratic restrictions would not apply as the unit had to be set up as quickly as possible. The question of its ultimate command was left open, but nonetheless it was a considerable display of confidence in Amedeo. As well as recruiting the men, Amedeo had carte blanche in selecting the officers, and would be provided with his own depot and quartermaster.

Amedeo left the office in a conflict of emotions. He was proud of the honour done to him, shaken that Frusci was resigned to war and appalled that his marriage plans were indefinitely postponed. The crisis that Balbo had talked about so openly at dinner, to which Aosta often hinted, had finally arrived. The last time he had stayed with Uncle Amedeo – when he had gone to Rome to see De Vecchi – the general had referred to the plans he had had to draw up for the invasion of Jugoslavia. Amedeo had thought of them simply as a theoretical exercise, convinced that sanity would prevail. But he had been wrong. Mussolini – risk-taker and self-dramatist – was no more likely to stay out of a European war than an alcoholic could resist that last little drink. Italy, Amedeo realised, would soon be at war. And if the Patria were to fight, she had to win.

The unit was a *gruppo bande*, a less formal levy than the regular colonial regiments, but an essential component in the forces of Italian East Africa after the conquest of Abyssinia. Although the *bande* wore uniform, their military discipline was loosely applied. Many recruits were mercenaries, serving for a few months. Martinets on the staff disliked these units, one complaining that 'their informality ended in the moral ruin of their officers too'. Yet they had spread Italian authority, in an acceptably diluted form, to the remote fastnesses of the empire, and provided useful employment for what would otherwise be marauding bands of armed men.

Amedeo's *gruppo bande* was to be more formal than most. Its nucleus would be 100 Eritrean NCOs, including those from the garrison at Amba Gheorgis. Half the troops were to be Eritreans, the Prussians of East Africa, as Amedeo always thought of them. The rest would be recruited from the villages of the Amhara province and Tigre. There was no shortage of volunteers, the profession of arms being a dignified occupation. The soldiers looked forward to putting a little money aside and then returning to their villages, rejoining their unit again when funds ran low. The force was to be called Gruppo Bande Amhara a Cavallo (the Amhara Cavalry Group), as it was formed at Gondar, although every ethnic group in the empire was represented, whether Muslims or Copts: Eritreans, Tigreans, Amhara, Yemeni mercenaries and even a number of Arab smugglers from the Sheik Rasciaida tribe on the Sudanese border. Except for the Yemenis, most of whom would be on foot, Amedeo mixed the various peoples together, relying on the Eritreans to provide the core. The individualist Amhara, whose loyalty to the Italian cause might prove more questionable, would need careful handling.

For officers, Amedeo chose half a dozen lieutenants in their early to mid-twenties. His second-in-command was Lieutenant Renato Togni, the son of his commanding officer at the Military

Academy at Modena. Six years younger than Amedeo, he was good looking, popular with women, adored by his men and irreverent to all forms of authority. When the Fascists banned the use of *lei*, the polite form of address – on the grounds that it was not Latin in origin – substituting *voi* instead, Togni decided only to use the previous respectful form to his troops, coupling it with the most delicate use of subjunctive and conditional tenses. Mystified Eritrean *ascari* waiting for orders would be asked whether they would mind standing to attention, be so good as to turn about or be kind enough to quick-march. Soon his NCOs began imitating him and Togni had one of the best-mannered platoons in the army. He hesitated to accept Amedeo's offer, until he was assured that he would have his own men to command, and would not be the unit's administrative adjutant.

On Togni's recommendation, Amedeo recruited Guido Battizzocco, a reserve lieutenant in the Alpini, to command the 200-strong camel corps. The other squadrons were given to Filippo Cara, a former secondary school teacher from Rome, the 'blond commander' Alberto Lucarelli and Ambrogio Mattinó, a dour Sicilian of few words. When news circulated throughout AOI that Amedeo Guillet, the war hero and champion rider, was setting up a new unit, he was deluged with requests and recommendations from officers who wanted to serve. He understood how Major Ajmone Cat had felt when Amedeo had been imposed on him by his uncle five years before.

Carlo Call, the deputy director of Asmara's Istituto Sierovaccinogeno, which had achieved wide fame in Africa in breeding European livestock, became the unit's vet. A huge man from the German-speaking South Tyrol, he was nicknamed Gondrand by the *ascari* after the enormous lorries of the freight company. Finding a suitable doctor, however, proved more difficult. One applicant could not ride, while another was so corpulent that during a march his sweating figure had to be doused with water to prevent his succumbing to sunstroke. Amedeo doubted whether he was up to riding fifty kilometres a day through the Sudanese lowlands at 40° centigrade. He was relieved to be approached by Dr Pietro Bonura, chief surgeon at the hospital in Agordat. As a young man, the doctor had fought as a private soldier in France during the Great War, but his patients in the lowland town did not want him to go to war again. Amedeo had to appeal to Frusci for him to be allowed to join. Another recruit was Angelo Maiorani, a lawyer in Asmara, who had a dubious reputation as a critic of Fascism. A fierce patriot, he wanted to fight, even though he was forty years old and his wife was expecting a second baby. His knowledge of Arabic and Tigrinian, as well as his talents as an amateur topographer, made him a useful recruit, and Amedeo raised him to corporal. Finally, the Gruppo Bande was allocated five Italian farriers, who would keep the unit mobile.

While Togni and the others began drilling the men, Amedeo set off to buy horses in Beghemeder. He bought many at the village of Danghila, south of Lake Tana, where the local commissioner, Signor Cigala, had the reputation of being an eccentric, extravagant character. He invited Amedeo to stay at his comfortable villa, which had a swimming pool. The building and compound were surrounded by barbed wire, as the area was full of *shifta* and rebels. Entering, Amedeo was taken aback to see lying on the dining-room table a fully grown leopard, which was treated as a family pet and allowed to go wherever it liked.

Over the next ten days, Amedeo bought a couple of hundred Dongolai ponies, famed for their stamina and resilience, and had the word passed around outlying villages that he was in the market for more. He then returned to the commissioner's villa, where he came across the leopard in a cage outside the front door. This was just how one shouldn't look after animals, Amedeo thought, letting them roam free one moment and then incarcerating them the next. He opened the cage door and approached the animal, which seemed out of sorts. Although it bristled and growled, it allowed him to give it a few reassuring strokes. A window opened above and a woman screamed: '*Via, comandante*! Run for your life! That's not our leopard!' Amedeo froze, gave it a final, hesitant pat, and edged back out of the cage. The Gruppo Bande had nearly lost its commanding officer before the war had even begun.

However, Amedeo soon had cause to be grateful to the commissioner at Danghila. His growing herd of horses would be tethered at night within a barbed-wire enclosure in circles of twenty, with a few soldiers camped in the middle. One night, while the men were sleeping, hyenas broke in and began attacking the horses. In panic, they broke their ropes and jumped the wire, galloping off into the darkness. It was an embarrassing setback. Such things happened, the commissioner said, advising the lieutenant to offer a reward of ten thalers each for any animals that were returned. Within a few days most of the horses had been found, and he then told Amedeo to account for the others, and the extra expense involved, by writing them off on paper during his return journey to Gondar. Various diseases and injuries should account for a plausible number, the official said, and in that way no questions would be asked. Amedeo was impressed to see a consummate bureaucrat of AOI at work.

Five hundred camels were bought to serve as pack animals from the Beni Amer tribe on the Eritrean–Sudanese lowlands, whose ruler, the Diglal, had long been a friend of the Italians. Centuries before, word of Venice – or Bundukia, 'the place where muskets are made', as the Arabs called the city – had reached even this remote desert and the Diglal wore a hat consciously styled on that of the Doge. As well as the camels, Amedeo came away with 300 recruits.

Within two months after the meeting with Frusci, the Gruppo Bande had 800 horsemen, 400 Yemeni infantrymen and 200 camel corps. A training base was established in the cool highlands above Keren, and a large suburb of camp followers soon grew up. Amedeo had seen little of Khadija since he had thrown himself into the task of setting up the Gruppo Bande, but at Keren their former intimacy resumed. She took charge of the *campo famiglia* just as she had at Amba Gheorgis. Her dream had always been to have a chief, but her Italian *comandante* had proved far more than that. With so many men under his command, and an immense wealth of horses and camels, he was a *ras*.

But Khadija remained a tempestuous spirit. Early one morning, some of the Gruppo Bande's Yemeni troops led their horses down to a stream to drink, where a regular Eritrean battalion was bivouacked. A *shumbashi*, or senior NCO, brusquely told them to clear off, as his colonel was asleep in a tent nearby. When he called them *facchini*, or porters, the Yemenis took offence. Many of their fellow countrymen did, indeed, work on the docks at Massaua. Before long scuffles broke out and the two sides were hurling stones at each other. Furious, Amedeo jumped on an unsaddled horse and rode into the mêlée, using his riding crop freely on both sides. At this moment, the Eritreans' colonel emerged from his tent in his pyjamas. As Amedeo began explaining that it was all the fault of the colonel's men, another shower of stones fell about them. It was Khadija, at the head of the women from the *campo famiglia*.

'What do you think you are doing?' he demanded furiously.

'Should the women stand still when their men are being attacked?' Khadija replied, unperturbed.

'Get the hell out of here!' Amedeo yelled, struggling to compose himself. He turned back to the colonel, who was looking Khadija up and down with a roué's smile. The two officers decided that it would be best to let the matter rest.

To give the unit its own *esprit de corps*, Amedeo allocated a banner to each squadron. At the points of a metal semi-circle were the cross and the crescent of his men's religions, and below it dangled a tail of horse hair tied with a bright ribbon, a different colour for each of the four squadrons. His own banner had five horse hairs, and above them flew the Italian flag with the Cross of Savoy in the centre and the motto which had been Uncle

Amedeo's, *Semper Ulterius* (always onward). To remain clearly visible to their men, and with a perhaps imprudent disdain for enemy fire, all the officers were mounted on greys. When the 800 horsemen moved off, kicking up clouds of dust on the Eritrean lowlands, they resembled a mongol horde rather than a unit in a modern European army.

In the early summer of 1940, General Frusci arrived in an open-topped staff car to inspect the Gruppo Bande Amhara. They rode past in formation and then saluted the general with their heavy chopping scimitars, which Amedeo had specially imported from Italy. The general was impressed. At the end of the review, Frusci drew Amedeo aside and told him that on the Duke of Aosta's insistence he was to remain in command of the Gruppo Bande. When the Viceroy had announced this decision, some on the general staff questioned the wisdom of entrusting a force of nearly 1600 men to such a junior officer who was still, technically, only a lieutenant. The duke had brushed their quibbles aside.

'I know what this man has done in the past, and I know what he is capable of doing in the future,' he said. 'This is not a command to be given to a middle-aged colonel with a paunch.'

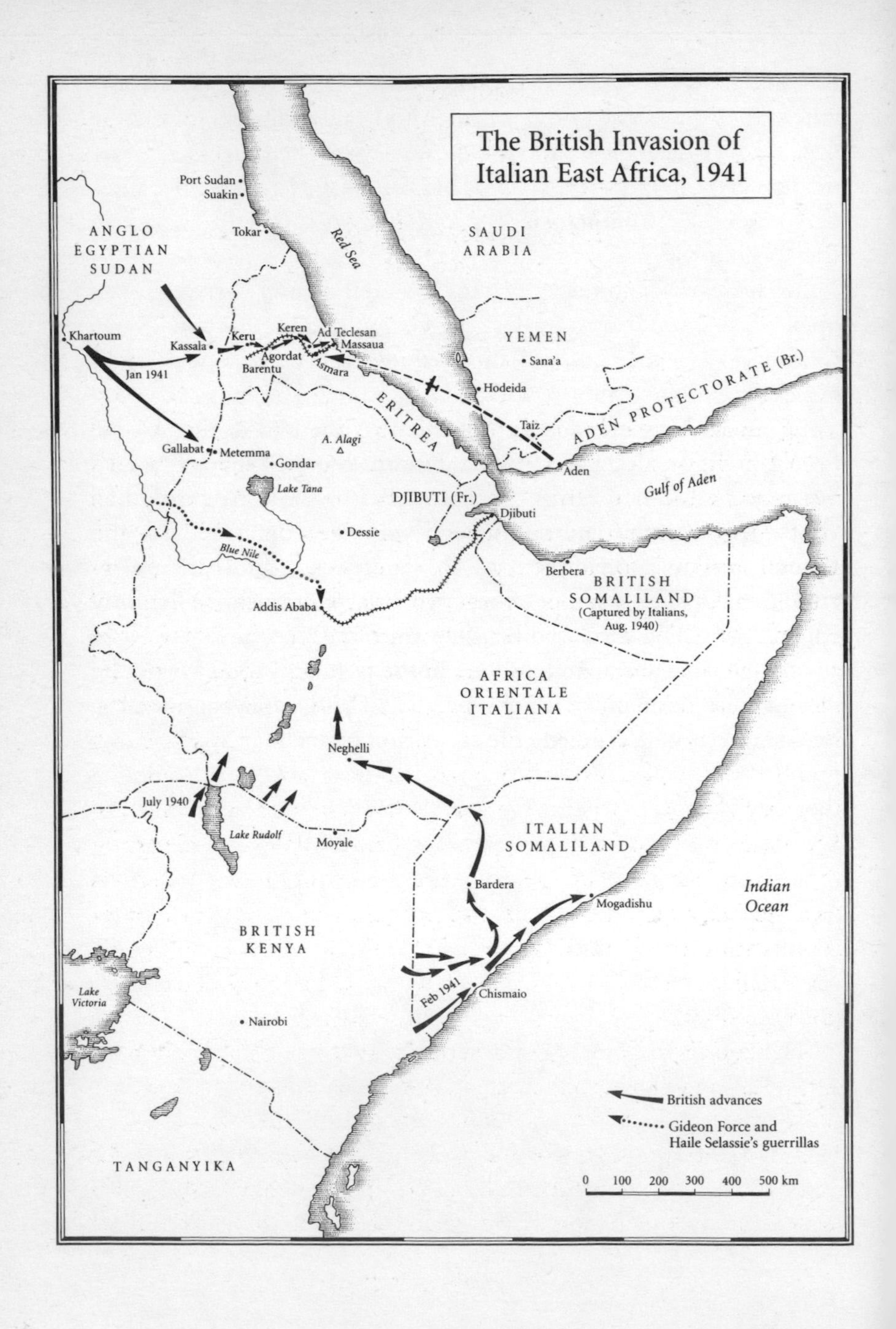

The British Invasion of Italian East Africa, 1941
Port Sudan
Suakin
Tokar
Red Sea
ANGLO EGYPTIAN SUDAN
SAUDI ARABIA
Khartoum
Kassala
Keru
Keren
Ad Teclesan
Massaua
Agordat
Barentu
Asmara
Jan 1941
YEMEN
Sana'a
Hodeida
ADEN PROTECTORATE (Br.)
ERITREA
Taiz
Aden
Gallabat
Metemma
A. Alagi
Gondar
Lake Tana
DJIBUTI (Fr.)
Gulf of Aden
Djibuti
Dessie
Blue Nile
Berbera
BRITISH SOMALILAND
(Captured by Italians, Aug. 1940)
Addis Ababa
AFRICA ORIENTALE ITALIANA
Neghelli
July 1940
Lake Rudolf
Moyale
ITALIAN SOMALILAND
Bardera
Indian Ocean
Mogadishu
BRITISH KENYA
Feb 1941
Chismaio
Lake Victoria
Nairobi
British advances
Gideon Force and Haile Selassie's guerrillas
TANGANYIKA
0 100 200 300 400 500 km

ELEVEN

# *Lightning War*

Amedeo never doubted for a moment that the British would fight on alone. Like everyone else, he had been astonished by the news from Europe. The German Blitzkreig had cut through northern France in May 1940, sending the British and French armies into full retreat. Within weeks, the British were falling back to the Channel ports and France was on the brink of collapse. Amedeo took no pleasure in the fact. To him, it seemed as though a column of Latin civilisation was crumbling to the ground. He never believed the propaganda from Rome that the British defeat would shortly follow. Although their army was being bombed and strafed on the beaches of Dunkirk, and had abandoned their stricken ally to the Germans, Amedeo was sure that the European war was far from over. He had no deep knowledge of the British, nor could he speak their language, but from his earliest days he had marvelled at the vast stretches of pink on the atlas representing the British Empire. In common with many upper-class Italians, including the Duke of Aosta, he overestimated its power and vitality. But the 'tired sons' would fight on.

The defeats in France set the rumours stirring again throughout Africa Orientale Italiana that the Duce was about to declare war. For those officers who had fought with Britain and France in the Great War, it was a depressing possibility. Major Saroldi, a dashing camel corps officer and one of AOI's more flamboyant characters – celebrated for walking down the crowded streets of Asmara followed by his pet lion – expressed the common view when, a week before war was declared, he wrote to a British friend across the border: 'Although things are looking very black, I hope that my country will be spared the shame of fighting alongside those barbarians who I myself fought as a boy of eighteen.'

Even at this late stage, there was still no widespread enthusiasm to go to war on either side. But there were exceptions. Relations between the British at the tiny Sudanese frontier fort at Gallabat and the Italians at Metemma, only separated by a dried river bed, had always been good. Colonel Castagnola, a highly regarded officer from Sicily – or, as one British officer preferred to put it, 'a small, fat, swarthy, but genial individual; very astute and quite a good game shot' – was a frequent and popular guest at Gallabat. With the British now evacuating the beaches of Dunkirk, Castagnola crossed the border to remonstrate about the number of British troops on the frontier. On this occasion, he was greeted by a fierce Wilfred Thesiger, the celebrated desert explorer who had spent his childhood in Addis Ababa and was godson to Haile Selassie. The colonel complained that war between Italy and Britain had not been declared. Bimbashi Thesiger – a lieutenant in the camel corps – brushed the matter aside, and then apologised for not inviting the Italian to dinner. It was on account of 'manoeuvres', he growled.

A week later, on 10 June 1940, Amedeo had just finished lunch at a small fortified post on the Gondar road when there was a sudden shout for silence and everyone edged closer to the radio. Over the whistles and crackles came Mussolini's distinctive voice addressing the crowd from the balcony of the Palazzo Venezia: 'An hour marked by destiny now rises in the heavens above our country . . . The hour of irrevocable decisions.' Italy was at war with Britian and France. After hearing the broadcast in Addis Ababa, the Duke of Aosta turned to General Nasi: 'For six months we will be able to thrash them. But after that, God help us.'

Amedeo made his way to Keren as quickly as he could, where

the mood of Togni and the other officers was sombre. Such restraint was a feeling common to both sides, although the British partisans of the exiled Haile Selassie appeared delighted that their imperilled country had acquired another foe. 'On hearing it, the exuberance of Wilf Thesiger expressed itself in a savage war dance,' wrote the diarist of the Eastern Arab Corps. 'At last,' declared Sylvia Pankhurst, 'the long agonising vigil is over.'

Later that evening, two British police officers at Moyale, on the Kenyan frontier, who unfortunately had not caught the BBC evening news, strolled over the border to have a drink with the Italian *residente*. This time, instead of a glass or two of chianti on the veranda, they were arrested and led away by an armed guard. They were the first British prisoners in the war against the Italians.

In Asmara, the Italian population was convinced Mussolini would bring off another dramatic victory. Loudspeakers were erected in the piazzas so that the latest victory bulletins could be broadcast directly to the populace. Greeks, Indians and Jews were rounded up and interned in the Adekamre camp, where they had to spend the night (although during daytime they could continue their normal affairs). And schoolboys arrived for their lessons singing:

> *Se non andremo a piedi, andremo in ferrovia*
> *Vogliamo Nizza e Corsica, Savoia e Tunisia!*
> (If we don't go by foot, we'll go by train,
> but we want Nice and Corsica, Savoy and Tunisia!)

But the day after war was declared, the RAF from Aden put a dampener on the rejoicing by bombing Asmara's airport.

The surrender of France a week after Mussolini's declaration of war revealed an unpalatable truth to the British. Their security on land in the Middle East and East Africa depended in large measure on the considerable French forces in Tunisia and Djibuti. With

France out of the war, and Britain fighting for its survival in the skies above southern England, the position in Egypt, and the Suez Canal, looked desperately vulnerable. A large Italian army was being concentrated on Libya's eastern border, while far to the south the small Sudan Defence Force faced the might of Africa Orientale Italiana. Douglas Newbold, a senior civil servant in Khartoum, wrote in despair: 'Those who don't know the facts say they are only Dagos and a few hearty Sudanese with spears can see them off . . . [but] Kassala is theirs for the asking. Port Sudan probably, Khartoum perhaps. Bang goes forty years of patient work and we abandon the trusting Sudanese to a totalitarian conqueror.'

For four days ominous quiet settled along the frontier. At Gallabat and Metemma each side awoke every morning to see villagers driving their cattle down to the water to drink. Finally, at dusk on 14 June, one British soldier could bear it no longer and loosed off a round. Others followed his example, firing a furious fusilade. When this ceased, there was stunned silence from the Italians for ten minutes. Then they too began shooting back, keeping up continuous fire for two hours. The only casualty of the noisy exchange was a Greek civilian in Metemma. But the war had now begun in earnest.

A fortnight after these first shots, Amedeo rode into the encampment where Togni was waiting, looking unusually subdued. He had just heard on the radio that Italo Balbo had been shot down over Tobruk, in Libya. Although he had been killed by friendly fire, the following day an RAF plane dropped a wreath into the water to honour the man who had flown across the Atlantic. His death was more than a tragedy for his family and friends – Italy had lost its strongest independent political figure. The Duce, who perplexed Italians at the time by making no public expression of sorrow, acknowledged this fact much later in a laconic tribute. Balbo, he said, was 'a fine Alpino, a great aviator, a true revolutionary – and the only one who would have been capable of killing me'.

Ironically, in an outburst of genuine grief, it was Ciano, far

LA DOMENICA DEL CORRIERE

Si pubblica a Milano ogni settimana

Supplemento illustrato del "Corriere della Sera"

Uffici del giornale: Via Solferino, 28 - Milano

Anno XXXVIII — N. 13

29 Marzo 1936 - Anno XIV

Centesimi 30 la copia

*Right* Amedeo's pursuit of the Ethiopian stragglers responsible for the Gonrand massacre, which outraged Italian public opinion, is given cover story treatment. Far from being 'exemplarily punished', as readers were assured, the rebels escaped when reinforcements forced the Spahys to withdraw.

Amedeo on Sandor, photographed immediately after the charge at Selaclaclà on 25 December 1935. The wound to his left hand was the most painful of all that he suffered in war.

After the disastrous pitched battle of Mai Ceu, a defeated Haile Selassie abandons the front with his escort. He spent three days in prayer at the rock churches of Lalibela.

The Spahys di Libya stage a dramatic re-enactment at the celebration in Rome on the first anniversary of the founding of Italy's African empire, June 1937.

*Above left* Antonio Ajmone Cat.

*Above* The tall figure of the Duke of Aosta (left) dwarfs the king, Vittorio Emmanuele III. The appointment of the comparitively unknown duke as viceroy of Italian East Africa in 1937 surprised many leading figures of the regime.

*Left* Princess Jolanda, the eldest of the royal children, was a close friend of Amedeo (right) as well as his equal as a rider. By 1937, when this picture was taken, she too was settled in Italo Balbo's Libya.

THE SWORD OF ISLAM,
MARCH 1937

*Above* Mussolini rides into the film-set capital of Tripoli before the Sword of Islam ceremony. Amedeo, who bought and trained all the horses, is on the grey in the background.

*Left* Mussolini (centre), Balbo (left) and other Fascist dignitaries salute the Italian *tricolore*.

*Below* Libyan crowds line the streets to greet the visiting Duce, accompanied by Italo Balbo, the governor.

Flanked by a Libyan escort bearing the Roman *fasces*, from which the Fascist Party drew its name, Mussolini adopts a final pose on the horse Amedeo bought for him in Germany. Italo Balbo, on the grey, ensures he is not out of the frame.

*Right* The Duce raises aloft the Sword of Islam and proclaims himself defender of the world's Muslims. The sword was made in Florence.

*Below* Italo Balbo presenting the Bronze Medal to Amedeo.

Amedeo (right), amid a squadron of the two-man Fiat Ansaldo tanks – the 'sardine tins' – of which he had such a poor opinion, outside Santander in 1937.

The general's adjutant visits the Italian front line during the bitter fighting on the Ebro.

*Left* General Luigi Frusci, Amedeo's benefactor, wearing the curious uniform of the 'Black Flames' division. Italian involvement in the war was ostensibly clandestine.

*Below* One of the Russian armoured cars captured from the Spanish republican forces by Amedeo and his *arditi* volunteers outside Santander, August 1937.

Hardly the stage-management of Nuremberg . . . During his visit to Rome in May 1938, Hitler has to stand beside the king, while Mussolini looms awkwardly in the background. White-bearded Marshal De Bono is behind Queen Elena, while a miserable Ciano is surrounded by Hess, Ribbentrop and Goebbels, all of whom he disdained. Fascist women complete the scene, swathed in stoles. But Italy's pretensions as a great power are revealed *below* in a picture of 1937 chosen at random. Barefoot, malnourished children, their heads shaven against lice, turn out for a civic ceremony in the southern city of Salerno. 'You have enough to colonise in Calabria and Basilicata,' Mussolini was told by his Jewish mistress, Margherita Sarfatti before he embarked on his adventures in Ethiopia in 1935.

from being a friend, who scribbled in his diary the epitaph that Balbo himself might have agreed with:

> He had more dash than talent, more vivacity than acumen. He was a decent fellow, and even in political clashes, in which his temperament delighted, he never descended to dishonourable and questionable expedients. Balbo's memory will linger long among Italians because he was, above all, a true Italian, with all the great faults and great virtues of our race.

When the Duke of Aosta heard the news he had difficulty composing himself. Mourning the loss of a close friend, he was outraged that Fascist propaganda tried to pretend that the British had killed Balbo. 'It's enough to make one die of shame having to listen to such balls,' he wrote to his wife. 'Sadly, we are still such buffoons and mountebanks . . .'

In July, the *guerra lampo* – the lightning war that Mussolini had talked about for years – finally began. After much dithering, Africa Orientale Italiana attacked. The fort of Gallabat on the Sudanese frontier was captured and Frusci sent 12,000 men to seize Kassala, held by 600 Sudanese troops. He felt no enthusiasm in doing so. Kassala's strategic value was negligible. When Frusci had questioned the wisdom of this course, Mussolini personally urged him on with exhortations recalling an Italian colonial hero who had been killed at Kassala fighting the Mahdi sixty years before: 'The shade of Carchidio Malavolti is awaiting you,' the Duce radioed portentiously. The general shrugged his shoulders and obeyed.

When Amedeo called in at headquarters, the general told him flatly: 'We have just pointlessly extended our front on the lowlands by another 200 kilometres.'

Nonetheless, these Italian victories provoked deep anxiety in Cairo and London. With Marshal Graziani back in command in Libya after Balbo's death, the British nightmare was a co-ordinated attack on Egypt from both the western desert and the Sudan. The 'wasp waist of the British empire' at Suez would be pinched. 'If you lose Khartoum,' Churchill told Anthony Eden, now the War Minister, 'your name will live in history.'

Just as the Italians greatly overestimated British strength, so London misread their aggressive intentions. None of the Italian generals, from the Duke of Aosta downwards, had any confidence in an all-out offensive. Leaving aside the delicate issue of the calibre of the troops, the empire was entirely cut off, and its supplies of fuel, tyres and ammunition could not be renewed. Even if the Italian army managed to reach Khartoum, it would never be able to march on to Cairo, more than 2000 kilometres across the desert to the north.

On the prompting of Rome, and despite the scepticism of Aosta and his generals, the Italians, under the command of General Nasi, invaded British Somaliland in August. Greatly outnumbered, the British decided to evacuate after a brief resistance in which they suffered 260 casualties. It was not a bloody defeat, but the Italians were jubilant. They had overrun a part of the British Empire, perhaps not quite its jewel, but in a clear victory nonetheless. For the British public, led to believe that their soldiers would be easily able to see off the Italians, it was a galling blow. Amedeo, like most senior Italian officers, was unimpressed by the conquest of this barren land, which had cost a third of AOI's fuel and a high quantity of tyres. There seemed little point in the lightly armed Italian troops acquiring any more deserts, or digging in on the lowlands where the superior British equipment, particularly armour, would win the day. He was convinced that the fate of AOI would be settled in the highlands of Ethiopia and Eritrea, and that it was there where the army should concentrate its energies. But his younger subordinates were delighted by the campaign's turn of events and seemed to believe that they would be in Khartoum before the month was out. Amedeo poured out his frustration and anxiety in a letter to his father, who quickly discouraged him, for in Italy such talk was becoming dangerous. 'Unfortunately, what I most feared has happened, but I ask you not to speak to me of these things. Do your duty as a good officer as you always have done.' Whatever reservations Amedeo felt about the war, he kept his thoughts to himself.

Churchill took the loss of British Somaliland badly, and began heaping scorn on Sir Archibald Wavell, the Commander-in-Chief of the Middle East. In September, the luckless Wykehamist and scholar – neither point a great recommendation to the Prime Minister – had no sooner reassured London that there was no immediate threat to Egypt from the south, than Graziani crossed the Egyptian frontier in the northwest. There was another moment of panic, until the Italians unaccountably stopped at Sidi Barrani, and dug in.

London's patience was exhausted, and its wrath descended on Khartoum. Eden himself arrived by aeroplane, with Wavell, to assess the situation. When General Sir William Platt, the Kaid (commander) of the Sudan Defence Force – for the British were as fond of exotic Egyptian titles as the Black Shirts were of ancient Roman ones – announced that he was confident he could stop any further Italian advances, the mood turned ugly. The War Minister had arrived to hear plans for attack, not further preparations for defence. There were now 28,000 troops in the Sudan and some tanks. Then there was the question of Emperor Haile Selassie. Since his arrival in Khartoum on the outbreak of war, the Negus had been snubbed by British officials, who had very nearly put him back on an aeroplane to London. He would set the natives off, stir up a hornet's nest and provoke the Italians, the colonial officials complained. As patiently as he could, Eden reminded the meeting that that was the whole point. Platt, a good but conventional soldier, was admonished, the governor-general sacked and, in early November, Major Orde Wingate arrived with a million pounds in gold and orders to foment a full-scale guerrilla war in Ethiopia.

It was not quite the fresh start the British had hoped for, however. Surprisingly, given his future brilliant career in Burma, Brigadier William Slim's attack, the first of the campaign, proved an utter disaster. At Gallabat the Italians had taken up excellent defensive positions. When troops from the Essex regiment attacked at night, the Italians waited until they were within twenty metres before opening fire. They were then lightly shelled. Panic set in when the attackers mistook smoke for gas. The men of Essex turned tail and fled.

Events finally swung towards the British on 9 December 1940. Wavell, at last adequately supplied with armour, attacked Graziani's fortifications at Sidi Barrani, which were laid out as though for a nineteenth-century colonial war. The British swept over the Italian positions, capturing 38,300 prisoners, 237 guns and 73 tanks for the loss of 624 men. In Rome, it was a devastating awakening. 'News of the attack on Sidi Barrani came like a thunderbolt,' wrote Ciano in his diary; the pretensions of Fascist Italy to be a great power were revealed as empty posturing. Mussolini held his bald head in his hands and lamented: 'It's the material that is lacking. Even Michelangelo needed marble to make his statues. If he had only clay he would merely have been a potter.'

After long months of failure and defeat, the British had won their first great victory of the war. But instead of finishing off the Italians in north Africa – a decision they would later come to regret – Wavell, with the ill-fortune that dogged his wartime career, was ordered to send the excellent IVth Indian Division down to the Sudan to join the Vth.

Africa Orientale Italiana braced itself for attack.

## TWELVE

# *The Man on the White Horse*

21 JANUARY 1941

It was evening when Amedeo and the Gruppo Bande returned to their camp at the wooded oasis of Awashait on the Eritrean lowlands. They had been reconnoitring deep into the Sudan for four days. The men were tired and fed up after yet another futile mission. It was the third time they had penetrated enemy territory, always heading northeast towards the Red Sea, where they expected the British to arrive. But they had seen nothing, apart from enemy fighters flying over to strafe and bomb Kassala and other positions on the frontier, while aircraft of the Regia Aeronautica, with the distinctive Cross of Savoy on their tail fins, flew in the opposite direction, towards Khartoum. But on the ground, there was nothing. They were surrounded in every direction by hundreds of kilometres of empty sand and scrub.

It occurred to Amedeo that he could probably capture the little ports of Suakin and Tokar. But he doubted whether the Gruppo Bande would be able to hold them for long. Somewhere out there in the Sudanese desert the British were mustering, and with their fast trucks and armoured cars they would be able to race across the barren landscape, striking at will at the exposed Italian positions. Not for the first time he was pleased to have recruited the smugglers from the Sheik Rasciaida. No one knew the desert as they did. Where to Amedeo it simply appeared to be unvarying and flat, they could find deep wadis and cover which could shelter the horsemen by day. With so many enemy aircraft in the sky, the unit travelled in strength only at night.

He was pleased with his men. Over the past nine months they had become a highly disciplined body, who depended on each other and carried out orders exactly as required. Above all, morale was high and there was a strong determination to get to grips with the enemy. It was sometime during the winter of 1940/41 that a journalist from the magazine *Azione Coloniale* came to visit the Gruppo Bande. Struck by Amedeo's theatrical nickname, *comundar-as-shaitan*, the 'devil commander', and warming to this theme, he described the young officer as 'a desert corsair, thin, sunburned and with a face which seemed to have taken on the enigmatic, and slightly absorbed expression of the Arabs, with whom he had lived for a long time and whose languages and dialects he knew'. An ox hide was stretched over the floor of his tent, and a rolled up mat and burnous served as a bed. Beside them were an earthenware oil lamp and the Vatican edition in Latin of Tacitus's *Germania*. The officer's rifle and scimitar, stacked in a corner, completed the furnishings.

There were other diversions among the Gruppo Bande's officers apart from reading Latin, which perhaps failed to strike the appropriate note with the correspondent of *Azione Coloniale*. In the evening, Togni would pluck away at his guitar and the others would sing ribald or irreverent songs they had made up. With Amedeo weighed down by the burden of command, Togni was the cavalrymen's most extrovert spirit. The two friends would often have long conversations under the stars, where the younger man would unburden himself of his complicated personal life: the young Italian widow in Asmara, as well as obligations to his native mistress, who was at the *campo famiglia* at Keren.

Amedeo eased himself out of the saddle, relieved to be back at base after four days. A groom ran up to lead the horse away, but the *comandante* insisted on checking his mount over for sores. For at last he was reunited with Sandor. Ever since his return to Africa, Amedeo had been keen to buy back the Barbary Arab he had so painstakingly schooled. But he had always been turned down by his new owner, Lieutenant Marchese Francesco Santasilia. When the Italians seized Kassala in the first weeks of the war, Santasilia had been one of the casualties, and his commanding officer, knowing of Amedeo's attachment to Sandor, had offered him the horse. Amedeo had been happy to accept; there were very few horses of the quality of Sandor in the whole of Africa Orientale Italiana.

As the animal was led away, an orderly approached to say that General Ugo Fongoli needed to see the *comandante* immediately at the fort of Keru, three kilometres away. Amedeo groaned inwardly. He had nothing to report – again – but he set out immediately on a camel with an escort of two men.

On arrival, Amedeo was met by an excited officer urging him to hurry to the general, who was waiting for him in his office. Amedeo entered the little room and began his report, but was interrupted. Everything had changed, the general explained. Amedeo had not come across the British because they had headed straight for Kassala, further south. Italian aerial reconnaissance had seen them on the move, and the oasis had been quickly abandoned. The enemy were advancing fast with motorised infantry and armour, and their vanguard included the formidable Mathilda 'I' tanks, which no Italian armoured vehicle could match. Pointing with his amber cigarette holder, Fongoli indicated that 10,000 Italian troops, who had been on the frontier, were now falling back towards Keru. They would then be sent further back still to Agordat, where a new front would form. The speed of the British advance, after months of inactivity, had taken everyone by surprise and these troops, precariously strung out along the road, were sitting ducks. There could not be another Sidi Barrani, the general said. What he needed was time: to get the troops from the frontier on the way to Agordat and then to abandon the fort and get his own men underway. It was vital that the enemy did not learn how desperately exposed the Italian position had become. Having no tanks, no armour of any kind, the only mobile troops Fongoli had at his disposal were the Gruppo Bande Amhara a Cavallo.

'Guillet, do you think you would be able to hold them back for a day?' the general asked hesitantly.

Amedeo paused. He thought of his weary men and their horses. What could he possibly do against the British with only 1500 lightly armed men? He could sense that the general hated asking him to stage this diversion, which could easily end in his death and the decimation of his horsemen in their first action. But Fongoli's rationale was right. Thousands of Italian infantrymen were marching through the night over the exposed lowlands, knowing that the next day the enemy could fall upon them.

'I'll do whatever is necessary, general,' Amedeo replied.

Without saying a word, Fongoli stretched over and took his hand. When he released it, the general unconsciously made a little gesture that seemed to Amedeo like a form of benediction.

All his officers had turned in by the time he rode back into the camp at Awashait. He had them woken up and they assembled quickly in his tent. The British, he explained, were somewhere on the plain before Keru. In three hours' time, and before sunrise, the entire Gruppo Bande, accompanied by the 400 Yemeni infantry and the 200 camel corps, would attack them. Every effort was to be made to make the unit appear to be the advance guard of a far larger force, threatening the British flank and supply lines back to the Sudan. All the men were to carry two days' rations and a good quantity of ammunition.

'How exactly are we going to do it?' asked Togni laconically, his voice hoarse with an incipient cold. They would have to exploit the opportunities as they presented themselves, Amedeo replied. It was an answer that discouraged any further discussion. As Togni and the others rose to leave, Amedeo picked up his poncho, a souvenir from Spain, which his orderly had laid out on his bed.

He gave it to his friend, saying that he could not afford to have his second-in-command falling sick.

Alone in his tent, Amedeo spread out a map of the lowlands and pondered Togni's question. Nothing mattered except the battle the next day, and he forced down thoughts of Bice, his mother and father, and the risks involved. These he knew were far higher than any he had faced before. The image of the Cossacks harrying the Grande Armée flashed through his mind, though his enemy were advancing not trudging home through the snow. In his own fashion, he had to make the same brutal calculations as had Fongoli, but with single soldiers or platoons, not entire regiments. It was inescapable logic that the sacrifice of his unit was a price worth paying to save 10,000 infantrymen. He could only hope he did not lose too many men.

Call, the veterinary surgeon, had come back into the tent quietly, carrying a mess tin filled with cold *polenta*. He left it on the side of the table as Amedeo stared fixedly at the maps. Then, seeing that the *comandante* was not eating, Call gently spooned the *polenta* into his mouth as though feeding an infant. Amedeo was lost in thought. But he did not really need the maps. His men had ridden over the plain of Aicota many times before. He offered thanks under his breath in both Arabic and Latin that he was not facing the enemy in the Sudan, where the desert proper began. On the Eritrean lowlands there were rocky hills and patches of woodland, and of course, there were deep wadis criss-crossing the map. These had possibilities. Some were wide and several metres deep, and all would be dry in January. At last, he stretched himself out on his bed and tried to sleep. Call blew out the lamp and silently left.

Corporal Mohinder Singh of the 4th battalion of the 11th Sikhs also slept badly that night. It wasn't that he didn't feel tired. Ever since his captain had been seconded to Gazelle Force, the mobilised

British vanguard, they had hardly stopped moving. For four days they had been pushing forward at breakneck speed, first attempting to surprise the Italians with a strike at Kassala, and then to catch them on the road, when they had disappointingly fallen back. In the deserts of Libya, where he had been fighting the month before, and in the Sudan, Mohinder had always been able to sleep well, wrapped in his groundsheet on the sand. But Eritrea was different. His officers had said the climate would be just like the Punjab's, but out of the sunlight, in the shadows of the hills, and at night, it could be bitterly cold with a heavy dew in the morning. And this was only going to get worse. Ever since they had crossed the frontier the land had risen and before them were the mountain ranges of the Keren massif. In the misty half-light, the Sikh began preparing for the ritual ablutions that marked the start of his day. Mohinder undid his hair, letting it fall loosely down his back, and plunged his face into a basin of freezing water. When he emerged, much of his listlessness was gone. The water was cold, but at least there was plenty of it. In the Libyan desert he had had to resort to the uncomfortable necessity of cleansing himself with petrol.

As he tied back his beard and began binding his turban, Mohinder counted himself lucky yet again to be with Gazelle Force, which was named after the troops' main source of fresh meat. Most of the officers were familiar – even celebrated – names from the best of the Indian army. The Sudan Defence Force had pitched in a handful of armoured cars, and there were some British gunners of the 25th Field Regiment and the Surrey and Sussex Yeomanry. All felt reassured by their outstanding commanding officer, Colonel Frank Messervy, a tough, wiry cavalryman from the elite regiment, Hodson's Horse. Now the knife blade was prodding the Italians in the back, he was determined to keep it there, hoping to turn their well-organised retreats into a rout. Messervy would roar past the column in his heavy open-topped Chevrolet, equipped with a machine gun, its bonnet decorated with a pair of gazelle's antlers, urging his men forward, 'Bum on you lot! Bum on!'

War widened a soldier's prospects and Mohinder hoped that if he did his duty well he would return a sergeant, wealthy and respected, as his grandfather had. For Ethiopia had made his fortune, when in 1867 he had been part of General Napier's expeditionary force to punish Emperor Theodore for imprisoning the British consul and assorted missionaries. Mohinder's family still cherished the medal his grandfather had won at the battle of Magdala. Like everyone else in the invading force, the Sikh did not expect the fighting to be fierce. He shared the general low opinion of the Italian army, having driven his captain past the long columns of prisoners, rounded up after the fiasco of Sidi Barrani. Their withdrawal from Kassala without a shot fired seem to confirm that the enemy had no stomach for a fight.

Mohinder set about making tea for his captain, who was sitting huddled in his greatcoat studying a sketched map showing the heavily defended Italian position at Keru. Most of the Sikhs in Gazelle Force had been moved forward that night, ready to attack. As soon as the sun rose, the British artillery would begin their pounding. Mohinder poured the tea and opened a can of condensed milk. The camp around them slowly came to life. Although there was a heavy mist, it was getting lighter. He could hear sounds of stirring from a company of Rajputana Rifles behind them and the armoured cars of Skinner's Horse.

Less explicable was the drumming noise coming from in front of him, which was followed by large dark shapes pushing through the sparse trees. Only when they were out of the brush did their pace quicken and Mohinder comprehend with horror what he was seeing. Barely a hundred yards away and galloping straight towards him was a spectacle of war he imagined was long obsolete. Still holding his captain's tea and the tin of milk, Mohinder stood rooted to the spot. Gazelle Force, with its armoured cars and machine guns, was being charged – literally charged – by men on horses. As they came on, they were shouting bloodcurdling cries, some firing carbines, others waving scimitars. Mohinder dropped the tea and ran back to his rifle propped against the lorry, while the captain jumped out of his seat, scattering the maps. Both grabbed at the rifle which the officer wrenched from Mohinder's fumbling fingers. The horsemen were among them now, slashing at running men and hurling their red grenades – 'like cricket balls' said one British officer – into the lorries and milling men.

On every side there were clouds of dust and to the sound of gunfire and explosions were added the cries of wounded men and screaming horses. And then, as quickly as they had appeared, the horsemen were gone, skirting in front of the Skinners, and galloping straight towards the gun batteries pointing towards Keru. Major Ian Hossack, second-in-command of the Skinners, grabbed a rifle and shot at a 'young fair-haired officer on a grey horse' – Lucarelli – who had come at him with his sword at the engage. But the Italian dived forwards out of the saddle behind his horse's neck – which took the bullet – and hung on grimly until the charge came to a halt. Another rider of a grey horse, an Eritrean NCO called Araya Zeben, was not so lucky, leading to competing – and inaccurate – claims among those who believed they had shot the leader of the charge. Still at a gallop, 'the riders continued with great gallantry on to the gunlines of two troops of 390 Battery of the Surrey and Sussex Yeomanry', according to the regimental account, as well as towards the Gazelle Force HQ itself.

Messervy, well forward of his troops, was with a few other officers engrossed with the problem of attacking Keru, when an armoured car of Skinner's Horse burst on to the scene. 'Look out! They're on us!' shouted a young officer. First they heard the gunfire and grenades behind them and then, thundering through the stunted trees, the enemy could be seen.

Frantic cries of 'Tank alert! Tank alert!' roused the gunners, who flung themselves on to their 25-pounders, and began turning them 180 degrees, away from the fort of Keru and towards the charging enemy. 'Troop, gunfire! Troop, gunfire!' shouted an officer at the top of his voice; while clerks, orderlies and signallers of the Brigade HQ dived behind boulders and fired at the horsemen with pistols and rifles. With astonishing parsimony, only one rifle had been allocated for each artillery truck. Gunners grabbed everything available to fire at the horsemen, which included an ancient Lewes gun, flares and a Boyes anti-tank rifle. All of a sudden there was an ear-splitting boom, as the first of the 25-pounders opened up at a target barely two hundred yards away. The line of the horses rippled, but then came galloping on. All the guns began firing – some straight through the batteries in front of them – creating a furious noise and covering the plain in smoke. Armour-piercing shells were fired over open sights into the mass in front. No one had imagined the Italians would be mad enough to come at them on horses. Shots scudded over the ground at a height of two to three feet, cutting a swathe through the legs of horses without exploding. To Amedeo's side, one was hit in the chest by a shell that had bounced off the ground; its quartered body was tossed like a child's toy high into the air, while the rider was nowhere to be seen.

The commander of the Gruppo Bande had no idea of the extent of the mayhem he was causing. Skinner's Horse had been responsible for providing a protective screen in front of the artillery and Gazelle Force HQ. But Risalder-major Nur Mohammed 'lost his head', and fled back to the guns thinking that the horsemen were only a diversion for a bigger assault by proper troops. (It was conduct that had him sent back to India.) Meanwhile, the furious cannonade of the artillery men was passing through the enemy horsemen and falling on to their own lines to the rear.

Sheltering in a shallow trench 600 yards away, Captain Douglas Gray, of Skinner's Horse – the regiment's champion pig-sticker who had also ridden in the 1938 Grand National – at first thought that he was on the receiving end of an Italian barrage. One shell landed right in front of him. Had it been filled with high explosive rather than an armour-piercing round, he would certainly have been killed.

Also keeping his head down was Captain Philip Tower, of the 25th Field Regiment RA, who threw himself into a dip in the ground, and stayed there – less worried by the horsemen than by the shells fired by his own gunners that were whizzing over his head. 'I fancy they did not do much damage to the enemy,' he wrote later, 'but it was a splendid noise and very frightening for a short time.'

Struggling to stay on his horse – for even Sandor was unsettled by a 25-pounder firing at fifty yards away – Amedeo wheeled off to the left, digging in his spurs until he reached the safety of the dry river bed of the Washamoia. The whole charge had lasted only a few minutes. But it was an experience that would live in the memories of Mohinder Singh and the others who witnessed it for the rest of their lives.

Amedeo's squadron and Togni's regrouped first in the wadi. Adrenaline was surging through their veins and their horses were covered in sweat. They grinned at each other, amazed that their daring had paid off so handsomely – and relieved that neither was among the dead. Amedeo told his friend to get the Yemeni infantry into position and start firing, and then defend the Gruppo Bande's right with his squadron. After Togni had galloped off, he saw to the rear that Battizzocco, in full view of Gazelle Force, was manoeuvring the camels on a hillside. The sound of more shots and grenades accompanied the arrival of the squadrons of Cara and Lucarelli – the latter sliding down the bank of the wadi still clinging desperately to his horse, whose neck was streaked with blood.

'Find something else. That one's finished,' shouted Amedeo, who had dismounted and was scanning the plain from the brink of the wadi to see how the British were reacting to the interruption of their breakfast.

Gazelle Force broke off from their preparations to attack Keru, turning its attention to the new threat, while three Mathilda 'I' tanks were sent forward from the main battle group. Togni was first to notice the new danger. The tanks were working their way round far to the right of the Gruppo Bande, who were now two or three kilometres away from their first charge. Once they realised how flimsy the Italian forces ranged against them were, the rest of the faster British armoured cars would follow. The tanks had to be stopped, or at least delayed. Togni ordered the bulk of his men and the Yemenis on foot to fall back and rejoin the *comandante*. He then scribbled a note on his cavalry pad, which he gave to Dr Call. He would charge with only thirty of 'my marshals', he informed Amedeo, and try to hold up the Mathildas, giving time for the Gruppo Bande to pull back and reform. He did not add that he would lead the charge himself, as none of his men would be coming back.

Still wearing his friend's Spanish poncho, Togni waited until the tanks approached a wadi. As soon as they tipped over the edge, their guns pointing at the ground, he charged. Through binoculars British officers saw the astonishing sight of horsemen attacking these vast mastodons. The riders were hurling grenades onto the armour, making a fearsome noise and disorienting the crews, but doing no damage. As soon as the tanks were clear of the wadi, they swivelled their machine guns round to deadly effect, bringing down horses and riders in ghastly heaps. Of the thirty-one who charged, only two made it back to Italian lines. Togni himself was shot as he galloped high above a tank along the bank of the wadi. Another burst of fire brought down his horse, which crumpled with its dead rider, rolling off the bank to land on the roof of a Mathilda.

Amedeo was still scouring the plain with his binoculars when Dr Call galloped up. In his heavily accented Italian, the Tyrollean explained what Togni was trying to do. As Amedeo read his note, they heard the sound of exploding grenades, machine-gun fire and, finally, silence. Dr Call bowed his head and shut his eyes. The other officers, suddenly sombre, looked at the ground.

'Well, no one was ever born in battle,' Amedeo told them bluntly.

He ordered Dr Call to gather up the wounded and set off for Agordat immediately. Then he turned to the others, telling them to fall back along the network of wadis, well away from the tanks. He was grateful to his friend. Again a cavalry action had succeeded in confusing the British and Togni's sacrifice had saved the Gruppo Bande from being outflanked.

The British halted and pondered their options, not wishing to stray too far beyond their guns. It was midday, hours after the first charges, when infantrymen and light armoured cars were cautiously sent forward in a badly strung-out frontline six to seven hundred metres across the plain. Armoured cars of Skinner's Horse were on the right, in the middle were the infantry of the 4/11th Sikhs and on the left were other armoured vehicles, of the Sudanese Defence Force. As he watched them come on, Amedeo noticed a rare opportunity presenting itself. If he charged straight through the infantry, the armoured cars on either side would be able to do very little without firing on their own men. Nor would they be able to give chase at any speed, thanks to the wadis breaking up the land. He felt very calm, as he ordered the squadrons to get ready, and then spurred Sandor up and out of the wadi, where all could see him. Behind him came an *ascaro* carrying his horsehair banner with the tricolour and Cross of Savoy. Amedeo raised himself in his stirrups and pointed at the enemy infantry.

'*Savoia!*' he shouted, ordering the charge.

The 250 horsemen scrambled up the bank onto the plain, quickly gathering pace as they galloped towards the infantry. The Sikhs fired a few shots and then ran to the cover of the armoured cars, which tried to manoeuvre. Once through the infantry, Amedeo kept going, still at a fast gallop, gathering twenty riderless, panic-stricken horse behind him. He urged Sandor on, putting as much distance as he could between himself and the armoured cars. But above the pounding hooves he could hear machine-gun fire which he knew would be thinning the ranks of the horsemen behind him. As he galloped, Amedeo suddenly saw that he was heading straight for the guns of some Indian artillery. Again he wheeled away – at a greater distance than the first charge – and the guns fired a loud but harmless volley. With relief, Amedeo saw some woods in front of him and galloped into them to safety.

Keeping to the wadis, he eventually worked his way back to the place he had started from. At about three, he received a radio message from General Fongoli, one of the very few occasions when this horse-mounted transmitter actually worked. The immediate danger was over, as the infantry from the frontier had passed through the Italian lines at Keru and were now well on their way to Agordat. In front of him, the British were cautiously redeploying their heavy armour and artillery. It was time to leave. Keeping well away from the main road to Keru, the Gruppo Bande made their way back to the wells at Awashait on their exhausted mounts.

Deafened by their own gunfire and still uncertain whether the Italians were poised to launch a major attack, the British only slowly recovered from the confusion of these extraordinary actions. It barely seemed credible that on the lowlands of Eritrea, the British army had, for the very last time, faced the cavalry charge of an enemy they viewed with disdain. Strewn over several kilometres on the plain of Aicota lay the corpses of two hundred of Amedeo's *ascari*, with an equal number of dismembered mounts.

'The damage to the wretched horses pierced by our shelling was horrendous,' wrote Captain Gray, who set about shooting the wounded animals. Skinner's Horse had traded in their mounts for armoured cars only fourteen months before and the emotional resonance of a real cavalry charge was not lost on them. Many loose horses were rounded up and Sowar Richpal Singh, an excellent trainer of polo ponies, was unable to resist mounting one and doing figures of eight at a trot and canter.

'His paces are good,' he shouted to the captain, 'but he's a bit stiff on his near fore.'

But mingled with their admiration for the enemy's courage, were recriminations among the officers of Gazelle Force. The attack had taken them by surprise and come close to over-running their headquarters. With everything else in the British advance being crowned with brilliant success, no one chose to dwell on this unfortunate incident at Keru. Far better to write it off as an irrelevant *folie de guerre*, another Balaclava, that had been brave, certainly, but had also been brushed aside with ease. The fact that Gazelle Force had wasted an entire day before Keru dealing with the Gruppo Bande Amhara was quietly forgotten.

At the wells of Awashait, Dr Pietro Bonura was excelling himself. With his medical orderlies, he had created an efficient mounted first-aid team, riding out to retrieve many fallen riders. The doctor arranged for his patients to be carried back by camel to Agordat along the safe mountain tracks, two or three wounded men to each beast.

Before resting, Amedeo had to report to Fongoli, and he rode a camel alone down towards the Italian lines at Keru. Signs of the fort being evacuated were everywhere. At the command post, Amedeo began very stiffly to make his report, but was silenced by the general's embracing him with great warmth. He had left two hundred men dead on the plain of Aicota, Amedeo said, among them Togni. His friend's wounded orderly, who had feigned death after the charge and had managed to reach Italian lines after dusk, had seen the British take his body down from the roof of the tank. They had laid him out on the ground and saluted.

It was time for everyone to pull back, the general gently told Amedeo. The Gruppo Bande had succeeded brilliantly. The general was only awaiting final orders to abandon his position and fall back to Agordat, where the Italians would make a stand. What was left of the Gruppo Bande was to keep to the hills and protect the brigade's left flank. They would meet again in a couple of days, Fongoli said, leading Amedeo to the door.

So far the Italians had extricated themselves from their pointlessly exposed positions on the lowlands with success. But while Fongoli prepared the evacuation of Keru, a fatal blunder was made further to the south. A unit of the Polizia d'Africa Italiana took up the wrong position on the plain from Barentu, leaving a gap in the Italian line undefended.

At dawn, two days after the charge at Keru, Amedeo was horrified to hear shooting from the plain below. He galloped down a slope with some of his men to see several hundred panic-stricken Italian soldiers from Fongoli's 41st Brigade running towards him. Behind them, some distance away, loomed the British armoured cars, which had worked their way behind the Italian line. Amedeo had his men fire in the air to stop the rout, and ordered the infantry to follow his horsemen into the hills. The armoured cars pursued them for as long as they could, and Lieutenant Mattinò maintained a fierce rearguard, which discouraged the Highland Light Infantry from giving chase. But Fongoli, among the last to leave Keru, was captured with seven hundred men. He was the first Italian general to fall into British hands during the campaign. He was a fine officer, Amedeo reflected, but he had lacked that essential ingredient in war – luck.

## THIRTEEN

# *Keren*

The Gruppo Bande and the infantry they had rounded up during the retreat were among the last Italian troops to reach Agordat. For two days they had followed the mountain contours back to the town, which was the largest on the Eritrean lowlands. Everywhere there were signs of a hasty defence being prepared. With some misgivings, Amedeo saw the 15,000-strong Italian infantry digging in and preparing to make a stand on the plain in front of the town. He knew Agordat well. It was a typical neat Italian colonial town, laid out in the same grid as those built by the Romans two thousand years before. But although there were mountains scattered in front of the town, and a range behind, its natural defences were not ideal. The wisest course would have been to abandon it altogether, but now it was too late. Guns, armour and supplies were already in place and the British were expected at any moment.

General Frusci was in divisional headquarters, keen to inspect this sector of the front, which would almost certainly be under attack the next day. 'The Gruppo Bande has returned, *Eccellenza*,' Amedeo reported. 'Decimated, certainly, but not broken.'

The general was moved to see him. He had heard of the heavy casualties and he embraced the younger man. Frusci explained that the defence of Agordat had been entrusted to Colonel Raimondo Lorenzini, an outstanding officer in the Alpini. The Duke of Aosta had appointed him personally, ignoring the claims of more senior officers. The viceroy was losing patience with the ill-informed 'advice' from the army command in Rome. It was thanks to their orders that the Italians were still attempting to hold the lowlands, with barely a single sizeable tank in their armoury.

Lorenzini could see little need for a cavalry unit to stay at Agordat. Amedeo kept the three hundred Yemeni infantry, Battizzocco, the most experienced of his Eritrean NCOs and twenty horsemen, and sent the rest of the unit, including the camels and the wounded, back to their base behind the massive natural fortress of Keren. He turned in early that night to recuperate from almost a week spent in the saddle. At dawn, he was ordered to report immediately to headquarters. Lorenzini had been appalled to discover that Mount Cochen, which dominated the southern approach to the town four kilometres away, had yet to be occupied by Italian troops, although there were defences to its sides. He told Amedeo to establish a position on the summit, which rose 1500 feet from the surrounding country.

Taking an NCO of the Alpini with them as a guide, Amedeo and his men set out on foot for the mountain. They passed briefly the 9th Eritrean battalion, which by chance had camped at the base of Cochen, but he did not delay. He and his men then began to climb, intending to make the summit before sunset. An hour later, he was making his way along the edge of a ravine when he noticed a column of men doing exactly the same on the other side. He quickened his pace in order to reach higher ground before his adversaries, but some had arrived there before him. A few minutes later, the rocks were splintering with machine-gun bullets, quickly followed by mortar fire. Armed only with his Austro-Hungarian Mannlicher cavalry carbines and the loud but ineffectual Italian grenades, Amedeo would need to get higher to inflict any damage on the enemy. He and some men circled the mountain and kept climbing, while the platoons of Battizzocco and the Alpino provided cover. But the British above them could see their weakness. Before Amedeo had gone very far, his entire force was being attacked by

Indian troops, the 1/6 Rajputana Rifles, charging with the bayonet. Fighting in and around the rocks of Mount Cochen – 'as big as furniture pantechnicons,' according to one British officer – descended into a savage hand-to-hand affair. The first assault was driven off, but the prospects were looking very bleak for Amedeo's Yemenis. Ammunition was low and the casualties were mounting. He sent a note with an *ascaro* to Lorenzini asking for immediate reinforcements, knowing that by the time they arrived from Agordat, it might well be too late. But suddenly an immaculate Eritrean shumbashi of the 9th Eritreans was standing before him, saluting. The battalion commander, Major Zoppis, and the rest of the officers were at HQ in Agordat, he explained. Could the six hundred *ascari*, lined up at the base of Mount Cochen, be of any assistance?

Amazed that a humble Eritrean NCO had taken the initiative to volunteer his entire battalion, Amedeo almost embraced the man. He told him to bring the men up as quickly as possible. Once reinforced, they began driving back the Rajputana Rifles and troops of the 14th Punjab Regiment. A furious Brigadier Reginald Savory, in command of the 11th Indian Brigade, climbed Cochen himself to see why his men were making so little headway. Savory – 'always well turned out and never without his pipe and stick', according to one of his officers – feared the mountain was lost. He grabbed a rifle and bayonet and joined in the fight. More troops poured in from both sides, including the officers of the 9th Eritreans, whose CO outranked Amedeo and now took charge. Shortly afterwards two more brigades followed. For the next forty hours, the Gruppo Bande fought without a break, charging forward, holding a few rocks and then being driven off again. Finally, Amedeo was ordered to take his exhausted men off the mountain and get the wounded back to Agordat.

But almost as soon as they arrived back in the town, the British broke through. A minefield had been cleared allowing the Mathilda tanks to squeeze past Mount Cochen, overrunning the Italian infantry positions. The British were on the plain before Agordat.

Eleven of the light Fiat Ansaldo armoured cars – 'the sardine tins' – suicidally drove out to face them. Through tears of frustration, Amedeo watched as one after the other was blown to pieces. Incredibly, a unit of Black Shirts led by Colonel Luziani of the Bersaglieri, supported by a handful of German merchant seamen volunteers, then left their trenches and advanced towards the enemy. The British did not fire at first, thinking the men were surrendering. Only when they began hurling grenades at the tanks, did the British machine guns scythe the men down.

It was the end. The carnage was complete. Agordat was as good as lost and every moment wasted would be to the enemy's advantage. The Italian front was crumbling and troops, though still in good order, were pouring down the road to Keren. As Amedeo and his men remounted, he suddenly realised the folly of this. If the British had got past Cochen, they could easily be blocking the road to Keren further on. The retreating infantry would be cut to pieces if they encountered armour. The thought hardened into certainty. Instead of going by road, the troops should retreat along the railway line higher up, which clung to the mountains above the town, beyond the reach of the British tanks. Sending Battizzocco to the head of the column, Amedeo galloped down to the mass of troops still in Agordat and shouted at them to get off the road. Heavy equipment should just be abandoned. It was all lost anyway. When senior officers questioned his authority, he explained the danger in terms that discouraged argument. No one disputed the possibility of a British trap for long and soon the entire column was climbing up the embankments to the railway line. Amedeo's men maintained a rearguard, firing down on the first Indian troops to enter the town. Then they scrambled up the slope and galloped off between the rails.

Agordat may not have been the decisive victory the British were hoping for, but it was a serious setback for the Italians. As well as losing nine medium-weight tanks and fifteen light ones, they had left behind 196 pieces of artillery and 1200 dead. Several hundred indigenous troops, mainly those recruited from the lowlands, had also been captured or had deserted. 'Our situation is grave, but certainly not desperate,' Aosta openly messaged the army. 'It is enough to want to stop the enemy to do so.'

They would hold them at the mountain stronghold of Keren. Eleven peaks, the highest 5900 feet, dominated the approach to this prosperous little town. The only way to reach it was by road and railway that passed through the narrow gorge of Dongolaas. High explosives had been used to bring down the cliff faces and it was blocked by massive boulders. To either side, the mountain range continued for 150 kilometres.

On the afternoon of 2 February 1941, Amedeo and his men arrived at Keren, having ridden the entire 96 kilometres from Agordat along the railway line. At precisely the same time, Colonel Frank Messervy, with Gazelle Force, roared up to the blocked pass of Dongolaas. To his fury, his advance had been held up by the four-span bridge, the Ponte Mussolini, having been blown up. There were going to be no easy victories for his armour this time.

The next day Savoy's 11th Brigade arrived, and promptly attacked up the almost vertical slopes of Mount Sanchil, on the northern side of the pass. The Cameron Highlanders, Rajputana Rifles and Punjabis led desperate charges against the Italian positions, won some ground and were then driven off. After three days of this, General Platt called the attacks off. The conquest of Keren needed a more subtle approach.

In the baking heat of the day, the British were having to climb rockfaces and over boulders, carrying both munitions and water. When a soldier was wounded on Sanchil, it could take nearly a dozen men up to an hour to bring him down to the plain. The dead were left where they fell, which meant flies swarmed around the front line and the stench was overpowering.

These mountains, with their dramatic peaks and lush plateaux, had always struck Amedeo as an idyllic landscape, and in the past he had dreamed of living in Keren with Bice. Its beauty was marred now. On the slopes facing Keren were the neat orchards and orange groves planted by settlers, while those on the other side, facing the British and the lowlands, had always had abundant wildlife. From the heights above, the bodies of lions and antelopes could be seen in the British minefields. Once during the fighting, a family of baboons, caught in no-man's land, were mistaken for the enemy, and repeatedly shelled by both sides as they ran frantically from one to the other.

The Italians, who had an excellent vantage point, were well entrenched and reinforced. The Duke of Aosta, although assailed both by Orde Wingate's Ethiopian 'Patriots' within Abyssinia and General Alan Cunningham's invasion from Kenya, had moved the crack 11th Granatieri di Savoia, under Colonel Corso Corsi, from Addis Ababa to Keren. He appointed General Nicola Carnimeo in overall charge of the army of 25,000.

The Italians had the advantage of occupying false crests just beneath the mountain peaks, which meant that if these positions were taken, they could retreat even higher and rain down grenades, mortar and machine-gun fire onto the attackers below. Well dug in behind huge boulders, only their forward positions were vulnerable to British artillery. Machine guns sited amid the rocks took a heavy toll on the attackers, and barbed wire was often left undamaged by the enemy fire. After the easy victories in Libya and the Eritrean lowlands, the British had been inclined to despise their Italian adversaries, and ridicule their lack of martial valour. But now their officers' reports became more respectful. The mortars were 'accurate, well-sighted and well-handled' and 'counter-attacks were characterised by bold and clever infiltration, with sniping, by small parties supported by fire'.

* * *

On 6 February, the arrival of the viceroy himself at Keren strengthened morale. Among the officers the duke wanted to see was Amedeo, who arrived at headquarters as Colonel Lorenzini was leaving. The duke congratulated him for his spectacular action at Keru, an act of daring that had seized the imagination of soldiers in both armies. He lamented the loss of Togni, saying that he had written personally to his family and was recommending him for the Gold Medal, Italy's highest award for bravery.

All day the duke had been attempting to raise the spirits of the troops, but to Amedeo he spoke frankly. The seams that held Africa Orientale Italiana together were coming undone. Haile Selassie, with Orde Wingate, had crossed into Ethiopia and was rallying the Amhara. Much of Ethiopia had turned against the Italians and was impassable except in well-armed convoys. The almost complete destruction of the Regia Aeronautica meant no position was invulnerable to the RAF's air attacks, including Massaua and Asmara. While in the south, General Cunningham had advanced into Italian Somaliland, where the resistance had been pathetic.

Morale was the key issue, even more so than the shortages of supplies, the third-rate equipment and the poor training of the troops. Increasing numbers of Italians were disenchanted with this war. Few could see the point in it, and many were convinced that, in Africa, the war was already lost. General Gustavo Pesenti, the commander of the Somali–Kenya sector, made no effort to defend himself for his failure to stop Cunningham's invasion from Kenya. An educated man, a well-known musician and author, he bluntly told the duke that the campaign was lost and that he should seek a truce as a prelude to a separate peace. Pesenti then told the viceroy that the king had not wanted war, and that the Fascist regime in the empire should be dismantled before its collapse in Italy, for 'everyone was fed up with it'. The duke had made several efforts to silence the general, declaring that they both deserved to be shot: Pesenti for saying what he had, and he for listening. He then sacked him and had him repatriated to Italy, although he did not report his seditious sentiments. 'I, a Savoy, shall never betray my king,' the shaken viceroy recorded in his diary.

Yet he believed that something of Italy's empire could be saved, if only the troops fought on and held the line at Keren. Indeed, there was the possibility of complete victory. The British were overstretched in the Mediterranean, having poured troops into Greece, which the Italians had invaded in October 1940 (albeit with disastrous results). If Egypt were threatened again from Libya, perhaps by this new German general, Erwin Rommel, the British would have to abandon the campaign in Eritrea. Their supply lines stretched hundreds of kilometres behind them and if the garrison at Keren held on until the great rains of July and August, the British would be washed away. Even if they could keep their army supplied under such conditions, when the roads would be unpassable, malaria and other diseases would soon decimate their ranks.

'Whatever happens here,' said the duke, 'we must carry on to the end, no matter how hopeless things become. Even beyond the end. For every British soldier we can tie down here will help our army in Libya.'

The duke had little idea of the sense of obligation his words inspired in the younger man. Being given command of the Gruppo Bande was the greatest single honour ever paid him. Amedeo would follow the viceroy to the end, and beyond. Whatever happened at Keren, he for one would never surrender. For a few moments there was silence between them, and the handsome features of the duke seemed cast in melancholy. Few even of the twentieth century's follies quite matched the pointlessness of the British and Italians going to war in Africa. He was a commander fighting a war he did not believe in, for a dictator he viewed with disdain, as everything he held dear was disappearing forever. The duke's dreams for Ethiopia were over now. The schools, hospitals and roads, and a country rejuvenated by Italian colonists were never going to happen. Indeed, everything he had achieved was being swept away. No one knew what the final reckoning of the war would be, but all that remained were duty and honour. The duke sighed, smiled at Amedeo, and then rose from his seat and towered over the younger man. They embraced, holding each other closely for a moment. Then Amedeo saluted and left. They were never to meet again.

On 10 February, the British began a ferocious air and artillery bombardment of the Italian positions at Keren, which lasted several hours. In the late afternoon, the battle-hardened 4th Indian Division, commanded by General Henry Beresford-Peirse, attacked both to the north and the south of the Dongolaas gorge. On Sanchil, to the north, troops of the 11th Indian Brigade, supported by Cameron Highlanders, captured one of the peaks from *ascari* who had found the aerial bombardments impossible to bear. A fierce bayonet charge by the Bersaglieri pushed them off, but they were, in turn, driven back. At the end of nearly two days' continuous fighting, the peak was back in Italian hands.

To the south, Gazelle Force, the Royal Fusiliers and the Rajputana Rifles attacked the Col d'Acqua, the smallest and most vulnerable of the mountains, being slightly set forward from the rest of the range. Unfortunately for them, it was held by the 4th Toselli Eritreans, commanded by Colonel Siro Persichelli. The unit was named after Major Toselli whose column had been wiped out to a man at Amba Alagi in 1895. It had been the Thermopylae of Italian colonial history, and on the night before their annihilation the officers reputedly had sung Gounod's *Ave Maria*. Ever since, the 4th Eritreans had been the élite of Italy's colonial troops, wearing a distinctive black cummerbund in permanent mourning for that day.

The British attack was badly co-ordinated and confused. Over forty-eight hours, the fighting degenerated into a ferocious hand-to-hand struggle, characterised by acts of astonishing bravery on both sides. It was here where Subadar Richal Ram, of the Rajputana Rifles, won a posthumous Victoria Cross. Four Medaglie d'Oro were issued to officers of the Toselli, which had five hundred dead, including twelve officers. Reinforced by the Granatieri di Savoia and the 11th Black Shirt Legion, made up of tough colonists many of whom had fought in the First World War, the remaining Toselli counterattacked, screaming their terrifying Tigrinian battle cry '*Ambessa! Ambessa!* Be lions!' As British troops tried to scramble to safety up the slopes of the neighbouring mountain, Bulucbasci Uoldesilassi ripped off his black cummerbund, and cried out that he would dye it red in the enemy's blood.

At midday on 12 February, Platt called off the attack. 'Keren is proving a tough nut to crack,' Eden reported to London from Cairo.

For the next month, no further attacks were mounted against the Italian positions, as the British licked their wounds. The Gruppo Bande, dismounted and reduced to four hundred men, were holding a sector of the front, some distance north from the fulcrum of the Dongolaas gorge. Amedeo used this time to have the women, horses and camels taken to a small village in the hills above Asmara, which would be their new base. Khadija had been pleased to be reunited with her *comandante* and relieved that he had survived the fighting without a scratch. But this was not war as she had known it, chasing *shiftas* around the Semien. Entire mountains could disappear in the cauldron of aerial bombardment and many of her friends in the *campo famiglia* were widows now. Amedeo told her to take the remaining women to the new camp, ordering a wounded *ascaro* to accompany her. One of the oldest men in the Gruppo Bande, Amedeo had called him Talmone, from an Italian drinking chocolate whose advertisements depicted an elderly couple. Shot in the groin during the fighting, the old warrior's repeated lamentations that he could no longer have children had, in spite of themselves, amused Amedeo and Khadija, for he was well past sixty. Three army lorries arrived to take the women to the new camp, but before they left, Amedeo sought out Togni's woman and gave her a large sum of money. It was a forlorn convoy that pulled out of Keren, but Amedeo was relieved to see the women go. He did not want them around, if the British broke through at Dongolaas.

Apart from the constant bombardment and aerial bombing, the section of the front held by the Gruppo Bande Amhara was quiet. Every so often Amedeo sent out patrols to reconnoitre the enemy positions. The unit's anti-Fascist lawyer, Angelo Maiorani, felt bad for not having charged at Keru and eagerly volunteered for every hairbrained plan aired around the camp fires. When he suggested he go down to the plain dressed as an Arab to check on British troop movements, Amedeo finally agreed, so long as an *ascaro* went with him. Maiorani was perhaps too unworldly for the task. In the middle of a busy intersection, where British lorries were constantly passing up to Dongolaas and down to the frontier with Sudan, he got out his notebook and jotted down their markings, making no effort to disguise what he was doing. Being short-sighted he even walked over to some of the trucks so that he could copy their lettering accurately. Astonishingly, he got away with it, but when the two men returned, the shaken *ascaro* announced: 'Send me on any other mission, *comandante*, but never again with *Avucato* Maiorani.'

On 14 March the British attacked again. This time, supported by the Free French, they tried to force the Italian lines at Cub-Cub, sixty kilometres to the north. Lorenzini, newly made general, rushed off to beat this threat back. But the next day, Platt again attacked the mountain defences, after the heaviest aerial bombardment yet inflicted on Keren. 'It is going to be a bloody battle against both the enemy and the ground,' he declared. 'It will be won by the side which lasts the longest.'

Fifteen battalions of Indian troops were sent forward, the cream of the Raj army, backed up by three English and two Highland battalions. For two days there was incessant fighting on the mountains on both sides of the gorge. The peaks disappeared under clouds of dust and smoke. Everywhere the British were beaten back, except immediately south of Dongolaas where the extraordinary Messervy won a toehold at the old Italian fort of Dologorodoc. General Lorenzini appreciated the mortal danger that this presented, and ordered one counterattack after another. During the seventh of these Lorenzini himself was decapitated by British artillery fire. 'It was a severe disaster for the Italians,' said Platt, correctly assessing its effect on Italian morale. The casualties were rising among their best men: Colonels Corsi, of the Savoy grenadiers, and Persichelli, of the 4th Toselli, were also down, the latter, though, urging his Eritreans on from a litter.

The eyes of the world were fixed on Keren. Churchill anxiously asked Eden in Cairo whether he needed reinforcements, 'as the battle seems rather evenly balanced'. Hundreds of miles from their supply depots, the British were running out of ammunition, having fired 110,000 shells. Nowhere had the Italian line been broken, although Messervy was still clinging to Dologorodoc. In their desperation to dislodge him, the Italians even sent in a detachment of Alpini, who climbed down the sheer rockface at night and were gunned down only yards from his command post.

Wily new tactics were adopted by the British. One morning, the Italians woke up to hear what sounded like Italian opera resonating from the gorge. At first, they assumed their shell-deafened ears were playing tricks. In fact, it was Italian opera blaring out through loudspeakers linked up by Lord Corvedale, the son of Stanley Baldwin, the former Prime Minister. In between pacifying arias, he interspersed news of Italian defeats in Somaliland and southern Ethiopia.

Thanks to Messervy providing cover, British sappers were able to begin clearing the blocked pass of Dongolaas. On 27 March, the Matildas at last drove through into Keren. It was deserted. Carnimeo had pulled his troops out during the night. He could do no more and against the British armour he had no defences.

'The Italians have fought at Keren as they have done few times in their history,' said one British report. 'They have fought superbly!'

Amedeo's orders were to fall back to the gorge of Ad Teclesan, only fifty-two kilometres from Asmara, where the Gruppo Bande were to be placed at the disposal of Colonel Borghese of the 10th Granatieri di Savoia, with whom they would hold part of the line. They took up position on a small hill, well below the level of the vital Keren to Asmara road. The pursuing British feared briefly that they were in for another prolonged siege, with the Italians dominating the surrounding heights. But Ad Teclesan had nothing like the natural fortifications of Dongolaas pass. Again parts of the hillside were brought down with explosives partially blocking the road, but Italian morale had sunk low after the loss of Keren. After early clashes, the high ground fell into British hands, and it would not be long before the rest were cleared. For the first time, Eritrean regular soldiers began to desert.

The situation was desparate. But in the heat of battle Amedeo's mood would swing from black despair to utter confidence. On the morning of 29 March, he was standing beside Colonel Borghese when he saw three British light tanks trundle along the broken road three hundred metres above his position. The British were becoming arrogant, if they thought they were just going to drive into Asmara. Amedeo strode down the lines of the Gruppo Bande, summoned thirty men randomly – among them a handful of the Ethiopian rebels he had spared at Amba Gheorgis more than a year before – and told them to bring two petrol bombs each. From their position, they could make their way to the bottom of the steep valley and then climb unseen through the scrub and rocks up the other side to the road. Approaching the tanks from below, they began hurling their bombs. Two began to burn furiously and the third reversed back to the British positions in flames.

Loud cheering along the Italian lines greeted Amedeo when he

A stricken Graziani, above and right, is carried away after the assassination attempt in Addis Ababa on 19 February 1937 during the celebrations of the birth of the Prince of Naples. Mussolini sacked him, because of the inefficacy of the repression that followed.

*Right* On the same day, Beatrice Gandolfo paraded in a mediaeval carousel through the streets of Naples.

The fortified outpost at Amba Gheorgis on the vital road from Gondar to Asmara, with euphorbia candelabra in the foreground. Fear of brigands, and guerillas loyal to the deposed Haile Selassie, meant lorries (right) always travelled in convoy.

*Above* Amedeo talking to his subordinate Landolfo Colonna, before the Second World War. It was Colonna, when a prisoner in India, who discovered from the British that Amedeo had survived the Italian defeat and had found a refuge in the Yemen.

*Left* Amedeo in 1939 with an important Ethiopian chief, wearing the lion mane head-dress.

*Far left* Amedeo is welcomed by a crowd of dancing women at a remote village in the highlands of Beghemeder, 1938.

Amedeo drilling his garrison at Amba Gheorgis, followed by Landolfo Colonna, 1939.

The viceroy's visit: The Duke of Aosta towers over Amedeo during his inspection of the fort at Amba Gheorgis. Beside them stands General Frusci, wearing sunglasses.

*Above* The garrison at Amba Gheorgis rides out, with Amedeo saluting. Thanks to Marshal Graziani's repression, rebel activity in Ethiopia was widespread in 1937–38.

*Left* Amedeo and the other officers at Amba Gheorgis are carried in triumph by their men after a succesful operation against Ethiopian rebels. All the NCOs in the garrison were Eritrean, though the figure in white is Amedeo's Libyan Spahy orderly, Salem Kaskas, whom Italo Balbo had allowed to accompany his *comandante* to Italian East Africa.

*Top* The Gruppo Bande Amhara a Cavallo in full charge, as the British were to see them on the Eritrean Lowlands in January 1941. The cavalrymen were drawn from every tribe in the north of Italian East Africa.

*Left* Amedeo on manouevres with his Gruppo Bande on the Eritrean Lowlands, 1940.

*Below* Summer 1940: General Frusci arrives to inspect the Gruppo Bande Amhara a Cavallo, Amedeo riding beside his car.

*Left* The infantry of the Gruppo Bande were made up of Yemeni mercenaries.

*Below* The Gazelle Force on the move as the British invade Africa Orientale Italiana from the Sudan.

*Above* The West Yorkshires at Dologorodoc, whose hold of the vital ridge allowed British sappers to breach the defences at Keren.

*Right* General Nicola Carnimeo.

*Below right* General Frank Messervy, photographed in Burma later in the war.

*Far right* General Lorenzini, the 'Lion of Keren', who was decapitated during his desperate efforts to dislodge the West Yorkshires off Dologorodoc.

returned from this exploit and Colonel Borghese impulsively ran over to congratulate him. It was a generous, but ill-fated act for British infantry had moved forward to avenge their losses. A burst of machine-gun fire caught the Italian colonel in the chest. Rather than proudly embracing Amedeo, he breathed his last in the young officer's arms. For the rest of the day the opposing sides kept up constant fire, almost equal in ferocity to Mount Cochen. Amedeo's report recorded sixty-five dead that day, and a further thirty-one wounded.

The next day, 30 March, was dedicated to Sant' Amedeo, and it began with British mortars and machine-guns opening up on the Italian positions. At midday Amedeo had cause to bless his patron saint. A shell burst just beyond the Gruppo Bande's trenches, while he was standing beside one of the smugglers of the Sheik Rasciaida. He heard a slight groan and turned to see that the *ascaro*, still standing upright, had been neatly decapitated by the crown of the shell. He was struck by how slowly, even gracefully, the body crumpled and fell. A furious barrage followed, after which British infantry charged the Gruppo Bande's trenches, hoping to take them with the bayonet. They were beaten back with heavy losses, the corpse of a young, fair-haired British lieutenant lying immediately in front of Amedeo's trench. With evening, he allowed the enemy stretcher-bearers to remove the wounded and dead under a flag of truce. Sant' Amedeo's day accounted for another thirty-eight dead in the Gruppo Bande, and forty-one wounded.

On the third day of resistance at Ad Teclesan, the British brought up heavy artillery and the Italian line was swept by machine-gun fire from several different positions. Amedeo was scouring the ground for the enemy with his binoculars, lying behind a rock outside his trench. A machine-gun fixed on to him, peppering the rock with fire. Flattening himself against it, Amedeo suddenly felt a searing pain in his left foot and knew he had been hit. He waited until the machine-gun racked the rest of the line and then fell back into the trench, where he cut away his boot, which was filled with blood. With astonishing good luck, the bullet had passed between the Achille's tendon and the bone, without seriously damaging either. It was a painful wound, but he could still walk.

His men were desperately short of ammunition, and further handicapped because their various rifles had different calibres. Some were equipped with the Italian infantry's Model 91 (from the year 1891), while others had Mannlicher carbines. He still had enough for the latter, but he needed 91s for his equally antiquated Fiat 14, water-cooled machine-guns. He sent Lieutenants Cara and Lucarelli back to the grenadiers' lines for more.

Frank Messervy was also well forward of the British positions when day broke. To push through the Italians at Ad Teclesan he sent forward the 2nd West Yorkshires, a unit destined to be involved in more continuous frontline fighting than any other British infantry battalion in the Second World War. It was with them that Messervy had held his position under ferocious fire at Dologorodoc, and together they would later fight in the Western Desert and in Burma.

Messervy watched appalled as dawn lit up the West Yorkshires climbing up the ridge of Ad Teclesan, while on the other side the 10th Granatieri di Savoia lay in wait.

> The Italian guardsmen looked fat, fierce and bristling, a real warlike lot,' he recalled. 'They were obviously all ready for the West Yorkshires and I dreaded the moment when they would catch our fellows in the light on the brow of the ridge. But there was just nothing I could do about it. Then the attackers reached the ridge and their flat tin hats rose above it. Immediately, almost as one man, the ferocious attitude of the Grenadiers changed into the amiable aspect of hokey-cokey vendors and they flung their arms wide in surrender.

The position at Ad Teclesan was by now hopeless, and the Italian command ordered further resistance to cease. Within an hour the

West Yorks had taken the position and rounded up 460 prisoners, including 19 officers. By the time Cara and Lucarelli arrived on the scene the Italian front at Ad Teclesan had collapsed, and they too were captured.

Far below, enemy firing on the Gruppo Bande's trenches unaccountably came to a halt. Everywhere along the Italian line positions were being abandoned and troops had fallen back. It took a while for Amedeo to realise that he was completely alone, cut off from the rest of the army and, seemingly, forgotten by the enemy. The road was cleared of boulders, and columns of British lorries began lining up in full view. The carcasses of the light tanks Amedeo and his men had destroyed were pushed over the side. As soon as darkness fell, he gathered the able-bodied among his men, who numbered around a hundred. They crept out of their trenches down to the dried-up stream below and slipped away, following its course until it joined the shallow river Anseba.

Beside it, a company of Indians was settling down for the night around a fire. With the Italian army fleeing down the road to Asmara, or into Ethiopia, they had not bothered to take any precautions. A salvo of shots and a few grenades had them diving for cover. Amedeo ordered his men to cut their land telephone lines and destroy any transmitters. What remained of the Gruppo Bande Amhara a Cavallo ran across the shallow river, helping their hobbling *comandante*, and vanished into the darkness.

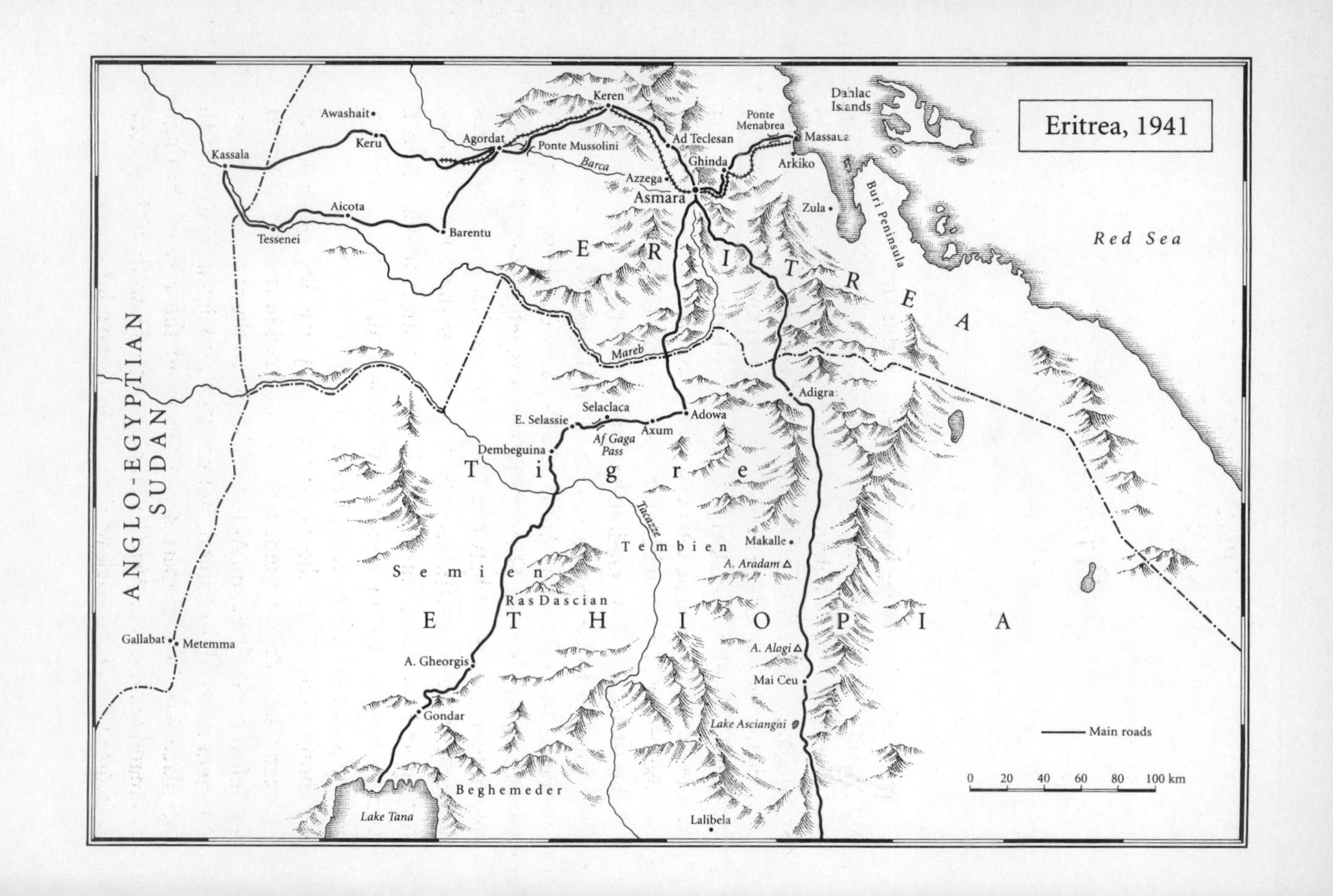

Eritrea, 1941
Red Sea
Buri Peninsula
Ponte Menabrea
Arkiko
Zula
Keren
Ad Teclesan
Ghinda
Asmara
Azzega
Barca
Ponte Mussolini
Agordat
Keru
Awashait
Kassala
Aicota
Tessenei
Barentu
E R I T R E A
Mareb
Adigra
Adowa
Axum
Selaclaca
Af Gaga Pass
E. Selassie
Dembeguina
T i g r e
Tacazze
T e m b i e n
Makalle
A. Aradam
S e m i e n
Ras Dascian
E T H I O P I A
A. Alagi
Mai Ceu
Lake Asciangni
A. Gheorgis
Gondar
B e g h e m e d e r
Lake Tana
Lalibela
ANGLO-EGYPTIAN SUDAN
Gallabat
Metemma
Main roads
0 20 40 60 80 100 km

FOURTEEN

# *Private War*

Amedeo lay on the bed staring up at the straw roof of the tukul. It was all over. Even he could not deny that. Asmara, the centre of Italian power in Africa for sixty years, was in British hands. After Ad Teclesan, they had streamed down the road towards the capital, which Frusci had declared an open city before he pulled out. On the outskirts, Archbishop Marinoni and the other civic leaders had met the enemy's armoured cars, which, in error, had opened fire, luckily without tragic consequences.

The Italian civilians made no secret of the fact that they were eager for the British to take over as soon as possible – just as the Europeans in burned-out Addis Ababa had welcomed Badoglio's troops six years before. Throughout the campaign, there had been a complicit agreement between the two sides that order must not break down lest the Africans run amok. So far there had been no looting and the Carabinieri were keeping matters under control. But every hour saw the arrival of more armed, confused and disorderly *ascari* on the streets of Asmara.

Among them were the two hundred weary and demoralised Eritreans the Gruppo Bande had encountered in the country after the defeat at Ad Teclesan. Amedeo had urged the major commanding them to avoid the capital. But he refused to listen. Even though the place was falling apart and Frusci and the rest of the high command of *Scacchiere Nord* had retreated to the south in Ethiopia, he insisted on going back to the city to receive his orders.

Exhausted and wounded as he was, Amedeo had the presence of mind to know that this was a mistake. Instead, the Gruppo Bande made for the village of Azzega in the hills, whose chief, a *fitaurari* named Gebreyesus Geremeddin, was an old friend. They received a cordial welcome and while the remaining troops were fed by the villagers, Amedeo was served fried eggs by the chief's wife. Gebreyesus insisted that Amedeo, feverish and in pain, rest on the cast-iron double bed that filled his tukul.

The next night Amedeo, still in uniform but unarmed and alone, cautiously walked to Asmara, eight kilometres away. Using the back streets, he made his way to the centre. It was heart-breaking for him to witness the capital passing from Italian to British rule. The patrols of British troops were vastly outnumbered by thousands of disarmed but aimless Italian soldiers, who were simply waiting to be rounded up. As he watched from the shadows, tears coursed down his cheeks. Never had he thought Italy would be reduced to this.

Avoiding everyone, he worked his way to the back door of the house of Giovanni Rugiu, a family friend and manager of the city's Banco di Roma. The Rugius quickly took him in, removed his filthy clothes and ran a warm bath so that he could wash off a fortnight's filth from the battlefield. Exhausted, yet still reeling from the collapse of his world, Amedeo sat motionless in the bath until Signora Rugiu came in to wash him like a child. She cleaned and dressed his wound, and then led him to a bed, easing him between the fresh cotton sheets.

They were good people the Rugius; considerate people who had not hesitated to help him, even though the enemy occupied Asmara. He was proud to be one of them, proud to be Italian, in spite of the bewildered flock of sheep outside that had once been the Italian army in Africa. *Brava gente*, good people, he repeated to himself, the words echoing in his head. The Rugius. They were Sardinians, naturally, with a name like that. *Brava gente*.

* * *

Amedeo slept until the late afternoon of the following day. Signor Rugiu told him what he knew of the general situation; that the British were taking control of the city, but there were still Italian troops on the streets. Once it was dark, Amedeo left the house wearing one of the banker's suits, which Signora Rugiu had pinned up as best she could for the shorter man. Before he left Asmara, Amedeo wanted to see Frusci's wife, who had always been so friendly and encouraging, to make sure that she was being looked after. She had evacuated the opulent *palazzo* her husband had occupied as governor, which the British had taken over, and moved into the smaller Villa Roma, the Asmara residence of the Duke of Aosta. Standing guard in a sentry box beside the high cast-iron gates was a carabiniere, rather than a British soldier. It was a sensitive touch on the part of the conquerors, Amedeo felt, to have the wife of Italian Eritrea's last governor guarded by her own people. Claiming to be Signora Frusci's lawyer, he was led up the gravel drive past the circular ornamental fountain and into the main drawing room of the villa, where in former times dancers had glided over the mosaic floor, their reflections caught in the huge art deco mirrors on the wall.

Signora Frusci, a cashmere cardigan draped over her shoulders, tripped across the floor of the empty room to Amedeo, whom she kissed on both cheeks. She was being well treated, she reassured him. The British had even sent her some flowers, which was a kind gesture, even if they were from her own old garden. And cigarettes, too. Amedeo could not help noticing that she was smoking a great deal of these, turning over in his hands the unfamiliar packet with a picture of a Viking-like, bearded sailor. Her husband, she explained, had joined the viceroy, at Amba Alagi in Ethiopia. The name meant nothing to her, but Amedeo recognised it immediately as the mountain where Toselli's column had made its doomed stand.

What was he going to do, Signora Frusci asked. He did not know. He could not reach the duke deep in Ethiopia through the

British lines. For the same reason he could not reach Massaua, which was still holding out, although he doubted it would be for much longer. He would do something, he told her, and he certainly would not be taken prisoner. Signora Frusci wished him luck and kissed him, before opening the French windows so that he could leave through the garden.

As he headed down the hill to the main Corso, Amedeo could see that the conquerors were getting on top of the situation. One of the first orders imposed on the confused citizens was that all traffic would henceforth drive on the left. Vehicles of all sorts were, in fact, pounding through the city down towards Massaua, the last position of any significance in Eritrea still in Italian hands. There were more British soldiers on the streets than the night before. A group of them – including some Scots in khaki kilts – were loudly drinking at the Bar Diana just beyond the opera house.

There was little overt animosity towards the conquerors, who had already made a good impression on Asmara's Italian population with their orderliness and magnanimity. Indian troops gave up their milk rations so that the children of Asmara did not do without. For the battle-weary troops, this European city with its temperate climate and population of European women, was a welcome contrast to the wilderness of the Sudan. When officers of the 5th Indian Division held a celebratory dinner at the Hotel CIAAO, they were delighted by the welcoming little flourishes, which the manager had learned years before at the Savoy. However, the city's bordello of Italian women, behind the Cinema Impero, was closed on patriotic grounds, and the request that it open for the use of British officers was indignantly refused.

Amedeo could see patrols of British troops led by military policemen in red caps rounding up the remnants of Frusci's army. The Italians were told to report to Fort Baldissera, on the outskirts of the city, where they would be fed. Amedeo was not tempted to accept the hospitality. In the days that followed the water supply to the fort broke down, and the incarcerated men suffered desperately from thirst. With the whole of the Italian population staying firmly indoors, Eritrean women of the city lowered water to the men below. '*Masakin, masakin*,' they cried. Poor things, poor things.

Still wearing the banker's suit, Amedeo limped painfully back to Azzega, turning over the Duke of Aosta's words to him at Keren. Eritrea might be lost but he had to fight on, just as the duke was doing at Amba Alagi. The surrender of thousands of Italian troops did not mean he should meekly give up his arms. The more British troops he could tie down, the fewer they could send back to reinforce their army in Egypt. The sun had disappeared behind the mountains, and it was beginning to get cold. But Amedeo did not feel it. The idea was growing firmer in his mind that he would continue to fight. And he would do so in Eritrea. Time and again the *ascari* of Italy's oldest colony had proved themselves to be among the bravest and most disciplined troops of the entire army. Now that the Italian empire was coming to an end, what was to become of them? The crude propaganda dropped over their lines at Keren by supporters of Emperor Haile Selassie made Ethiopian feelings clear: Eritrea should fraternally reunite into an enlarged empire ruled by the Negus Negusti. It was an arrangement which the British, indifferent to Eritrea's fate, would probably go along with. But Amedeo knew that Eritreans viewed union with repugnance. For centuries, the country had been on the shifting frontier between the Coptic world and the Islamic one. Only after Italy's arrival had Eritrea known a state of relative peace and stability and, remarkably, in the seventy years of its colonial rule, a sense of nationhood had been created. Eritreans might not have been able to define exactly what this involved, but they knew they did not want to be at the mercy of others, particularly not that of the Amhara, against whom they had fought so many times.

When he arrived back at Azzega, Amedeo shared his thoughts with Gebreyesus. The old warrior was deeply attached to the Italian flag, which he had served since fighting the Senussi rebels of North Africa in the Twenties. The Italian presence seemed the natural order of things, and he was disturbed that it had broken down. But what he found even more alarming was the prospect of the colony being handed over to the Ethiopian emperor. His fears were shared by all the Eritrean chiefs, particularly those whom the Italians had allowed to retain a degree of autonomy. If Amedeo were to fight on, Gebreyesus assured him that he would be helped.

In the meantime, the old man gently suggested, the *comandante* should get rid of his European clothes. He could never pass himself off as an Eritrean, but no one would suspect another rootless Arab caught up in the collapse of Italy's African empire. The next day, Amedeo folded up Rugiu's suit neatly on the iron bedstead and dressed in Arab clothing. When he emerged from the tukul, he did so as Ahmed Abdullah al Redai, a Yemeni stranded far from home.

To fan the Eritrean chiefs' patriotic fervour, Amedeo added some material inducements. Dr Call was looking after several hundred horses, mules and camels of the Gruppo Bande in a mountain clearing six kilometres away. The friendly chiefs would make much better use of these than the enemy, and so Amedeo began sharing them out, along with a large quantity of saddles, rifles and ammunition. For his remaining men, he kept back thirty camels and half as many mules. And he couldn't bear to part with Sandor, who had carried him at the charges of Selaclaca and Keru. Besides, he needed a horse; his wounded ankle meant he was unable to walk for long.

The division of the spoils was the last time Amedeo saw the large, good-natured Dr Call. Nostalgic for civilian life, he returned to Asmara and took to sleeping at the Istituto Sierovaccinogeno, where he had worked before the war. In time the British caught him and he joined lieutenants Mattinò, Lucarelli and Cara in prison. Battizzocco evaded capture until he was finally discovered hiding in Asmara. The only one of the Gruppo Bande's former officers who remained at liberty, apart from the *comandante*, was the lawyer Maiorani, who quietly returned to his civilian duties. But with the imprudence that had characterised his brief military career, he took to holding meetings in his house where like-minded friends would join him in rousing patriotic songs. The British eventually decided it was safer to place the fiery patriot behind the walls of Fort Baldissera. But before he was taken away, he managed to burn the banners of the Gruppo Bande, which had been entrusted to him, in his oven.

After the women of the *campo famiglia*, and the venerable Talmone, drifted back to their villages in Beghemeder and Tigre, Khadija alone remained. She loved her *comandante* and could never leave him, and he was grateful that she stayed. Cut off from everything that was familiar, he drew closer to her. As he fell asleep in her arms in the iron bed at Azzega, Khadija would stroke his head gently. He seemed more her man than ever before, having shed his fellow countrymen as he had his clothes. He was no longer a *ras*, nor even much of a chief, merely the fugitive leader of eighty *shifta*. But he was hers at last.

By April 1941 the viceroy of Africa Orientale Italiana was living in a cave on the mountain range of Amba Alagi. Here, he decided, the Italians in Africa would fight their final battle. Like Toselli before him, Aosta's remaining forces were entirely cut off, their fate only a question of time. British artillery and aircraft pounded his lines and the surrounding countryside was swarming with hostile Ethiopian irregulars. Yet he held on. There was just a chance that Italy could be extricated from Mussolini's disasters, saved by the Nazi allies for whom the duke had so little appetite. The Italian invasion of Greece, which he thought both squalid and unprovoked, had been a fiasco. But when the Duce, humiliated in the field, had implored the Germans for military help, the result had been two more British defeats and evacuations in mainland Greece and Crete. Meanwhile in Libya, miracles were expected from Rommel who, the duke found it difficult to forget, had made his early reputation by his daring breakthrough of the Italian lines at Caporetto in the First World War. The German general's tanks and the motorised Afrika Korps had regenerated the Italian forces, and he was advancing with breathtaking speed towards the depleted British defences in Egypt.

The British position was such that, the moment Massaua fell, the 4th Indian Division was sent back immediately to the Western Desert. Colonial units from Africa, such as the King's African Rifles, the Gold Coast Regiment and the Congolese Defence Force continued the fighting in Ethiopia, alongside the swelling number of Ethiopian 'patriots'. British intelligence officers were much amused to pick up panicky Italian radio reports that they were now fielding troops with 'cannabilistic tendencies'. An irreverent ode was penned:

What a heavenly thought
To sit down to a sort
Of 'Italiens au naturel'.
To know that the chops
Are just slices of Wops,
Tasty in spite of the smell.

Fricasséed Frusci,
Compôte Granatieri,
Angelini on Horseback, of course,
A savoury dinner of General Pinna
Is a joy to the Congolese Force.

Aosta, my man,
Make peace while you can
In a normal and usual fashion.
It is better by far
To remain as you are,
Than to end as a military ration.

Nowhere had the Italians fought better than in Africa Orientale Italiana, but with the defeats of Keren and loss of most of Ethiopia to the south, confidence in the remains of the army had sunk. Under Frusci, a half-hearted attempt was made by 5000 troops to make a stand at Dessie. One moment the general was reassuring the viceroy that his men's spirits had been revived with the news of successes in Libya, the next there were alarming signs that terminal demoralisation had set in. At one point, he had to complain directly to the duke that two senior officers, a general and a colonel, were so infatuated with a couple of native women lodged at the HQ that they were refusing to do their duties. When the South African division arrived, Frusci assured Aosta that he would fight on but, to both their surprise, an hour later Dessie surrendered. Italian civilians had taken matters into their own hands, deciding that further resistance was pointless. Once they began waving white flags, and marched out in front of the troops, the will to fight collapsed. For once, the Duke of Aosta did not control his temper. 'The loss of Dessie is the most ignoble end one can imagine and it is clear that it surrendered without fighting,' he radioed the unfortunate Frusci.

At Amba Alagi the viceroy bravely continued to fight off his besiegers for another month. But on 19 May, the hopelessness of his position was clear to all, as the last of the key defences on his perimeter was blown away by British guns. To avoid pointless loss of life, the duke at last surrendered. Accorded the full honour of arms, he reviewed the troops of his enemy, accompanied by Sir William Platt. Towering over his captors, in his elegantly tailored uniform, the duke saluted the British and Indian troops who had defeated him. For those British officers who witnessed the scene, and would later fight the Germans or the Japanese, the surrender at Amba Alagi remained remarkable. The cleanest, the most anachronistic – perhaps also the most needless – campaign of the Second World War ended on an appropriate note of chivalrous courtesy. The British troops could congratulate themselves on a job well done; the empire of Africa Orientale Italiana was no more. Few then realised that within only a few years so too would be theirs.

A year later, the Duke of Aosta died of tuberculosis a prisoner of war in Kenya aged forty-one. He had declined repeated British offers to repatriate him to Italy, in order to stay with his soldiers. Again it was Ciano, in his diary, who best summarised the duke's tragedy:

> [Aosta] did not want war. He was convinced the empire would only hold out for a few months. Besides, he hated the Germans. Concerning the issue which is covering the world in blood, he feared more a German victory than an English one. When he left for Ethiopia, in May 1940, he had a sense of his destiny: he was determined to face it, but he was full of sadness. I communicated the news to the Duce, who briefly expressed his regret.

FIFTEEN

# *Major Max*

Major Max Harari's heart was not in his job. When he arrived in Asmara, he had welcomed a rest from the rigors of the Western Desert. The war there seemed to have been won, and his duties as head of military intelligence in the former Italian colony were unlikely to be onerous. Here, too, the Italians were beaten, and it was simply a question of rounding up the prisoners. Two months after the surrender of Asmara, most had been packed off to India, Kenya and South Africa. General Frusci had the good fortune to be sent on to the United States, after it entered the war. The Americans were eager to parade a few high-ranking enemy officers, whoever had captured them, and the former commander of *Scacchiere Nord* much enjoyed being fêted as a noble adversary.

Like the other British officers, Harari found Asmara delightful; a piece of Italy in the midst of Africa, with its shops, churches and monuments to Risorgimento heroes and the founders of the colony. It reminded him of visits to Rome before the war to watch the horse shows in the Piazza di Siena and of warm evenings spent sitting in the pavement cafés of the Via Condotti. There was even polo, after a fashion. The Italians had levelled excellent playing fields outside the city, and all the ponies had been found in their neat stables when the British arrived. It was difficult for a high-goal player like Harari to get a good game, however, once the Indian regiments had returned to Egypt. Most of his fellow officers in the Occupied Enemy Territory Administration were happier with croquet.

But all these comforts and diversions had begun to pall by the summer, when the war in the desert took a different turn. Rommel's panzers had erased the memory of Wavell's triumph at Sidi Barrani, and the news from Egypt was very black. The 8th King's Royal Irish Hussars, Harari's regiment, was in the thick of it and he wanted to be back at the front, fighting at their side.

There was another reason, too, why he was so eager to return. Egypt was his home. His father, Sir Victor Harari, was a banker whose fortune had been made under Lord Cromer's administration of Egypt. In the years of British dominance in the Middle East, the Hararis, like other families of Cairo's *haute juiverie*, had become more British than the British. Max, 'a legendarily charming and dapper clubman' according to one friend, had been sent to Charterhouse and had gone on to Lincoln College, Oxford. He did not stay to complete his degree, however. Cosmopolitan, rich, fluent in French, German as well as Italian, which was widely spoken in Alexandria, Harari soon tired of university life, and many other activities before the war. There was a flat in London and a house in Le Touquet, as well as the pleasures of the Riviera, Italy and Cairo itself, then at its most fashionable.

Harari had volunteered when the war began and was offered a commission in a suitably fashionable cavalry regiment, whose traditions and lore made it just the kind of British institution he most loved. When the Irish Hussars were posted to Egypt, Harari held dinner parties for his fellow officers at the family mansion in Cairo. Surrounded by puppyish subalterns and their pretty English girlfriends, he would hold court in the heavily gilded, French dining room, where liveried Sudanese servants would wait at table. In his dress uniform, Harari would be seen languidly resting one elbow on the table, supporting the burden of his cigarette, an attractive companion always at his side. In his mid-thirties, Harari was older than the others, and the only one with an air of calm assurance. Much later, when the Eighth Army finally arrived in Naples and required a military governor for the playground island of Capri, Major Max Harari was felt to have all the necessary qualifications. Immense style and charm were not his only attributes, however. He was an excellent officer, and his bravery at El Alamein was to be mentioned in dispatches.

If his subordinates in military intelligence in Asmara found fault with Major Harari, it was because he was too indulgent towards the vanquished Italians. All manner of unsavoury characters would turn up in his office; narks, informers, time-wasters and the aggrieved. Many were members of the swiftly formed Unione Antifascista Italiana, trying to ingratiate themselves with the British military administration. More worthy of consideration were the mothers and wives who begged Harari to intercede for their sons or husbands incarcerated in Fort Baldissera. He would admit all, listen to their petitions sympathetically and then offer what reassurance he could, for the war had not changed his feelings for Italy or the Italians.

Some British officers might worry about a few Europeans hiding in the hills trying to avoid internment. But most were harmless, frightened souls, who simply did not want to leave their homes and families for a prison camp in South Africa or India. When a subordinate reported that an Italian woman was seen leaving Asmara for a nearby village every day to take food to her husband, Major Harari declined to take any action. One frightened clerk was hardly likely to bring down the British Empire. A certain elasticity was usually needed in dealings with Italians, and Harari was not a man to go looking for trouble. Besides, it was not as though the British required any more Italian prisoners.

More important, though, to the point that they were intruding on the pleasure of his evening rides at the manège beside the polo field, were the activities of a man whose name was being heard ever more frequently at British headquarters: Amedeo Guillet. Convoys coming up from Kassala had to be well guarded now.

Four attacks had been made on them, during which a number of soldiers had been killed and three lorries looted and burned out. One had been carrying a large consignment of whisky. But although empty bottles had been found in several Coptic villages in the hills, no one could account for how they had got there. On another occasion, the Asmara to Agordat railway had been sabotaged. The rails had been thrown down a gorge and the train fired upon. Telegraph lines were being cut; a road bridge, the Ponte Aosta, near Ghinda, had been damaged by a mine; and lorries travelling down towards Massaua had been shot at. The attacks were never pressed. Every time patrols were sent out, the guerrillas disappeared into the hills.

All these actions had been led by Guillet, Harari was informed, a cavalry officer who unaccountably had refused to surrender with the rest of the Italian army. With less evidence, other acts of sabotage and theft were soon attributed to him. One moment, Guillet was in the north of the country, then at Massaua, or over the border in Ethiopia. Brigadier Savory, briefly the military governor of Asmara, was informed that Guillet was going to attempt to kidnap him. The guards at the governor's palace were doubled, and for a while the gardens and menagerie were closed to the public.

When the British arrived in Asmara, chaotic efforts had been made by Italian functionaries to destroy sensitive papers. A huge pile had been set alight outside the headquarters of the Partito Nazionale Fascista, a similar bonfire blazed in front of the post office. But the military records of AOI's army had been captured intact, and from these, coupled with questioning civilians and soldiers who knew Guillet, Harari had accumulated a thick dossier on the Italian officer. All Amedeo's medal citations were included, as well as the confidential comments of his superiors. Harari knew of the charge at Selaclaca, of the captured Russian armoured cars at Santander, of the three bridges on the Codoñera and, of course, of the Gruppo Bande Amhara a Cavallo and the charges at Keru.

This last episode was still talked about in the British mess, elevated in the retelling to the scale of Balaclava. Guillet, Harari was told more than once, had been decapitated riding a magnificent horse, his sabre falling from his hand as he charged the guns. Heard it from a chap in the King's African Rifles, who was told it by an officer in the Skinner's before they were sent back to Egypt. Harari would listen, and say nothing. He discouraged talk about Guillet; the last thing he wanted to create among Asmara's Italian population was a full-blown folk hero.

Other Italian officers were also fighting on, most notably General Nasi and his army at Gondar. Outnumbered and cut off by a joint Anglo–Ethiopian force, he held out until November 1941, finally surrendering after bitter fighting. Others had become guerrillas. Colonel Di Marco was leading a fugitive existence on the vast, waterless plateaux of the Ogaden, towards Somalia; Major Lucchetti was still uncaptured around Addis Ababa, and Major Gobbi at Dessie. Captain Bellia, a follower of D'Annunzio, and veteran of the nationalist poet's seizure of Fiume after the First World War, was having some success convincing Ethiopians close to the emperor that they ought to hedge their bets with the British, who were about to lose Egypt and be kicked out of the Middle East. But all these officers and their men were cut off in Ethiopia, and most were only holding out in terror at surrendering to the Ethiopian 'patriots'. Even Nasi's sizeable force posed no serious threat, its defeat merely a matter of time. All were rounded up and sent into captivity.

Amedeo Guillet was a different problem. He was leading a well-organised and devoted band of indigenous fighters, the remnants of his Gruppo Bande. Furthermore, his activities were confined to Eritrea, which was still overwhelmingly sympathetic to the Italians. With good reason. When Orde Wingate and Brigadier Dan Sandford began organising the Ethiopian resistance, there had been a heated split between those who believed Haile Selassie should be restored to the whole of his empire, and those who supported the rights of its recently subjugated minorities. Before the Italian conquest of 1936, the British consul in Gore, home of the Galla people, had talked of 'the despotic Tafari [Haile Selassie] regime, and the supineness of the self-seeking treacherous smooth-spoken and bigoted Amhara officials'. In Wollo, too, the scene of bitter fighting during Ras Tafari's rise to power, the population were not overjoyed at his return. These complications were ignored by the emperor's British propagandists, notably Sandford and Sylvia Pankhurst.

In Eritrea, the antipathy felt towards Haile Selassie was even greater than in his rebellious provinces. The Eritreans watched with dismay as Ras Seyum, the duplicitous lord of Tigre, rode into Asmara at the head of 7000 men to join up with Platt. (After declining the usual requests for money and arms, the irascible British general suggested that Seyum's men discharge their tardy patriotic energies by acting as porters.)

The eventual fate of Eritrea was a matter of very little importance to the British military administration. The first priority was to keep the Italian infrastructure in place and have the colony resume producing food, which it did very efficiently. As to the future, there were those who dabbled with the notion of turning Eritrea into a Jewish homeland for Europe's refugees; others favoured partition, with the lion's share going to the Anglo–Egyptian Sudan, and the rest to the emperor. With Sylvia Pankhurst and her friends cheering on the Negus at every opportunity, Eritrea had the singular misfortune of falling foul of both the tidy minds of British colonial officials and the ill-informed sentimentality of the British left.

On one point everyone seemed agreed: the wishes of the local Eritrean population were not a consideration. The colony was occupied Italian territory, to be disposed of as its conquerors saw fit. The Eritreans, in short, were to pay for the sins of their masters. Yet Harari was aware that there were faint rumblings of an emerging national sentiment. After four months without pay, the *Zaptie* colonial police revolted and a couple were shot. A gathering of

Eritrean policemen, chiefs and intellectuals assembled at the Red Sea Hotel, not far from Asmara's mosque, and set up the Mahber Fikri Hager, the 'love of country' organisation. Its aims were as yet unfocused – some, out of genuine conviction or because they were on the emperor's payroll, wanted union with Ethiopia, others, especially the Muslims, wanted Eritrean independence – but it became a rallying point for Eritrean national feeling.

Inspired by very different motives, Amedeo was encouraging similar sentiments. An agitated and suspicious Eritrean population would serve the needs of Italy. He encouraged *ascari* to ransack military magazines scattered around the country and take their weapons back to their villages, rather than let them fall into British hands. Once the Axis armies arrived at Cairo he hoped to rally thousands of well-armed ex-*ascari* against the few British troops remaining in Eritrea and drive them out. Or even sooner, if the moment seemed opportune. If the British were pushed out of the Middle East, would they really wish to mount a new invasion of Eritrea, or even be in a position to do so? As for the Ethiopian 'patriots', Amedeo had no doubt that Eritrean *ascari* could see them off without difficulty.

He roamed the country maintaining the pretence of Italian power. He spoke to the Assaorta, the tribe from which the 4th Toselli were drawn, the Muslim Ad Shek, the Bileni around Keren, the Maria Rossi and the Maria Neri, the Giaberti Muslims of the littoral and, down on the lowlands towards the Sudan, the Beni Amer. He even resumed contact with the Muslim Mirghani clan in the Sudan, headed, after the death of their female chieftain – unique then in the Islamic world – by her son, Sherif Sayyed GaFar, who was similarly anti-British. To the north of Eritrea, he made contact with Muntaz (corporal) Ali, who kept up a continuous war against the British – and their Sudanese troops. Every morning, he would raise the Italian tricolour outside his tukul. For him, it was the symbol of Eritrea's independence, particularly independence from the emperor.

Amedeo told the chiefs of victories in the deserts of North Africa and encouraged the idea – for which he had no authority – that if Eritrea were to rise it would become an autonomous part of the Italian empire. He cited Libyans being given the right to Italian citizenship by Italo Balbo. Similarly, he issued promises of titles and rewards, which would be made good once the Italians returned. As would the backpay of his men. And everywhere he went he raised fears about the wrathful, predatory Negus Negusti, Lion of Judah, back on his throne and coldly coveting an Eritrea which had never been his.

# SIXTEEN

## *A Horse Called Sandro*

Three times the little aeroplane flew low over the column, seeming to slow down almost to a halt every time it circled. It was obvious that the pilot was suspicious. He would not be able to make out any weapons, but eighty men led by one on a grey horse was an unusual sight in the Eritrean countryside. Amedeo cursed his luck. It was always risky to venture out on to the bare Asmara plateau. Far better were the mountains or the green valleys and gorges below the city towards Massaua, where he could hide ten times that number of men without difficulty, especially when there were clouds.

Amedeo made rapid calculations. They were on the barren plateau midway between Ad Teclesan and Keren. There were few British troops in either place, so if they came after him, they would be driving out from Asmara. He doubted whether anyone would move on account of the pilot's radioed message; he would have to convince his officers personally that he had seen a guerrilla band. It would take twenty minutes to fly back to Asmara, half an hour to persuade his superiors, and then a further hour and a half before British troops from Asmara could be expected to show up, along the fast asphalt road. He had two and a half hours, maybe less. It would be mid-afternoon by then, with still plenty of light left in the day.

There was no point in returning to Azzega; if the aircraft tracked them that would mean leading the enemy straight back to his camp. Amedeo quickened his pace towards the distant mountains, where he had a rendezvous with the chief of the Maria Rossi. Once in the wooded foothills he would be safe, but for the next hour and a half his band would be in open country, almost parallel to the road.

He tried never to stay long on these visits to the chiefs. With much of the country on the brink of famine, a guest should try not to be a burden at such a time – particularly one who was a fugitive. He kept his stay brief and always brought presents, such as tins of corned beef, condensed milk or sacks of flour that he had looted from the British lorries. It had been a great disappointment when the band had held up a lorryload of cigarettes.

At British headquarters in Asmara, Captain Sigismund Reich came into Major Harari's office, in a state of unusual excitement. He had been passed the pilot's radioed report. It seemed a suspiciously well-ordered band, the pilot said, and they did not look like peasants or shepherds, still less pilgrims. Among them had been a man mounted on a horse; Reich was sure it was Guillet. He wanted to send out some patrols immediately.

Harari tried hard to disguise his feelings for his deputy. Reich was a diligent, driven man, and clearly rather brilliant. But they were opposites, and both recognised the fact. Urbane and charming, Harari was a Sephardic aristocrat who was perfectly at ease with his acquired Britishness. He was never deeply discomfited by occasional mutterings in the mess that he was just 'a damned oriental Jew'. The dependable virtues of the British, their elaborate social rituals and their complacency, all such a contrast to the quicksilver of his own Levantine background, made him forgive them their occasional oafishness and prejudices.

On the other hand, Reich was disliked and distrusted by his fellow officers. The son of an Ashkenazi engineer, born in Schonbrunn outside Vienna, he had been brought up in Palestine in the

Twenties. There, his name went through the first of its two changes during his life when Sigismund was Hebrewised to Susya. An outstanding linguist, Reich had studied in Italy and France before the war, where he had supported himself and earned a brilliant doctorate in Paris on Arabic and Aramaic civilisations. When war broke out he joined the British Army, but no one was in a hurry to offer him a commission in a fashionable cavalry regiment. Instead, he joined the Palestinian Buffs, which drew on Jewish volunteers from the British mandate of Palestine. Through sheer hard work and efficiency, he had risen to the rank of captain. But unlike Harari, he was never well liked. 'He was not always an easy colleague,' a friend admitted, 'because he had little patience with mediocrity and his tongue did not spare the inefficient.' His many enemies in the British administration found cruel amusement in his unfortunate name and initials: 'SS Reich'.

Bitterness had eaten into the soul of Sigismund Reich. The land of his birth rejected him and reviled his race, while he felt frustrated in the backwater of Palestine. Only Britain offered the prospect of a fulfilled life and yet, in spite of his efforts, which included speaking English without a trace of an accent, he would always be an outsider. To fit in, Reich concocted the most elaborate fantasies, although never in front of the shrewd Harari. He went too far when he let slip in the mess that he had been operating behind Italian lines during the campaign, working as a waiter in a hotel in Asmara. The untruthfulness of this claim eventually led to Reich leaving Eritrea under a cloud. He was posted to the Western Desert where, fighting the Germans, he changed his name again to David S. Rice, although he was known to his friends as 'Storm'.

Max Harari could not help admiring the Italian cavalry officer, whose brilliant military career and sporting achievements were recorded in a bulging file. He was a Don Chisciotte, Harari felt, vainly fighting for something which was already over. He admired Guillet's courage, obstinacy and pride. He would have shot him without a second's hesitation, of course, but he knew that in doing so something else would be lost apart from simply an enemy's life. Reich was unburdened by such sentiments. It fascinated and repelled Harari to see the enthusiasm with which he pursued Guillet. He had developed an obsession with this man, who represented everything that Reich despised. For him, chivalry in war showed contemptible weakness, or was mere self-indulgence. He wanted Amedeo Guillet dead, or locked up in Fort Baldissera, and he was not in the slightest bothered which.

Harari listened to his deputy and agreed to his request for a couple of hundred troops. Picking up his riding stick and white gloves – and noting his deputy's look of disapproval – he bid him good hunting.

Amedeo had a fair idea what the British would do. They would come by road as far as possible and then leave their lorries, fanning out into the country. His men were well out of sight of the road now, but still some way from the safety of the mountains through which flowed the Anseba. The land was covered with clumps of euphorbia and thin woods of wild olive and juniper, but no thicker cover as yet.

A sweating scout came running back to him. He had seen enemy troops, maybe a hundred of them, loosely spread out as they combed the countryside. They were in the plain beyond the woods, which meant they would be on them in ten or fifteen minutes. Amedeo had his men take cover behind a hillock, dismounted and handed Sandor's, reins to one of his men to lead. He gave the order to fix bayonets and those who still had grenades should get ready to use them. Crouching as low as he could, so as not to make an outline against the sky, Amedeo swept the ground in front of him with his binoculars. The enemy were about a kilometre and a half away, but behind them was a promisingly thick wood which marked the valley of the Anseba. The enemy were all Sudanese, he saw with relief, rather than a superior Indian unit.

They were still not concentrating in force, but advancing in a thin line, ten to twenty metres apart. Amedeo held his men back, as he watched the enemy approach, lying with one cheek pressed against the ground.

He gently slid back behind the hillock, put away his binoculars and slid a bullet into the chamber of his carbine. His men were silent, looking up at him intently. He gave it another two minutes. The Sudanese had to be almost at the hillock. He raised his arm, ordered the charge and scrambled over the top. He ran straight towards the enemy, firing and reloading as he went on. Behind him his men yelled bloodcurdling cries. Some of the enemy knelt to take aim, others fired wildly and ran, their bullets whizzing over Amedeo's head. He heard a shriek of pain behind him but did not look back. As they broke through, other Sudanese began concentrating their fire. But Amedeo kept his men running for the trees. Most had overtaken him by the time he at last reached their cover. He collapsed breathlessly in a shallow ditch, his ankle in agony. The wound had broken open again and was bleeding.

Faced with well-aimed fire, the Sudanese held back. But in the distance other figures were running forward to join them. Amedeo took several deep breaths and forced himself to rise. They had to keep moving, he said, deeper into the trees and up along the narrow valley of the Anseba. He looked round for Sandor. Two men had been killed, he was told, including the *ascaro* leading his horse. Someone had seen Sandor galloping away from the shots. Leaning heavily on his carbine, Amedeo began hobbling after his men. The horse that had carried him at Selaclaca and at Keru was lost forever.

Major Max Harari worked late in his office that night, waiting for Reich to return. Suddenly a door slammed and a stream of German obscenities echoed down the corridor of the *palazzo* that had once been the headquarters of De Bono, Badoglio and Frusci. He sighed, poured a glass of Scotch and leaned back at his desk. Reich was an odd character certainly, the major conceded, but he somehow doubted whether these guttural expletives augured good news. Nor was it going to reflect brilliantly on him. To borrow a couple of hundred troops and still come home empty-handed was going to take some explaining. He raised his glass, sipping the Scotch, and then called out to the captain. The sooner he knew the details the better.

The grey stallion, however, was some compensation. It was a lovely animal, and one of the best schooled horses Harari had ever ridden. He was slightly too tall and heavy for the little Arab, but the paces were fluid and he admired the horse's keen intelligence. Immaculately dressed in a freshly ironed shirt, white gloves and jodhpurs – little details which the Italian women of Asmara found so untypical in a British officer – he rode Sandor over jumps in the manège that would be high even for a much bigger animal.

Harari never understood why the Eritrean grooms, who recognised the horse, insisted on calling him Sandor, however. It was obviously a mistake, a mispronunciation of the Italian name Sandro – as in Alessandro – and so he was renamed by the British major.

SEVENTEEN

# *Captain Reich*

Amedeo always thought of Orlando Rizzi as an old pioneer, like a character in the Wild West. His efforts to make a life for himself in Eritrea since he arrived in 1911 had an epic scale to them. In a valley at Dorfu, twenty kilometres from Asmara, he had built from nothing a functional country villa and an estate with fields overflowing with maize, bananas and papayas. He even had a dairy herd, for the lush valleys below Asmara's plateau had good pasture.

Since his arrival, Rizzi had only once been back to Italy, and that was to volunteer in the First World War. He did not have to do so; the colonies were exempt from conscription. But Rizzi was a patriot, of a vigorous pre-Fascist stamp. To his farm workers, Copts from the Highlands, a few coastal Muslims and Yemenis, he was a patriarchal landowner, who considered himself firm but fair. He had a genuine love for the country and for the Eritreans – '*i figli nostri*', our sons – and he had deplored Graziani's conduct in Ethiopia.

Living as a fugitive, Amedeo avoided his fellow countrymen. They were more closely watched by the British than the indigenous population and they were, he conceded reluctantly, irredeemable *chiacchieroni* – chatterers. Orlando Rizzi, though, was a man he felt he could rely on. After prayers in the mosque one Friday, Amedeo walked into his office in Asmara. The landowner did not recognise the bearded Arab standing before him, until he began speaking

Italian. He wanted Rizzi to give some account to his parents and Bice of what he had been trying to do, and why he had felt he could not surrender. If Rizzi did not hear from him again, the likelihood was that he would be dead, caught by an unlucky shot while attacking some convoy or depot. The old farmer suggested that Amedeo hide out at Dorfu, where he could pass himself off as a farm-worker, eat well and rest. Amedeo was tempted as he needed a place where he could disappear completely, but he turned the invitation down. The risks were too great to impose on Rizzi; Italian civilians caught helping saboteurs faced a sentence of hard labour.

Four months after the British conquest his men did not keep camp any more, but were widely dispersed throughout sympathetic villages. Roaming the countryside was becoming more difficult too, as his brush with the Sudanese made plain. Positions were well guarded, convoys were protected and the British were rounding up Italian civilians not vital to the colony's administration. On one foray to the mosque in Asmara, Amedeo had had the unpleasant surprise of seeing his face on a British 'wanted' poster. It was an old photograph from his military files, very different from his present appearance, but it was a disturbing development, especially as there was now talk of a reward for his recapture.

A second unsettling encounter with the British made Amedeo reconsider Rizzi's offer. He was riding with eight of his men on camels one afternoon near Ghinda, where he had hidden a cache of arms. Khadija was sitting behind him, adding to the impression that they were a party of Eritrean civilians. They had kept away from the main Asmara to Massaua road as much as possible, but had no option but to ride along it for a few kilometres before crossing into the countryside below. While they were doing so, two converted Chevrolets with mounted machine guns drove up towards them through the haze.

The vehicles, covered in dust from the coastal desert heaved to a halt forty metres away. Amedeo kept the camels slowly moving towards them, feeling for the stock of his carbine under a blanket on his *rakla*, the saddle. In the front seat of the first car sat an unsmiling British captain, who was staring at him fixedly. For a few fleeting seconds their eyes met. The officer then suddenly reached behind him for a Thompson machine gun, stood up and started firing. The camels immediately panicked, lunging away from the terrifying noise. As Amedeo struggled to control his beast, one bullet passed straight through his turban. He heard Khadija cry out as another grazed her leg and then the camel and its two riders fell down the high embankment. Two other camels and riders came somersaulting after them. The rest, kicked on by their riders, managed to stay upright as they slid down the steep slope. British soldiers ran to the edge of the road, and took aim with rifles. Khadija recovered first, opening up with Amedeo's Mauser Marine on quick-fire. There was a scream from above, then the British ran back to their cars, which they drove forward so that they could fire down with the heavy machine guns. But it was too late. Amedeo and his men took cover in a dense clump of trees and returned fire on an enemy silhouetted and vulnerable on the road. They kept up a sporadic exchange for a few minutes, until Amedeo ordered his men to move off, lest any more enemy troops came along. Astonishingly, no one was badly wounded, and Khadija was still able to walk.

For days afterwards Amedeo was unsettled by this experience, wondering why the British officer had suddenly opened fire. He wondered if it had been so obvious who he was. The encounter finally made him accept Rizzi's offer. He was given a comfortable tukul in the workers' village at Dorfu where he lived with Khadija. Her half-brother, Asfao, stayed nearby. His presence was easily enough explained. Ahmed Abdullah was a Libyan who could not get home, the farm workers were told. A couple of Yemenis there were in exactly the same position. As a Libyan, it was not unusual that he could speak Italian, nor that his Arabic was accented. When Amedeo disappeared on his forays, Rizzi let it be known that

Ahmed Abdullah was away on his behalf. But attacks on convoys were less frequent now, with Eritrea firmly under British rule. Amedeo encouraged those of his men, who were in bad shape, to return home taking their arms with them, ready to be called on again when the need arose. Only thirty stayed with him, scattered in various villages around Dorfu and he did not take all of them together on his raids.

At first, Amedeo tried to do the same tasks as the other farm workers but, both emaciated and weakened by his wound, he was not strong enough. When cutting a maize field he started well ahead of the others, who were methodically pacing themselves, but by evening, when everyone else had finished, Amedeo, limping heavily, was still way behind with his share. His wound was a constant concern, and it astonished him that the infection simply lingered, without getting better or turning gangrenous. Rizzi urged him to see a doctor in Asmara.

'Do you trust him?' Amedeo asked.

Rizzi pondered the question for a moment. 'No,' he replied.

Iodine and clean dressings were to be the only treatment, but Rizzi also moved Ahmed Abdullah to the easier job of tending his wife's vegetable and flower gardens. And he was at last being fed properly. The farmer often invited Amedeo to join his family for Sunday lunch, prepared by Filomena, their Piedmontese maid. But Amedeo declined, feeling it better to avoid the attention such an invitation would bring him at the farm. One Sunday, however, reassured that Signora Rizzi and her three daughters would not be there, for he had no wish for them to know that he was on the farm, Amedeo finally agreed. There were four of them round the table: Rizzi, his nephew, Peter, the Swiss farm manager and cheesemaker, and Amedeo. The pasta had been cleared away, and Filomena was fussing over the main course of braised frogs. Peter excused himself to step outside. He opened the door and immediately closed it again. Turning round, he hissed that the house was surrounded.

Amedeo just had enough time to grab Filomena, seat her in his chair and grab a broom before a Sudanese NCO banged the door open. He ordered everyone to stand and raise their hands. Captain Reich then came into the room. Blond-haired and blue-eyed, he looked unsmilingly at each Italian in turn. He paid no attention to the Arab servant, the only person present who made no effort to put up his hands, and who began to clear away the plates on the table. Reich started speaking to Rizzi in heavily accented Italian. With Peter, he quickly changed to more fluent French, addressing his questions through him from then on.

In the kitchen next door, Amedeo washed the plates. Then he washed them a second time, looking anxiously through the door towards Filomena, who was frightened and jittery. When he returned to the dining room to clear more things away, he asked her in deliberately broken Italian to help. No one objected. In the kitchen, the trembling woman kept repeating that she was afraid for him. '*Ca'staga ciuta*, Filomena! *Ciuta!*' Amedeo whispered in Piedmonetese, telling her to keep quiet. Reich then pushed open the kitchen door.

In Italian, he told her to cook him a couple of eggs. He was bored now. The Italians here were obviously civilians and his men had found nothing suspicious in the outbuildings. A couple of fried eggs seemed legitimate plunder for his wasted day. He was amazed to see the flustered woman break an egg straight on to the stove. And then do this a second time.

'I do it, Filomena,' said the Arab, putting the pan on the stove.

While they were cooking, he cut some bread and made coffee, and Reich sat down at the kitchen table. Filomena quietly slipped back to the dining room, less frightened of the Sudanese soldiers than of the British officer.

Reich ate the eggs and began slicing a papaya.

'Do any Italian soldiers on the run come here?' he asked suddenly, in excellent Arabic.

'Of course,' Amedeo replied, surprised at how calm he felt.

'They often pass through, and the master gives them something to eat and then sends them on their way. He cannot do less, but he is a coward.'

'Does the name *Tenente* Guillet mean anything to you? Or his armed *shifta*?'

'Maybe, maybe not,' the Arab replied, for there had been many passing through the farm. 'Is there anything in it for me?' he asked ingratiatingly.

The officer told him to let him know if anyone suspicious arrived and that he would reward him well. He would find him in the centre of Asmara in the big building in the square where the British flag flew and soldiers guarded the entrance. He was to ask for 'Captain Reich', and the Arab made several attempts to pronounce the name.

When the British lorries drove off down the farm road out of Dorfu, Orlando Rizzi headed straight for his wine cellar. Amedeo's performance required a celebration. Over a couple of bottles of chianti the Italians relived their favourite moments, imitating all the expressions of the humourless Captain Reich. Ahmed Abdullah, either from Muslim resolve, or fear of being seen with a drink in his hand, declined the wine. But Rizzi in his enthusiasm insisted on photographing Amedeo in his Arab guise.

## EIGHTEEN

# *Le Maschere*

The two months Khadija spent at the farm were probably the happiest of her life with Amedeo. She had a proper home of her own at last, a large round tukul, whose thick straw walls were proof against Dorfu's peculiar microclimate. In this small, green valley below the Asmara plateau, the weather could change in an instant from hot sunshine to shrouds of cool, moist clouds, as impenetrable, Amedeo believed, as London's smog. She enjoyed being part of the community of farmworkers and their families. Every few days she would walk up the long farm road, past the large, walled cistern Rizzi had built to collect rainwater for the farm, to the small village three kilometres away. She would buy dried fish, flour and tea from its market, and find out what was going on in the outside world: the strange ways of the colony's new masters, and of the latest outrages of their detested Sudanese troops, who were prone to drunken brawling in Asmara.

Khadija invested Amedeo's wages in a goat and a few hens. As her man was earning ten *lire* a day, there was even a little left over for luxuries, an ornate comb and a second-hand pair of European shoes. The tukul was modest but comfortable. There was no furniture apart from the two wood and rope beds, but Khadija had a large wicker box, like a picnic hamper, in which she kept her prized possessions. A cracked mirror hung on the wall beside the cooking utensils, and she had pinned up photographs of Italian movie stars, torn from magazines. Outside, a rope stretched between two poles for wet clothes and drying meat, and there were a few large cans to store water.

Filomena had quickly adopted Khadija and they spent hours together at the big villa. She would often return to the tukul with her hair rearranged into new styles, and once Ahmed Abdullah was disconcerted to see her wearing a cast-off European dress. Her dark lips were a slash of red lipstick and hanging round her neck was the silver chain with the image of the Madonna that Amedeo had given her, but which, out of a sense of Muslim propriety, she usually kept hidden. Filomena also began teaching her the rudiments of Italian cooking, and occasionally Khadija would bring back warm pans containing her efforts at *pasta al forno* and *spezzatino*. For Ahmed Abdullah, they were a pleasing variation on the *zigni* stew that was the staple Eritrean diet.

Asfao, one of Amedeo's most devoted followers, would generally join them for supper. Seven years older than his half-sister, he would chat amiably about the day's work and the other labourers. Amedeo was fond of this simple, good-natured man, who seemed to bear no resentment towards his sister whom both their father and the *comandante* had raised to a position far higher than that of himself. When it was time to turn in, he would politely excuse himself and leave.

Life on Rizzi's farm settled into a pleasing routine, and it seemed to Khadija, watching Amedeo tending the grapes and papaya plants, or cutting flowers for Signora Rizzi, that her *comundar-as-shaitan* was beginning to settle down at last. Every couple of weeks, Amedeo would go off to find his men, taking Daifallah, who was also working in Rizzi's fields. Amedeo trusted him entirely. He had used him as his runner many times, at Cochen, Keren and Ad Teclesan. And the Yemeni had been at his side throughout his guerrilla actions. The latest had involved blowing a wide crater in the road at the Menabrea Bridge, encouraged by the exhortation on its arches: *Ca custa lon ca custa*: Let it cost what it cost. It would not take long for the British to make good the damage, but it would hold up their lorries for a while, and remind them that there were still those around ready to fight.

Every time Amedeo set off to meet up with his men Khadija tried to hide her concern. The longer they stayed at the farm, the more she preferred her settled life. She had tried to understand Amedeo's war against the other Europeans, and he had explained several times why he had to fight on. But she knew from her visits to Asmara that the British controlled the whole country, with no resistance from the other Italians, and they could do as they wished. Although it seemed disloyal for her to admit such a view, the newcomers did not look like an enemy facing defeat. In the past, she had always feared that Amedeo would return to Italy, to the woman with red hair whose photograph she remembered from Amba Gheorgis. But now it was more likely, she knew watching him limp up the farm road with Daifallah, that one day he would not return at all.

Amedeo was no longer recognisable as the commander of the Gruppo Bande. He had grown his hair and beard, and wore a futa around his loins, a torn shirt and a turban. Five times a day he climbed the hill behind the Rizzis' house, where there was a tomb of a long dead pilgrim of the Hadj that had become a shrine for the local Muslims. He received great comfort from repeating the Arabic recitations he had first learned in Libya, and when he went to Asmara on Fridays, he always visited the mosque. His prayers were sincere, for he believed in God and was unconcerned whether he addressed Him using the rituals of the Roman church or Islam.

His days had a rhythm at the farm that he too enjoyed. Each morning, he would water the grapefruit and papaya or prune the shoots off the banana trees, as he had been taught. In the afternoon, he would tend Signora Rizzi's garden and vines. At the day's end, when walking back up the hill to the farmworkers' village, he looked forward to seeing Khadija outside the tukul cooking supper over a fire in a circle of stones. It would strike him then how beautiful she was. At twenty, she was no longer the tomboy she had been at Amba Gheorgis. They had been friends, enjoying each other as life flashed by while Amedeo immersed himself in policing the Semien. But an empire had fallen since then, and their relationship had deepened. Amedeo trusted her more than he did any other living person. And, yes, he admitted to himself, he loved her. Khadija stood up and waved when she saw him approaching. The simple long cotton shift she wore emphasised her height and slender figure, imbuing her with an elegance far greater than that of the old European dress. He was proud of her, and of the fact that she was his.

One afternoon, a few weeks after Captain Reich's visit, Amedeo was watering the garden and noticed that the drawing-room window was open. All the Rizzis were in Asmara, and Filomena was airing the house. The landowner had often invited Amedeo to make himself at home whenever he was away. He had never taken advantage of this before but, hot and tired, he felt like a rest. He climbed through the window, put Mascagni's opera *Le Maschere* on the gramophone and stretched out on the sofa. Melancholy swept over him as he listened to the music. He wondered how his elderly parents were coping with the war, living in the musty palazzo at Capua, and he thought of the Gandolfos and Bice, and whether she was still waiting for him. Suddenly, he was being pushed roughly, and he awoke from his half-sleep to see Filomena standing over him.

'They've come back! They've come back!'

It was the Sudanese soldiers. Leaving the record grating on the gramophone, Amedeo jumped out of the window, ignoring the army lorry at the front of the Rizzis' villa. He began walking up the hill towards the pilgrim's tomb, forcing down an almost irresistible temptation to break into a run. Their sudden return had completely unnerved him. He was in no state to repeat the performance he had staged for Reich. He was deeply and irrationally frightened, knowing that he ought to have stayed in the house where at least he could have explained his presence.

Behind him he could hear shouting. A Sudanese sergeant was telling him to halt. The order was repeated, first in Arabic, then in English, but he kept on walking at the same pace up towards the pilgrim's tomb and its votive rags. A shot rang out and Amedeo heard it whistle just above his head. The sergeant aimed again. Abraha, the Coptic foreman at the farm, saved Amedeo's life by pushing up the soldier's rifle.

'Don't you understand, he is deaf?' Abraha shouted. 'Must I, a Nazerene, have to stop you from slaying one of your own Muslim brothers on his way to pray?'

Amedeo heard the argument behind him, but did not turn. He looked down at his hand in front of him. It was shaking violently, and he could not stop it. Never before, even in the heat of battle, had fear taken such a hold of him. Images of Rizzi being taken away to forced labour assailed him, and he thought of his wife and daughters losing their home. He knew that if the Sudanese troops stopped him, he would break down. They would search him. The British might even strip him and find that he was not circumcised, according to the faith. At last he reached the tomb of the pilgrim and prostrated himself on the ground.

The farm outhouses and the village were brusquely searched. The sergeant who had fired at Amedeo, furious at having lost face in front of his men, violently pushed Khadija away when he arrived at the tukul. He emptied her boxes on the earth floor. Wrapped in a piece of cloth, he found an empty bottle of Coty scent, an old present from Amedeo. He demanded to know how Khadija had obtained a European perfume. She threw herself on her knees and begged for mercy. If her husband found out that she had been given it by an admirer he would beat her to death. The sergeant burst out laughing, assuming that Rizzi or one of the other Europeans on the farm was sleeping with her. He crushed the bottle under his boot and grabbed the drying meat from the line outside as he walked away.

Only when it was dark did Amedeo come down from the hill. He was silent and morose when he arrived back at the tukul. Khadija began telling him excitedly how she had outwitted the sergeant, clasping his knees like a panic-stricken, unfaithful wife. But Amedeo didn't hear a word. He had in his hand a piece of paper, a note to Rizzi, he told her. In it, he said that he was leaving the next day. He would not wait for the farmer's return because he knew Rizzi would try to change his mind. He had so nearly been caught, he explained to Khadija, all because of a foolish yearning to listen to music. He had endangered her, Rizzi, Filomena, Peter and everyone else who knew that he was at the farm. Besides, even the Eritrean chiefs were urging him to leave. The last time he had been to Azzega, Gabreyesus Geremeddin, worried by his deteriorating physical condition, had told him that he ought to bring his resistance to an end. If Amedeo were shot or captured, his campaign would be over and that of the chiefs to remain free of the Negus would be weakened even before it had taken organised form. The net was closing in, Amedeo admitted. First, there had been that strange officer who had shot at them on the road, then the visit of Captain Reich. Now the British had come back again. They had been at the farm for long enough.

He had made another decision at the pilgrim's tomb. He was going to end the band. Those men who had stayed with him could achieve little more against an enemy who had so tightened their grip on Eritrea. It was time for all of them to return to their villages, and for him to attempt to reach neutral Yemen.

A few days later, in a clearing in the woods around Ghinda, a circle of men sat listening as though to a village imam, except that they had rifles over their knees. Addressing them as 'dear brothers', Amedeo told the remnants of the Gruppo Bande Amhara a Cavallo that they had done their duty with honour and courage, but that they had to go home. The struggle was not over, but it was suspended. He knew that his remaining *ascari*, a few Yemenis and Amhara, but mostly Eritreans, would never surrender. They should take their guns back to their villages and wait for the call. Gebreyesus Geremeddin had their names and where they could be found, and when the right moment came they would rise again. The Italian tricolour, which they had served so well, would never forget them, nor the thousands of others who had died defending it. And it would return.

The news from North Africa was good, he reminded them. The British had lost Tobruk and were being pushed back into Egypt. The time to fight would come again, and he would return to lead them. Amedeo saluted smartly, the others stood to attention, shouting '*Viva il re!*' They had only the haziest notion of what the Italian crown represented in Europe. But for sixty years the tricolour, with the red shield and white cross of Savoy in the centre, had flown over Eritrea. Its values were concrete; the benefits of its rule everywhere apparent. Whatever the future might bring, the point of departure was the red, white and green flag that had brought Eritrea into existence.

With this parade-ground ritual, the *ascari* reaffirmed their admiration and respect for the man who had led them into battle many times, and whose future was even less certain than their own. Amedeo embraced the men in turn, trying to fix something about each face in his memory. Then the men began to move away across the plain.

When he came to part with Khadija, he told her to get provisions from the farm, and stay at Azzega before her long journey back to the mountains of the Semien. In four or five days she should reach her father's village. His tone was brusque and free of emotion. Khadija listened, briefly nodded, and walked away without turning back, her head unbowed. Asfao hesitated a moment, then stepped forward and embraced his *comandante*. They held each other tightly, and then he followed his sister.

Only Daifallah was still with him, for he too was hoping to cross the sea to Yemen. They watched the two figures walking across the plain until finally they, too, disappeared. When they did so, Amedeo could hold back his emotions no longer. He covered his face in his hands and wept. The Yemeni beside him turned away.

It was late afternoon before Amedeo finally stood up. Together with Daifallah, he began limping down the road to Massaua.

NINETEEN

# *The Well*

In all Eritrea there was no better place to disappear than Al-Katmia. A slum of corrugated iron and brushwood shacks, it sprawled from the fringe of Massaua into the desert proper. A shifting population of coastal Muslims, disbanded *ascari*, Yemeni dockers and mercenaries trying to return home had crowded into Al-Katmia. No Europeans lived anywhere near the quarter, surrendering the few sea breezes of the coast that made life in Massaua tolerable, nor would they willingly visit the place.

Daifallah found a shack in the centre of the shanty town where the two could stay on credit. Improvised from driftwood, ancient corrugated iron and thatch, it stood in a courtyard with several others surrounded by a high brushwood fence. The interior was divided by wicker matting and Amedeo had his own private space, though little larger than the rope bed that filled it. A few chickens roamed the courtyard, and under a lean-to were communal cooking pots, and a fire. Not far away were a standpipe and narrow cesspit over which were stretched two rocking planks. After satisfying their needs, civic minded residents would throw down some sand to cover the mess, and so discourage the swarm of flies.

There were two ways of getting to the Yemen from Eritrea in the closing months of 1941. One was to obtain a permit from the British port authorities to travel on the large single-sail sambuk that plied between Massaua and Hodeida once a month. The other was to seek passage on one of the numerous smugglers' vessels.

While anonymous, a smuggler's boat would take longer and involve unpredictable dangers and complications. However, this seemed to Amedeo the better bet.

Both options required money, and he had none. All the wages he had earned from Rizzi he had given to Khadija and he had nothing left. Nor did he feel he could ask Rugiu for more, as he had already tapped that generous source in the past. Most of the others in the shack were dockers who made a living loading and unloading the British merchant ships at Massaua. It was backbreaking, poorly paid and there was strong competition, but it seemed the only work available.

In the midday heat, Amedeo and Daifallah waited to help unload flour from a cargo vessel. When it came to their turn, the Italian discovered how tough this work could be. He tied a rope of hemp around his head, protecting his kidneys by wrapping wads of cloth around his body, then heaved the sack onto his back. The laden dockers always moved at a trot, muttering '*Ala al ginni, ala al ginni*' (Shield me! Shield me from evil spirits!') under their breath. At the end of the day, there were deep red furrows on his forehead from the rope and Amedeo could barely stand upright. He could not decide which hurt more, his spine which had been twisted when a horse fell on him during a steeplechase in Udine ten years before, or the bullet wound to his ankle. Daifallah had to help him limp back to Al-Katmia, and he knew that he would not last many days on the docks.

Some relief came when he got a job as a nightwatchman. He was being paid indirectly by the British authorities to guard a warehouse confiscated from an Italophile businessman called Omar al Kekia Pasha. Amedeo had known him before the war, and was amused to find himself dressed in rags protecting his property. As soon as the sun went down, four watchmen were positioned at each side entrance of the building. Every fifteen minutes throughout the night a shout of 'Hah! Hah!' would pass around to make sure all the watchmen were awake. After working in the port all day,

Amedeo was desperately tired. Opposite his doorway was the shack of Um Aminah, an old woman, who sat outside smoking her *nargileh* and drinking *gishir*, an infusion made from coffee bean husks. Unable to sleep herself, she took pity on the exhausted figure opposite and invited him to share her brew and stretch out on her rope bed. Amedeo soon fell asleep, and when the nightwatchmen passed around their rousing calls, Um Aminah would answer on his behalf.

Amedeo and Daifallah survived on boiled rice and whatever vegetables could be found. Their weight fell away and, on the wages they earned, they were never going to save enough for the passage to the Yemen.

Sharing the shack was an elderly Muslim Eritrean, Salah, who acted as the *ad hoc* leaseholder. He had found lucrative employment selling water in the city, which he would collect with his donkey from a well about four kilometres away. He would then return to the centre of Massaua, spread over two islands that were linked in the 1850s by long causeways built by the Swiss adventurer Werner Metzinger, who had briefly ruled the city as an oriental potentate. The causeways had been heavily bombarded by the British, cutting the water supply. In the evenings, the old man would complain of his fatiguing work to the Arab he took to be a Libyan. Amedeo saw the opportunity immediately. He suggested to Salah that they form a partnership. The old man went only once to the spring, whereas he could manage at least two journeys. Why not rest, while Amedeo worked? And whatever proceeds there were in the evening could be divided between them.

The old man hesitated. Lending his donkey to a stranger in Al-Katmia was a considerable risk, and could the young Libyan be trusted to share the spoils honestly? Amedeo was subjected to a lengthy examination, and his origins and family in distant Libya, where Salah had once served as a shumbashi in Italy's colonial army, were closely scrutinised. But something about the younger man won the old Eritrean's trust, and he agreed – but not before another lengthy discourse on how to do the job properly and not lame the donkey. Above all, he warned, Ahmed Abdullah should beware of being swindled, for most of his customers would be women, and only a practised hand such as Salah himself knew how to deal with them.

On the first day, they set off together, following the track to the well. Its sandstone parapet was furrowed by ropes which had been lowered and raised to the water for centuries. Salah laboriously demonstrated his technique for filling the water skins and carefully loading them on the donkey, for he expected Ahmed Abdullah to follow him precisely, with no deviation from his tried and tested technique. The young man had to promise that he would ensure the burden was equally balanced on either side, or the beast would certainly go lame. They returned to the city over Metzinger's narrow causeways and Salah shook his head sadly when they passed British soldiers in their unfamiliar uniforms. How had the Italians, so rich and so cunning, been defeated by these people, and why did no one think that the newcomers would stay, as all their predecessors had done? There was talk that Eritrea might be handed over to the thieving Amhara of Ethiopia. How the world had changed, Salah lamented, giving thanks that at his great age he would soon be free from it.

The next day, Amedeo began to work in earnest. To make the water business pay, he had to make at least two trips to the well, which meant rising before dawn. As he was bringing more water into the city, he could afford to reduce the price – a strategy which his partner accepted very reluctantly, for the laws of supply and demand were another feature of the changing world that pained Salah.

As well as undercutting his competitors, Amedeo added a few marketing devices of his own as he hawked his water through the narrow Arabic streets.

'*Moia! Moia!* Water! Water!' he chanted. 'Fresh and sweet is my water, dear ladies, as is the warmth of your heart.'

'And what have you put in your water today, Ahmed Abdullah, to make it so sweet?' the women would reply.

'Honey, dear ladies, honey sweetens my water.'

The Muslim women, whether Eritrean or Arab, were amused by such rare flatteries, and flirting with Ahmed Abdullah became a pleasing diversion from their daily chores. When a customer bought water, Ahmed would often give her a discount, making her promise not to tell the other women, for the reduced price was in honour of her alone. At other times, he would give their children water for free, remarking loudly how pretty they were, and give them an approving pinch to the cheek. His business thrived, and Amedeo was convinced he was bringing in more money selling water in Massaua than he had ever earned as a lieutenant in the Italian army.

But it was tiring work. In the evening, he came back to the shack and hurled himself onto an *angareb*, exhausted. His partner sat smoking his *nargileh* and drinking tea, casting a critical eye over the younger man. The old Eritrean complained that Ahmed Abdullah was not taking due care of the firm's capital equipment. The young man had made himself some tea and stretched out to rest, before giving the donkey water and hay.

'Father, you are right, but leave me be. All day and most of the night I work, making more money for you than you had ever earned before.'

Salah put down the *nargileh*'s alabaster mouthpiece and tended to his beast, shaking his head in disappointment.

'Today, the youth are not as they were.'

Daifallah, also tried his hand at free enterprise. He took a thaler from Amedeo's hard-earned profits and bought flour, ginger, sugar and cinnamon to make little cakes. With mounting scepticism, Amedeo watched him assembling the unappetising mounds that he then baked and hoped to sell. He was very fond of Daifallah, but doubted whether he had the temperament to succeed in business. All day, no one approached to buy the Yemeni's cakes.

Then, late in the evening, a customer asked to buy the lot. When he suggested a discount for a bulk order, Daifallah was indignant and haughtily sent him away.

'These delicacies are wasted on vulgar stomachs,' he explained to Amedeo back at the shack, before eating them all himself. After tasting one, the Italian did not encourage another venture into this line of work. Instead, he urged Daifallah to find a smuggler who would get them to the Yemen, while he raised the necessary funds.

Weeks passed in Massaua, with Amedeo busy and prospering in the water business. In his few moments of relaxation, he would stretch out on the roof of his shack and doze in the dying sun of early evening. He would look down on a couple in the next courtyard, enjoying their moments of tenderness, which were so rare to witness between the sexes in the Islamic world. The intimacy between them made him think of Bice, and the life they might have expected together, had there not been the war.

One evening, he was climbing up to his secluded perch when a loud explosion ripped through the shanty town, making him lose his grip and fall to the ground. The whole of Al-Katmia had been shaken. Lumps of concrete began raining down on the shacks. There was a second explosion, followed by a third. And then they were continuous. In no time, the whole of Al-Katmia was on its feet. Everyone was panicking, pushing down the wicker fences of the enclosures as they ran away. Amedeo grabbed his few possessions, and put an arm around Salah.

'What about my donkey?' shouted the old man.

But, as he spoke, the beast pushed its way out of the courtyard, joining the stampede. It was obvious to Amedeo what had happened. The huge depot of captured Italian munitions, stacked alarmingly close to Al-Katmia, had gone up in flames. For three hours the whole of Massaua was rocked by explosions.

Some British officers suspected that the notorious Amedeo

Guillet was responsible for this outrage, which had killed scores of Eritreans in the shanty town and had done a lot of damage. Sylvia Pankhurst wrote in an article (later republished in her book, *Ethiopia and Eritrea: the last phase of the reunion struggle 1941–52*):

> A fire in the harbour of Massaua, though attributed to an unknown cause, was believed by the British authorities to be due to sabotage. The government property destroyed in the fire was valued at £1,000,000 and almost the whole of the native quarter was destroyed. Captain Amedeo Guillet . . . openly claimed to have had a share in the work and to have derailed a train at Nefasit.

The train was certainly his work, but blowing up the munitions dump risked his own life along with hundreds of others. It also served little military purpose. The Italian shells were valueless to the British, and the damage to the workings of the port was slight. Leaving the munitions open to the summer rains and then the searing sun were far more likely to have caused them to explode spontaneously.

As the last explosions died down, the residents of Al-Katmia hesitantly made their way back to their homes. Amedeo's shack had lost its roof, but was otherwise undamaged. In the days after the blast, the British began to show an undue interest in the shanty town. A medical officer and soldiers arrived to test the drain water for contamination, ostensibly concerned about cholera. They were asking questions about suspicious newcomers as well. But much to Amedeo's relief, the posters with his photograph, which he had seen in Asmara, never appeared in Massaua.

Shortly afterwards, Daifallah returned to Al-Katmia one evening accompanied by a corpulent figure with a piratical moustache and beard. A large *jambiya* dagger was stuck in his cummerbund, and he had grown both his little fingernails long so that he could pick at irritants in the orifices of his body. A smuggler was hardly likely to resemble a Franciscan, Amedeo felt, and in spite of the man's palpable dishonesty he seemed competent. The man assured the two fugitives that he would take them to the Yemen.

The price would be ten thalers each, with a non-refundable deposit of six, payable immediately. Amedeo counted out the money which was wrapped in cloth around his waist. Two of the heavy silver coins had the image of Umberto I, and the face of the pirate momentarily fell. But the other four showed Maria Theresa, her titles and domains listed in abbreviated Latin: Empress of Austria, queen of Hungary and Bohemia, duchess of Milan . . .' It amused Amedeo that these ancient thalers were still, after 200 years, the most reassuring currency in the Horn of Africa. The Italian colonial authorities had had to admit defeat and mint new ones showing the image of the long dead empress. The coins disappeared into the folds of the captain's clothes and a rendezvous was arranged at a small bay south of Massaua.

The night before they left, Amedeo bid farewell to Salah. The old man was sorry to see his partner leave, whatever shortcomings and follies he may have had on account of his youth. He embraced Amedeo, who respectfully kissed him on the forehead.

TWENTY

# *The Smugglers' Ship*

There was no sign of the sambuk. Amedeo and Daifallah had been waiting since dawn and, as the sun rose higher, sending the temperature soaring, they were grateful for the shade of a prickly zeriba bush. Amedeo's spirits lowered as the hours passed and the conviction grew that they had been swindled. He thought of the thalers he had lost, each one adding up to a dozen water-skins he had loaded onto the donkey. Wrapping a spare *suriya* shirt over his head, he dozed in the midday sun, resigned to returning to Al-Katmia that evening.

Daifallah remained more alert, reluctant to admit that the smugglers he had chosen had let them down. In any case, Daifallah was hungry, the two having left their shack that morning without eating. When he saw a herd of goats a short distance from the shore, he roused Amedeo and told him to follow. The Yemeni skirted the sand dunes, making sure that there was no sign of a goatherd. When he got close, he carefully examined the animals, letting most walk past. Then he leapt on top of one, pulling it away from the others with one hand over its twisting head. It was a female, with full, pendulous udders. Daifallah told Amedeo to hold up her back legs, while he slid underneath and clasped his lips over a teat. Once he had slaked his thirst, he offered to do the same for Amedeo, who hesitated a moment and then scrambled beneath the beast. It was hardly breakfast with the Aostas at the Little Ghebbi, but the sharp milk was very welcome. When he had finished, Daifallah released their violated victim, who looked back at her two assailants indignantly, and then ran off to rejoin the herd.

Back in the shade of the thorn bush, Amedeo pondered his likely reception if ever he did succeed in crossing the Red Sea to the Yemen. Little was known about this reclusive land, which discouraged visitors, although its dealings with the Italians in Eritrea had always been friendly. Before the war, an Italian medical mission had been established at Sana'a, the capital, and, so far as Amedeo knew, it was still operating. There were rumours, too, that a handful of Italians had crossed the sea before the collapse of AOI. Amedeo's Yemeni mercenaries from the Gruppo Bande, and Daifallah himself, assured him that he would be welcomed with friendship. It was the British the Yemenis distrusted and kept at a distance. Their presence in Aden was too close to be welcomed by Imam Yahia, the ruler of the mountain kingdom. But worse were their cordial dealings with the detested Ibn Saud family, whose territories of Saudi Arabia surrounded the Yemen to the north. The Arab kingdoms had fought briefly in the 1930s, and religion also divided them. For the Imam was more than simply a king, he was also the spiritual leader of Zaydia, a peculiar branch of shiism that was established with the dynasty in AD 901.

Amedeo felt himself being shaken. The sambuk had arrived at last, just as Daifallah had always believed it would, albeit nearly eight hours after the agreed rendezvous. It slipped quietly into the bay, its long single deck low in the water, the crew making no response to the two's excited waving. Amedeo ran down to the water's edge and swam out to the boat, as though fearing it might disappear again, leaving Daifallah shouting from the shore, for he could not swim. A small boat was lowered to bring the Yemeni and their two sacks of provisions aboard. No apologies were offered for the delay by the captain, who instead demanded, with unseemly haste, the rest of his thalers, which he counted slowly in his ungulate hands. He told them to keep out of the way, while the crew of five prepared to cast off again. Chewing leaves of semi-narcotic qat, to which almost every Yemeni male was addicted, they sullenly went about their tasks, paying no attention to the passengers.

For the rest of the day, and all night, the sambuk slowly sailed south, never straying far from the Eritrean shore, which Amedeo idly watched passing by. They were clear of the Dahlak islands outside Massaua and were skirting the Buri peninsula. He tried to get Daifallah to eat some of the crew's fish and rice, but the Yemeni had been struck low with seasickness from the moment he had stepped aboard. He could keep down no food and only a little fluid, and became listless and weak.

Amedeo woke up late the next morning, rousing himself slowly in the heat of the sun. The boat was not moving, but rolling gently in the water. Another sambuk had drawn alongside, and the captain was in deep negotiation with another man, as unsavoury as himself. After a while, the talk settled down; a deal had been clinched. The crew began bringing aboard bundles of Italian Model 91 rifles, probably looted from the arsenal at Assab. Worth only twenty thalers in war-torn Eritrea, a rifle would sell for a hundred and fifty in the Yemen. Once the merchandise was stored away, the sambuk got under sail again.

A couple of hours passed. Amedeo sensed that something was bothering the captain. Talking quietly to his chief henchman, he cast furtive glances over at his two passengers. He was obviously not pleased with what he saw. The atmosphere on board, never welcoming, darkened perceptibly, and the crew were evasive whenever Amedeo tried to engage them in conversation. He tried to share his concerns with Daifallah but, lying prostrate on the deck, the Yemeni could think of little beyond his own suffering.

The barren mountains of the Buri peninsula, which Amedeo had looked down on from the monastery at Debre Bizen six years before, were behind them and the shore was now the flat expanse of the Dankali desert. For some unaccountable reason, the sambuk began edging closer towards it. The captain approached and aggressively stood before his passengers, hands on his hips.

'You are *zaidii*, aren't you?' he demanded.

'What of it?' said Amedeo, cursing inwardly. This was not the moment to get caught up in the interminable squabble between Sunni Muslims of the *shafeit* rite and the *zaidii* shiites of the Yemen's uplands.

'You will tell the *amir al bahr* at Hodeida what you have seen!' the captain shouted accusingly.

Amedeo tried to placate him. He had seen and heard nothing, and he had no interest in the captain's affairs. Besides, they had chosen his vessel with care and the last thing they wanted was to draw attention to themselves, or make denunciations to the harbour master at Hodeida.

'Liar! You deceive like all your kind,' shouted the captain, kicking Daifallah.

Imam Yahia had been harsh to the Sunni Muslims of the coast, for they had proved tardy in recognising his authority after he had ejected the Turks at the end of the First World War. It did not take much for old grievances to surface. The captain wanted them off his ship. Amedeo pleaded with him not to dump them on the barren shore of Dankalia, which was a death sentence as it was virtually uninhabited and waterless. But the captain would not listen. The Italian then shouted that he would denounce the lot of them if they did not honour their agreement to take them to Hodeida.

'Did you hear what this dog says?' The captain erupted, turning to the crew, who were forming a menacing audience. 'Throw him into the sea!'

As they rushed him, Amedeo grabbed hold of the mast with all his strength. Kicking and cursing, he was seized by his arms and legs, carried to the side and tossed into the sea. When he surfaced, he saw the crew laughing and jeering at him. The shore was only about a hundred metres away, but the Red Sea was notorious for its sharks and barracudas, and he had been cut in the scuffle. Spitting out a final curse, Amedeo swam as fast as he could for the shore.

Daifallah was luckier. He sank to his knees and begged for mercy. He could not swim, he cried. Something must have stirred the conscience of the captain. A boat was lowered to take him to the shore. With an astonishing display of scruples, the smugglers even returned their fare and their sacks of possessions.

In spite of several strong contenders, this stretch of the Eritrean coast was the least hospitable place on the Red Sea. The Italians had never attempted to link the town of Assab to Massaua by building a road through the scorching desert. The few Dankali nomads who lived there were notoriously unwelcoming and, further south over the Ethiopian border, the area had claimed the lives of more European explorers than any other part of Africa. Only a few years before, Wilfred Thesiger had been the first European to explore the Dankali desert's hinterland, whose populace measured their manhood by gathering the severed genitalia of their vanquished rivals.

The choice before them was stark. They would have to walk back to Massaua over a hundred kilometres north – and pray that they found water within the next few hours. It was some consolation that Daifallah began to feel better on dry land. Throwing their sacks over their shoulders they began to trudge along the coast.

After a couple of hours, Daifallah cried out excitedly and pointed at goat droppings on the ground. Water could not be far away, possibly help as well, he said. Amedeo and the Yemeni quickened their pace, following the trail for another hour until they came across the herd. A group of fifteen Dankali shepherds were gathered around a well by the shore, letting their animals drink. Tall and strikingly good-looking, the Dankalis had heavy sticks and some were armed with long, straight swords which, unusually for Muslims, had a cruciform hilt. But although they shared the same faith, the Dankalis had little reason to like Yemenis, who for generations had crossed the sea to enslave their women and children. As the two strangers approached, the shepherds clustered together menacingly.

Amedeo called out a greeting, and asked whether they could have some water and maybe buy some milk.

'Milk you do not sell, but give to those in need,'

'Well, brother, we are in need, so could we have some?'

'You are no brother of mine, nor friend either,' the shepherd replied. 'Who are you and where are you from?'

Daifallah interrupted and began telling their story, of how they were pilgrims who had been abandoned and left to die by treacherous smugglers.

'So you are alone then?' said the Dankali, who seemed to be the leader. Before Amedeo could stop him, Daifallah confirmed that this was so, and began lamenting the lack of honesty in this world.

The Dankalis' leader interrupted him. Since the two Yemenis were here, they could return the sacks that they had stolen from his brother. Daifallah's blustering died away. When a shepherd grabbed at Amedeo's sack, he pushed him away roughly. Immediately the others came swiping at him with their long sticks. He was soon beaten to the ground and he covered his head as best he could as their blows flailed down. Out of the corner of his eye, he saw Daifallah run towards him, and then fall, hit heavily across the head by a shepherd's stick. After a while the blows stopped hurting, and Amedeo's body went limp.

Barely conscious, he was aware of the shepherds stripping him. He opened his eyes only when he knew they had gone. Every limb was cut and bruised, and he had a deep, unsettling pain in his side. The Dankalis had taken everything. The *taghia* around his head, his shoes and futa, his thalers and provisions were gone. With Muslim delicacy, the shepherds had left him only his long *suriya* shirt. Uncertainly, Amedeo rose to his feet. He tried to urinate; when he did so, it came out red.

Daifallah, also stripped, was lying awkwardly, his face turned towards the sun. He looked dead. Sadness overwhelmed Amedeo. There had been no need for the Yemeni to come on a smugglers' sambuk. Daifallah could have made his way home easily without the Italian or even stayed in Massaua, for no one was looking for him.

'Now even you I have brought to ruin,' he said, Daifallah joining the many others who had died obeying his orders at Keru, Mount Cochen and Ad Teclesan. A terrible sense of solitude seized Amedeo. For the first time, he was utterly alone and he felt the will to live draining away. It was some time before he could summon the strength to drag himself down to the sea and immerse himself in the warm, sticky water. He took off his sodden shirt and went back to the Yemeni. As he washed the blood and dust off his face, Daifallah moaned and his eyes flickered open. The salt in the water had stung his wounds. With renewed vigour, Amedeo hobbled to the well. A couple of rusting tin cans had been left beside it, and he brought one back to Daifallah, supporting his head so that he could drink.

The Yemeni was concussed from the Dankalis' blows, but after a few minutes he could raise himself and walk. The sun was going down and the heat had gone from the day. Amedeo knew that they had to make use of the cool, and begin at once to trudge back to Massaua. There were two options: they could follow the coast around the Buri peninsula, finding wells but perhaps also more Dankali, or bypass it taking the shorter, inland route. Amedeo knew the basic geography. It seemed pointless to follow the coast, when in a night march of twenty, or at most thirty kilometres they could bypass the peninsula altogether. When he asked Daifallah for his thoughts, the Yemeni demanded what was the point of the *comandante* studying and being able to read maps, if he did not know these things? Amedeo decided to head inland.

In the moonlight, large spider crabs crawled ashore. Amedeo upturned a dozen, smashing them open with a rock. But although they chewed and sucked at the shells, there was very little meat. Both men drank as much as they could of the slightly salty water from the well, sea water filtered and desalinated by rocks and sand.

They filled the two rusty tins, and carrying them in front of them, like choirboys bearing reliquaries, the two men set out across the desert, the stars and moon illuminating their path.

## TWENTY-ONE

# *Sayed Ibrahim*

The sun had only been up a couple of hours and they were already thirsty. The water from the well had not lasted long. Sloshing about in the leaky tins, they drank it rather than see it spill on the sand. But Amedeo was not concerned. They had made good progress during the night, keeping up a steady pace. The coast could not be more than three or four hours away, Amedeo calculated, and they continued striding on. Yet midday came and went and there was still no sign; no tell-tale cloud, or even haze, just flat, rock-strewn sand stretching out endlessly in front of them. Weakened from his beating, Daifallah faltered.

'Go on alone, Ahmed Abdullah. I am going to die here,' he declared.

The sun was burning down on their unprotected heads, and their pace had slowed to a listless walk. Burned bodies were preferable to sunstroke, Amedeo decided. He took off his *suriya* shirt and wound it around his head, telling Daifallah to do the same.

'But it is not proper to walk naked,' he complained.

Amedeo's parched lips cracked into a smile. 'Daifallah, I doubt that you are going to offer me any surprises.'

The Yemeni overcame his sense of propriety and the two naked men stumbled on. Daifallah fell to the ground several times. Amedeo pulled him to his feet, goading him to keep moving. But by late afternoon, it was almost impossible for either man to speak. Their tongues were swollen and dry. When Daifallah fell to the ground again, the will to rouse himself had ebbed away. Amedeo kicked and pulled at him.

'Leave me to die,' the Yemeni croaked reproachfully. 'I have followed you far enough.'

Forcing his tongue to moisten, Amedeo told him he could surrender to sleep and then, yes, he would certainly die under the sun. Muslims were fatalists who could resign themselves to the inevitability of death. But he was a Nazarene and he would believe in miracles to the end. His mother's family possessed an old reliquary that contained a thorn from Christ's crown, and every Good Friday it was carried in procession around Capua; the sick and the afflicted believed it could cure them. Periodically, a droplet of blood would form at the thorn's tip, and Amedeo would be taken by his mother to the convent where the reliquary was kept to see the miracle. He was thinking of the thorn with every step he took, he told the Yemeni. They must carry on until nightfall. Only then, when all hope was gone, would they lie down on the sand, hold hands as brothers, and face death with the rising sun.

'You believe in blasphemies, Ahmed Abdullah,' the Yemeni said disapprovingly, but pulled himself to his feet.

They kept going for another couple of hours, until the sun lowered and at last disappeared altogether. The two men fell gratefully to the ground and slept. The sand where Amedeo lay was still hot against his exposed flesh when he awoke. He rubbed his dry eyes with his hand, forcing them to open and saw that the desert was bathed in a strange orange light. For a moment, he thought he was losing consciousness, or that a blood vessel had burst in his eye, but then he realised it was the light from the full moon rising on the horizon. He lay watching the pale disc rise, marvelling at its beauty, as though nature were staging a spectacular finale to mark his end.

But then he noticed a curious black dot moving across the moon's surface. He pressed his fists into his eyes forcing them to look hard, until he was sure he was not imagining it. He roughly shook Daifallah awake. During the war, he had often passed his binoculars to the Yemeni who, like all Arabs, could see things in a desert landscape that eluded most Europeans. The Yemeni grunted and looked up, scrutinised the moon and then said that it was an evil spirit, a djin, coming to kill them and so end their suffering.

Amedeo felt almost inclined to accept this explanation. Then he slapped the Yemeni and forced him to look again. Was it possible that the spot was a moving figure, perhaps a man on a camel? Even if it was a man on a camel, Daifallah said eventually, he would probably kill them, finishing the job the Dankali shepherds had begun.

The Yemeni sank back on the sand, but hope began coursing through Amedeo again. The act of speaking, and the cool night air, helped him shake off his torpor. He slapped and kicked Daifallah. If a Dankali, the man deserved to die, after what the shepherds had done to them. And if they killed him he would have water, and they could take his camel and reach Massaua. Another chance at life was coming towards them at a steady trot. They had to seize it. They would hide behind a sand dune until he came close, then Amedeo would shout at him to halt or be shot. When the man climbed off his camel, he would seize him while Daifallah crept up from behind and hit him over the head with a stone.

'Where are we going to find a stone?' the Yemeni demanded. Amedeo cursed him under his breath but, as it happened, there were no stones to be seen. Eventually, Daifallah found a large piece of pumice, which looked big enough, but it weighed less than a kilo. The imminent danger was restoring Amedeo's vigour. With surprise, exceptional good luck, and Daifallah fulfilling his part – although he was dubious about the pumice – they might be able to murder this man. Anyway, they had nothing to lose. The outline of the figure on his camel was clearly visible now against the moon and the two men took up their positions.

Amedeo crouched down behind the dunes until the camel was

only a few paces away, and then shouted: '*Hoguf!* Stop! Or I'll shoot!' His dry throat made his voice deep and resounding.

The rider jerked his beast to a halt. 'What do you want?' he said, alarmed.

'Get down! Now!' Amedeo ordered.

The man made a guttural rasping command, and the camel slowly began to kneel on the ground.

'Who are you?' Amedeo demanded.

'I am Al-Sayed Ibrahim al-Yamani,' the rider replied.

A brother Arab, Amedeo understood, a Yemeni and a sayed, a descendant of the prophet Mohammed who, whether prince or peasant, was treated with respect by all Muslims.

'*Ia sidee, nahnu yamanain*,' Amedeo said, his voice breaking with emotion, as he sank weakly to his knees. 'My lord, we too are Yemenis.'

Daifallah stumbled out from behind his mound carrying his stone and then collapsed. The *sharif* looked down at the two figures, who were barely clothed let alone armed. He walked over from one weeping prostrate figure to the other. They were not frightening assailants, only desperate, dying men. He unstrapped the water-skin from his *rakla* and gently prised Amedeo's mouth open, making him drink a few drops. Then he did the same for Daifallah. He unstrapped another bag containing food and started chewing a little bread, softening it into a pulp before placing it in Amedeo's mouth. Then he gave him a little more water to help him swallow.

As the two men recovered, they sat before their saviour, whose *keffiah* covered his head to the shoulders and invested him with great dignity. In tones of respect, and remorse, Amedeo told the *sharif* how they had been left stranded on the coast by the smugglers and then beaten and robbed by the Dankalis.

'May God curse that *shafeit* captain!' he said.

'Do not curse anyone,' said the *sharif* sternly. 'I too am *shafeit*, and I have not killed you, though others might say I am generous not to do so. Your captain was a bad man, that is all.'

'Forgive me, *sidee*,' Amedeo said meekly, and kissed his hand.

While the men ate a little more bread, Sayed Ibrahim, as though thinking to himself, pondered their folly in attempting to cross the desert. It would have been difficult even for those who were fit and well provisioned. Good luck, or God's will, meant that he had found them while he was on his way to the market at Barasol. But now he had to continue on his journey to trade his dried fish and vegetables for flour and coffee. Amedeo interrupted these musings.

'*Sidee*, we are in your hands,' he said. 'If you have saved us, only to abandon us now, you will only have postponed our death.'

'But I must go to Barasol,' Sayed Ibrahim replied.

'You are a *sharif*,' Amedeo said. 'You know that there are very few occasions given by God to man to perform good deeds. Now you have been offered one of these occasions.'

'This is true, this is true,' he replied. After a long silence, he agreed that he would go to Barasol another time and told the two men to climb on to his camel. Throughout the night they rode towards the east, their saviour leading his beast.

By noon the next day, they had arrived at a little bay, where Sayed Ibrahim lived with his wife and daughter. There were a couple of huts, with stone walls and thatched roofs, a small boat and a well. In two neat fields, maize and watermelon were growing, and by the shore there were lines of drying fish. When the strangers arrived, Sayed Ibrahim's wife came out to greet them, curious to know why her husband had returned so early and with company. And their daughter followed her. Both women were unveiled, and the younger one was extraordinarily beautiful. Her head was covered, but the cloth did not hide the long curling black hair down her back; her eyes were bright and curious, and her smile a flash of white in her faultless, dark features. From the hell of the desert, it seemed to Amedeo as though he had arrived in the Bedouin's mythical oasis of Zerzura, which inspired the story of Sleeping Beauty, secure from the cares of the world.

Under a canopy of branches, the visitors sat on the stones while Sayed Ibrahim's wife made coffee with cardamom. The two women then moved a couple of *angarebs* onto the veranda, which were offered to the guests. Feeling completely secure, Amedeo smiled his thanks and fell asleep almost immediately.

Over the next couple of days, Amedeo and Daifallah recounted every detail of their adventure, without ever telling who they really were, or why they were so desperate to reach the Yemen. Sayed Ibrahim listened without questioning the truth of what was said to him. If he noticed the markedly different pronunciation of the two men, who claimed to be cousins from the same village in the Yemen, he made no comment. But he was curious about Amedeo, who seemed to be of a different calibre to the other man. Many times the *sharif* seemed on the point of saying something, but changed his mind and remained silent.

'Ahmed Abdullah, I have been observing you carefully,' he said at last, when the two were alone. 'I do not know who you are, but understand that you are not *ibn suk* – a son of the market. You are an *ibn nass* – the son of a good family. You can read and write, and you know what is right and wrong. Wait until this war between the Christians is over before you return to the Yemen, for you may not be so fortunate with other smugglers.'

He would then be able to leave on the big ship, as the *sharif* referred respectfully to the *Adua*, the small and ancient steamer that before the war plied between Massaua and Hodeida. On it, water came out of a metal tube – 'chuff' – and sweet orange juice, too.

'Or, at least, so people who warrant belief have told me,' Sayed Ibrahim said. 'I do not make mistakes in judging people, Ahmed Abdullah. If you want, stay here, where you will be safe.'

When Amedeo mentioned Daifallah, the old man said that, of course, he could remain as well.

'There is enough work for all. Peacefully, we will pass the time and you will be like a son to me. And when you return to your country, you may not return alone.'

Amedeo looked up, and the *sharif* held his gaze. He had not misunderstood him. Sayed Ibrahim had hinted that, if the arrangement worked well, then he might in time marry his daughter. The old man left him to his thoughts. Three days before he had faced death; now he was being offered the chance of a new life. Here was an opportunity to cleanse himself of his past and be reborn as an Arab, living simply on the shores of the Red Sea, protected by the *sharif* and comforted by the Faith. There would be no British soldiers, nor smugglers and, at last, he might find peace.

When the *sharif* left him, he suddenly felt very tired. War had overshadowed so much of his life. He could hear again the sound of an ancient machine churning out liquid lime. The men in the street below would pump the handle until, with a swoosh, a streak of milky fluid would smear the walls and trickle across the cobblestones. It was the winter of 1915, the year of Italy's entry into the Great War, and the town of Sassari, in Sardinia, was in the grip of cholera. The disease, introduced by Austrian prisoners, rampaged through the impoverished mediaeval alleys. His mother forbade her two sons and daughter to venture outside, but the six-year-old Amedeo could see what was going on in the piazza below. At night, mule-drawn wagons approached, their path lighted by flickering torches. The dead were being taken out of the houses and loaded on; they were so numerous the wagons had to be left uncovered. Amedeo had pulled the covers over his head, trying not to hear the lamentations outside, and the pleas not to take afflicted loved ones into quarantine in the *lazzaretto*.

He had always been lucky. He thought of that night on board the *Derna*, leaving Sardinia after the cholera epidemic for the mainland. An Austro–Hungarian submarine was prowling off the coast, and the passengers were gathered on deck in their lifejackets. The faces of the adults were pale and drawn, but to the young boy, attached by an umbilical cord to his mother's lifejacket, it had seemed an adventure. On the return trip, the *Derna* had been hit, going down with all hands including the officer who was his father's replacement. War had even followed him to school. His mother, the *baronessa*, decided to see out the conflict at Bari while her husband returned to the meat-grinder of the Carso. Here too his luck held. He had a cold on 24 May 1916, and so was at home when his school received a direct hit from German aeroplanes. The bombing raid – the first on an Italian city – had been carefully timed to coincide with the anniversary of Italy's declaration of war. Several of his classmates and a teacher were killed. He remembered watching his mother leaning out of the kitchen window, shaking her fist at the buzzing aircraft, her long black hair cascading over her shoulders.

Reaching the Yemen, which had been so important a few days before, seemed almost irrelevant now. Amedeo yearned for a life with no ambition or temptation. He would live with the *sharif*'s family from day to day, without enemies and confident that God would look after them all. And in this ennobling remoteness, he would not be alone either, but married to a young girl of breath-taking beauty.

But thinking about her brought him back to reality. His fantasy of a life of ascetic nobility and dignity suddenly made him feel ashamed. A wave of self-disgust passed through him when he thought of Bice. He had suffered during their years apart, but so had she, not knowing whether the man she had chosen to be her husband was ever coming home, or whether he was even alive. '*Sidee*,' he said to the *sharif* the next morning, 'Never has another man honoured me as much as you have done. The life you offer me is beyond generosity, and it humbles me. But please believe me when I tell you that I must go to the Yemen, whatever the cost.'

The *sharif* looked down at the ground and was silent for a long while.

'It was my dream for you to stay,' said the old man. 'But if you have to go, then go you must. But leave tomorrow. Do not stay longer, otherwise the parting will be difficult, and the regret unbearable.'

The next morning Sayed Ibrahim prepared his camel, again insisted his visitors ride it, and set off towards Arkiko, which was barely twenty kilometres from Massaua. It was late afternoon by the time they reached its outskirts, and the *sharif* stopped. Amedeo and Daifallah dismounted, knelt and kissed his hand.

'I am not rich but I have lived happily,' the *sharif* told Amedeo. 'Here are two thalers. Take them. I give them to you as though you were my son.'

Amedeo kissed the old man's hand again and they parted without further words. After walking some distance, both Amedeo and the *sharif* turned around at the same moment and waved farewell to each other for the last time.

TWENTY-TWO

# *Captain White*

Arkiko was a sprawling, nondescript village gathered around a desert spring. The threadbare tukuls were interspersed by a few ugly rectangular structures in concrete and corrugated iron, testimony to the village's proximity to Massaua. As the two strangers walked down the main street, villagers emerged from their houses and watched them closely. It was unusual for visitors to arrive from the desert to the south, especially on foot. A crowd, curious rather than threatening, surrounded them, demanding to know who they were and where they were headed. They were merchants, Amedeo explained, heading for Massaua. And no, they were not alone, but part of a large caravan which would be arriving very shortly. He would have been happy to end the discussion there, rest and pick up some provisions before pressing on to the port.

'What is that you are selling, brothers?' asked one villager.

'Flour,' said Daifallah suddenly, surprising the Italian.

The Yemeni did not have many ideas but this one was inspired. The crowd's interest rose appreciably. As in the rest of Eritrea, food was in short supply and the visiting merchants were suddenly made very welcome. Was there any chance of the caravan selling flour in Arkiko, they were asked, before it went into Massaua? Dishes of fish and vegetables were set before the strangers who, between mouthfuls, indicated that this might indeed be possible.

Using one of his thalers, Amedeo rented a small wooden shack that would serve as a shop. The two would stay there until their caravan arrived. For three days Amedeo and Daifallah enjoyed the hospitality of Arkiko, while they recuperated fully from their sufferings in the desert. Women asked them for precedence once the flour arrived, leaving little presents of dried fruit, or cups of warm *gishir*. The merchants kept a meticulous ledger of those who had asked first, although a little inducement might ensure that a name could rise higher up the list.

Yet, unaccountably, there was no sign of the caravan. Perhaps, Amedeo explained, the British, the *al inglis*, were holding it up, making sure – quite rightly, of course – that it had not been stolen. But it would be arriving soon, and, yes, a little more boiled rice to go with the fish would be very welcome. In spite of all Amedeo's loudly recited prayers, the caravan obstinately declined to appear. The two appreciated that their welcome at Arkiko could not be extended indefinitely. They announced that they would set out the following day to find out what had happened. Just before dawn they slipped away and set off as fast as they could towards Massaua, only a day's distance away. When they arrived at the shack in Al-Katmia, they were welcomed back warmly by their Yemeni friends. Salah, Amedeo's old partner in the water business was still there. He had sold his donkey to a young man who was plying the same trade. But Salah complained that he appeared to exhibit an even greater degree of youthful folly than Amedeo had, nor did he sell as much water. While they still had a little of the *sidee*'s money, they did not need to work, but they would require more to cross the sea. Amedeo overcame his scruples and wrote a note to Rugiu at the Banco di Roma begging the loan of fifty thalers. Daifallah took this to Asmara, while he set about finding another smuggler's vessel.

None seemed to be bound for Hodeida. But talk in Al-Katmia suggested that the British were allowing more regular legitimate traffic, hoping that they could rid Eritrea of its large Yemeni population for whom there was little work or food. All that was required was a pass from a British officer at the port to obtain passage on a large sambuk, already preparing to leave. Daifallah returned with the money after three days, some of which Amedeo shared with five other veterans of the Gruppo Bande who had also decided to return to their homeland. They resolved to travel together, this time armed with knives in case of trouble.

A British officer, who spoke passable Arabic, was interviewing all those who wanted to leave. Two of Amedeo's men went into the customs office, and emerged after five minutes proudly holding their permits to travel. Then Amedeo and Daifallah went in, followed by the three others.

Captain White was in his early thirties, running fast to fat and had greasy blond hair. Squeezed into his uniform, worn with shorts, he sat behind a desk discharging his tedious task with thinly veiled irritation.

'Name?' he asked.

'Ahmed Abdullah al Redai,' Amedeo replied, citing the place of his birth. He told him his tribe, where he lived in the Yemen, the name of his provincial governor – Qadi Mohamed Eshami – using information provided by Daifallah and the other ex-soldiers. His papers had long since fallen apart and been lost, he told the captain.

'Can you write?' he asked.

'Of course,' Amedeo said with some hauteur, and signed the papers presented to him.

'Why do you want to return to the Yemen?' the officer asked suspiciously.

'Because when the Italians were in charge there was work and food for all, but since you arrived we have all been dying of hunger.'

'Who are you to talk like that?' Captain White demanded angrily.

'I am who I am and everyone knows me,' Amedeo replied, warming to his role.

'Oh God, we've got another Napoleon here,' said the officer, turning to the other British port officials, who began laughing.

This name meant nothing to the short, painfully thin Arab standing before the Englishman.

'I say what I say,' he repeated.

At this point, Amedeo's men standing behind him began indicating to the officer that he was a little touched, laughing and tapping their temples. The officer stamped his papers and then dealt with Daifallah, the insolent halfwit's cousin. When asked whether he could write, Daifallah also replied that he could. Self-importantly, he took off his signet ring and dipped it into the captain's inkwell, upsetting the pot as he tried to pull it free. Captain White watched appalled as a black pool spread across his desk. Jumping from his seat, his face reddened in anger.

'You imbecile!' he shouted at Daifallah. 'And you,' he said turning to Amedeo, 'Just remember . . . Oh, get the hell out of here and don't come back!'

These were words Amedeo had been wanting to hear for months. Two days later the sambuk to Hodeida set sail with twenty-five passengers, Amedeo, Daifallah and the Yemenis among them. The voyage would normally last about six days, as the ship crawled down the Eritrean coast past Assab, the narrowest crossing of the sea, and then worked its way north clinging to the coast of Arabia. But almost as soon as it left Massaua, the wind dropped. For days the sambuk was becalmed, caught in the doldrums. The sea was as flat as glass and there was not even the suggestion of a breeze. One of Amedeo's soldiers had dysentery, and during the long hot, windless days his condition steadily worsened, and then became life-threatening. With the other veterans of the Gruppo Bande, Amedeo nursed him, holding him steady on the plank which jutted perilously over the side and served as the passengers' lavatory. On the tenth day when the sambuk was finally in sight of the Yemeni coast, the soldier died. He was wrapped in a winding sheet, stones from the bilges tied to his feet and, after a brief but dignified ceremony, his body was lowered over the side.

The days of languishing motionless in the water wore down the patience of the passengers; their irritation directed towards the short, stout captain. Immensely proud of his compass, and not relying only on the stars, he would scrutinise the instrument self-importantly. At first the passengers had been impressed by his technical expertise, but as the wind obstinately declined to blow, their respect turned to derision. Passengers jeered, telling him to ask the dolphins, which circled the sambuk, to pull them along.

They had more respect, however, as supplies on board began to run short. Calling all to order, the captain stood on the stern and announced that everyone's food was to be requisitioned for the good of all and allocated by himself. Amedeo watched quietly, curious to see how this instruction would go down. Much to his surprise, the captain was obeyed. The passengers were simple people who yelled and shoved to protect what was theirs, but in the end acted in the common interest. Food was distributed in an apparently haphazard, but ultimately effective way. The captain threw pieces of pitta bread to the multitude, who jumped up to grab them. Once they did so, they would run to the side of the boat, eating quickly and furtively like a dog afraid that another will take its bone. Daifallah was again badly seasick and Amedeo worried that he had been unable to get his share. When he knelt beside him and offered half his bread, the sick Yemeni smiled up at him and pulled out half of his own, which he had saved for Amedeo.

The passengers showed a delicate sensitivity, too. Whenever the only woman on board squatted on the plank, holding on to two ropes which were her only lifeline, everyone looked away. As he left the world he knew for the unknown, Amedeo was reassured by these considerations. At last, after twelve days at sea, the vessel arrived at Hodeida.

As the sambuk approached the beach, a white-bearded mufti was carried through the surf by two fishermen and climbed onto the prow. Before each passenger could disembark, they had to recite the Muslim profession of faith: There is no other god but

God and Mohammed is his prophet. Amedeo recited the words, then lowered himself into the water, holding his few possessions above his head.

Ahmed Al-Zabara, the *amir al-bahr*, harbour master, was an elegant man in his early thirties, who controlled the customs and government of Hodeida on behalf of Imam Yahia. Each passenger was questioned for a few moments and then waved through, including Daifallah and the five soldiers. They hovered expectantly, waiting to see what would happen to Amedeo. He announced that he was an Italian officer who had come to the Yemen for refuge. Al-Zabara's eyes widened, but otherwise his features were expressionless, and then he looked over the ragged figure before him who weighed little more than forty kilos.

'You look like an Arab and you talk like one,' said Al-Zabara. Amedeo assured him that he was an Italian cavalry officer, an *amir al-alai*, who had commanded 800 horsemen.

'Can anyone confirm that what you say is true?' the *amir* asked.

Amedeo indicated the five men, hanging back on the beach and watching the proceedings closely. They were his former soldiers.

'They are too close to you for me to be able to accept their word,' Al-Zabara replied. 'They are your friends. Worse. If what you say is true, they are your faithful followers.'

He summoned an assistant, and whispered some words to him.

With a polite expression of regret, Al-Zabara said that he was going to have to place Amedeo under arrest while the matter was examined further. They chatted for a while in the shade drinking tea, until Al-Zabara's assistant returned with some armed men. Daifallah and the others were taken away and questioned, while Al-Zabara and the soldiers escorted Amedeo to the town jail.

An Arab doctor bandaged his foot with a rag, and a blacksmith arrived to fit him in shackles. Under Al-Zabara's instructions, he placed the iron with great delicacy high above the wound to his ankle and then sealed it against the anvil. He tied string around the chains, and secured it higher around Amedeo's thigh, so that the metal would not slip down and chafe the wound.

Amedeo tried to read some meaning in Al-Zabara's eyes before he was led down the steps into the darkness.

## TWENTY-THREE

# *Arabia Felix*

The song of Aida and Radamés as the tomb closes over them had always been one of Amedeo's favourite moments in opera. Now he too was entombed but, instead of his beloved, he was accompanied by half a dozen petty criminals. Every three or four days, Ahmed Al-Zabara came to the gaol, and the Italian would be summoned to the office above. The *amir* would offer him cigarettes and *gishir* as they sat on cushions, undisturbed by conversing with a man in irons. He would ask Amedeo about his family and army career, and the latter would tell him how he had served in the conquest of the Negus's empire, in Libya and even in Al-Andalus, in Spain. Al-Zabara was fascinated by what was happening on the other side of the sea: would the British remain in Eritrea, would the Italians try to return, or the Negus be given the land, and, above all, who was going to win this war between the Christians? After an hour or so, Al-Zabara would rise to go, and Amedeo would follow a gaoler back to the gloom below.

He had been there for two weeks, marking each new day with a scratch on the wall, and knew that he was not going to last much longer. The wound in his ankle had become reinfected and his malaria had returned. The other prisoners could rely on a little extra food from their relatives or friends, but Amedeo's soldiers had been told not to approach the prison. Once, they pooled their savings to buy some cigarettes which Daifallah managed to throw down through the bars. He was spotted by the gaolers before he could drop down the matches, and warned that if he approached again he would be joining his commander inside.

But Amedeo had not been forgotten. Imam Yahia wanted to know more of this prisoner, the most senior Italian officer to have escaped from Eritrea. Al-Zabara sent lengthy reports of their conversations to the palace at Sana'a. Others too were interested in his case. Spies in Hodeida kept the British in Aden informed of unusual goings-on. The arrival of the notorious fugitive Amedeo Guillet prompted an official request to the Imam that he be handed over. He was a dangerous bandit, the British explained, responsible for numerous outrages. For the Yemeni ruler, however, the request only confirmed that his prisoner had been telling the truth, and that his value was all the greater.

One afternoon, Amedeo was lying on his filthy straw mattress when he heard the name Ahmed Abdullah called out. He raised himself and staggered towards the square of light, but this time the gaolers did not lead him upstairs to the office. Instead, the blacksmith was waiting to remove his chains; then Al-Zabara personally escorted him out into the bright sunlight of the street. A gaoler steadied him by the arm as he was led a short distance to the Dar-Al-Diafa, or government guest house, where the Imam received people of consequence who arrived in the port. Amedeo was shown upstairs to a large bedroom, with windows opening on to the sea. There was a large double bed shrouded in a mosquito net. He threw himself down on it, wondering whether this were not all a dream, and promptly fell asleep.

A little later he was woken, bathed and then dressed in a long white cotton *suria*, with intricate embroidery. A barber came to cut his hair and shave off the beard he had worn for more than six months. When the man held up a mirror, Amedeo gasped to see his reflection. He held the man's arm so that he could not pull the mirror away and then examined a face so thin and drawn it seemed like that of an old man. His grey-blue eyes were sunken deep into his head as though pebbles sinking on the shore.

Dr Luigi Merucci arrived from the Italian Medical Mission, sent from Sana'a by the Imam. He cleaned and dressed Amedeo's wounded ankle, and reassured him that his changed circumstances were permanent. There were other Italians in Sana'a and he would be looked after well. There were a thousand things Amedeo needed to ask Merucci, but for the moment he could not think of any. In a daze, he saw a servant lay a feast of meats, rice, yoghurt and fruit before him on a marquetry table, and he began to eat compulsively. He could hear Merucci, as if at an enormous distance, urging him to eat slowly, and felt bewildered and resentful towards this man speaking Italian who, with a look of concern, pulled the plates away from him. The doctor offered him some apricots instead, and after eating one Amedeo fell asleep again, his head swimming in the scent of the fruit.

The caravan assembled on the outskirts of Hodeida four days later just after dawn. Everyone was eager to be away from the stultifying heat of the coastal plain before midday. There were about fifty travellers heading for Sana'a, including Amedeo, Daifallah and the five men who were all that remained of the Gruppo Bande. No escort was considered necessary, although Al-Zabara had asked a Yemeni army officer in blue robes to look after the Imam's Italian guest.

Soon the road began to climb and, by the second day, the parched desert landscape around Hodeida gave way to the green, fertile valleys of 'Arabia Felix'. Neat, terraced fields, laden with fruit, vegetables and orchards, covered the hills and there were small shady woods, keeping down the top soil. The fresh mountain air seemed scented with fruit blossom. Peasants lived above their terraced fields in walled villages of remarkable beauty, then came out to work the land by day, just as they did in southern Italy. This was no Bedouin wilderness, but a sophisticated landscape made by man – though tended more often than not, Amedeo noticed, by women. He would watch them stooped over their crops, dressed in bright clothes and wearing necklaces of amber and silver thalers. Out in the fields, the women were unveiled and seemingly less inhibited than in the towns, scrutinising the travellers as they went by with kohl-black eyes.

As the caravan picked its way through the impossibly narrow streets of a village, the sounds of mothers shouting, the howls of young children and the scraping of kitchen pots, brought back Amedeo's childhood memories of Sardinia and Sicily. The caravan would halt at a village *funduk*, or inn, outside which would be clusters of chatting figures. Every man would have a large *jambiya* in his belt and most, even boys of only twelve, had a rifle. But Amedeo never felt any sense of threat due to the weaponry on display, which was borne with utter insouciance. At first the travellers would sleep on *angarebs* in the open after their evening meal, but as they climbed higher into the mountains they became increasingly grateful for warm, welcoming fires. It was bitterly cold after the sun went down and there was a heavy dew in the mornings.

Not long after dawn on the fifth day, as the muezzin's call echoed down the green valleys, Amedeo was walking ahead of the others when he caught his first glimpse of Sana'a, the city founded by Shem, the son of Noah. Through the mist, he could make out the walls, and the minarets and cupolas of the mosques. There were two hundred of them, he had been told. Houses of six and seven storeys were perched precariously on rocks, their delicately carved windows reminding him of Venice. As the sun rose higher, bringing the *Umma al Medain* (the mother of cities, 2,400 metres above sea level), into sharper focus, Sana'a seemed like something out of Marco Polo's '*Il Milione*': a magnificent, ennobling achievement of man. Tears began coursing down Amedeo's face.

The Yemeni officer left Amedeo at a guesthouse, where he had time to wash and dress in clean clothes before meeting the Imam's foreign minister, Qadi Mohammed Raghib. A distinguished-looking man in his seventies, the *qadi*, literally judge rose, politely from behind a large, ornate desk that mixed Louis XV with arabesque flourishes, and welcomed Amedeo in French. Qadi Raghib was a Turk, Amedeo discovered in the course of their long conversation, who had been sent to the Yemen, then a dependency of the Ottoman Empire, before the First World War. It was virtually an exile, the *qadi* explained, for he had once had a glittering career at the Ottomon embassy in Paris. Indeed, he had been one of the officials negotiating with the Italians after the war of 1911–12, when the Ottoman Empire ceded Libya, and he had served in Montenegro in the 1890s, where he had known the future Queen Elena of Italy, then in her teens. His involvement in the Young Turk movement, which sought to reform the moribund empire, had brought about his ruin, and he had been banished to its remotest corner. After the Ottoman collapse at the end of the First World War, Qadi Raghib decided to remain in the Yemen serving Imam Yahia rather than return home. There were many former Young Turks in Sana'a, the *qadi* explained. Later Amedeo saw groups of the soldiers, all in their sixties and seventies, gathering in the city's squares. Carrying swords and ancient firearms, they would sit, gossip and drink *gishir* – and peacefully knit socks. These they would exchange for tobacco and other luxuries, and those of the artillery men, Amedeo was assured, were particularly prized.

After Qadi Raghib had finished reminiscing, he coaxed from Amedeo his own story, listening without interruption as he explained his family background, his fighting in Abyssinia and against the British, and being wounded at Ad Teclesan. The old man leaned forward and gently stroked Amedeo's wounded ankle. He said that he had employed Yemeni mercenaries in his Gruppo Bande – 'like the Swiss at the Vatican', the old diplomat interjected – and then explained why he had fought on long after the Italian surrender. He was anxious about this part, emphasising his family's devotion to the Savoy dynasty and the king of Italy, for he had no doubt that the British had portrayed him as merely a brigand. He decided to be entirely truthful, and spared no detail of how he had organised the rudiments of a resistance movement and caused the British occupiers as much trouble as he could.

Qadi Raghib listened in silence, and then said: 'I doubt the Imam will be displeased to hear of this.'

The following morning, Amedeo again presented himself at the *qadi*'s office, and together they crossed the square to the Imam's palace, the Al-Magam. Sentries in blue burnous saluted smartly at the entrance. The two men walked down the corridors barefoot and were shown into a large drawing room. Windows of alabaster and stained glass filled the exotic interior with colourful light. The Imam was waiting, seated on a divan. Amedeo kissed the hand of the ruler, who invited him to sit on some cushions slightly below him. In spotless white silk robes, Imam Yahia was an imposing, refined man in his seventies, his grey beard neatly trimmed. He wore a distinctive silk turban, with a fold to the left, which fell below his ear, and in his belt was a large *jambiya* with a rhino-horn hilt. He told Amedeo that he was a great friend to Italy, and even noted that he shared the same birth date as King Vittorio Emanuele III. The Italian *amir al-alai* should consider himself his guest. Amedeo would be provided with a house, where his former soldiers could stay as well, if he so wished, and he would be paid the salary of a colonel, forty thalers a month. The only condition was that he must not involve himself in politics, nor the war against the British. So as not to complicate matters, he would continue to be called Ahmed, for his Nazarene name seemed so similar.

The Imam then invited Amedeo to tell his story, although he already knew much of it from Qadi Raghib and the reports of Al-Zabara. After an hour and a half, when the Imam signalled that the Italian could now take his leave, he said that they would soon speak again. The elderly Young Turk led Amedeo back down the palace corridors, and gave his arm an encouraging squeeze. His refuge in the Yemen was secure.

An official took Amedeo to the Italian Missione Medica, where he was greeted effusively by the eight staff, who were expecting him. Treatment began on his ankle, which was reopened, cauterised and treated with antiseptic. The hospital handyman even offered to make Amedeo a leather boot which would hold his foot firm, allowing it to heal at last. In the meantime, the word had passed around the twenty or so other Italians who had found refuge in Sana'a. They arrived at the hospital to welcome the new arrival. Most had heard of him, for his fame had spread widely in AOI.

There were over a dozen sailors who had escaped from Massaua before it fell, as well as a senior functionary, Dionisio, known to Amedeo before the war, who had calmly sailed over from Assab in a small boat once it was clear that the British would soon reach the isolated southern port. But no one had arrived so long after the British conquest, and Amedeo was bombarded with questions about friends and relations still in Eritrea. But as he had had few dealings with Italians during his months on the run, he was ill-informed of the gossip of Asmara. The Yemen's little Italian community seemed happy with what little he told them, and fêted his escape with a large lunch of Italian food, served with fine red wine made by the Yemen's Jewish community.

In the days that followed, Amedeo got to know the rest of the Europeans in Sana'a. Ten of the German merchant sailors, who had fought so bravely at Agordat, had escaped from Massaua in a motor launch. In the months that followed, Amedeo occasionally talked about returning to Europe with their first officer, by sailing a sambuk through the Suez Canal to Turkey. The obvious risks meant the plan never got beyond the theoretical stage. The seamen were pleasant enough company, although their National Socialist fervour throughout the excitements of 1942 became wearying.

Amedeo was more closely drawn to Hansen, a young German engineer, who had come to the Yemen with his wife and five-year-old daughter before the war. He had done so on the encouragement of his father who, for some reason that was never discussed, had fallen foul of the Nazis and been dismissed from his university post. Amedeo would often dine with Hansen and his beautiful wife, whom the Italian would defer to gallantly in Piedmontese as 'Madamin'. Afterwards they would tell each other stories and relate the novels they had read and loved as a way of remembering home, the Hansens exchanging *Effi Briest* for *I Promessi Sposi*. When the Imam decided he wanted to find sites for two new dams, Amedeo accompanied Hansen deep into the hinterland to help draw up the accurate maps required. They went panning for gold and found a small quantity, which they promptly sold in the market at Sana'a.

Of the British, there appeared no sign, beyond the occasional visit of an officer or an official from Aden with matters to discuss with the Imam. But Amedeo did not doubt that they were well informed about the enemy nationals in the Yemen. The only permanent British resident was Dr Petrie, an elderly Scottish doctor of such obvious piety and goodness that the Protestants among the German sailors asked him to lead them in their prayers. To Amedeo he was unfailingly polite and friendly, for it was an unwritten rule among the Europeans that the conflict elsewhere should not intrude on life in Sana'a. Amedeo saved some of his thalers to buy an old harmonium from the Scotsman and, working the pedals, he coaxed out wheezy arias from Verdi and Puccini, and the sonatas of Schubert and Schumann, which would carry through the night air of the *Umma al Medain*.

The Missione Medica had a radio and with it the Europeans followed the news from Radio Bari or the BBC's Italian 'Lord Haw-Haw', Colonel Stevens. They learned of more German victories in Russia and the Western Desert, and then, by the winter of 1942, of El Alamein and Stalingrad.

Amedeo was called upon by the Imam to comment on each of these events, and be given other tasks suited to his skills. He trained the royal bodyguard in modern battle drill, and taught the children of the Imam's daughter how to eat with knives and forks and sit at table in the European fashion. Amedeo carried out these tasks happily, eager to repay his host's kindness. But he did them with some trepidation, warned by the spectacle of the Imam's barber who, guilty of some minor transgression, spent a month wandering the streets of Sana'a loaded in chains. He carried them with immense dignity, almost as though they were part of his robes, so that whenever Amedeo greeted him he never had the heart to ask what had been his crime.

To keep his mind occupied – and bring in more funds, for his former soldiers were still with him and could find only occasional work – Amedeo tried his hand as a farrier and veterinary surgeon. Only the Italians, he was convinced, shoed horses properly in the Middle East, and he soon had a busy forge and even an apprentice, as riders sought his services. The only horses he never shod were the Imam's own Hamdanis, an ancient strain of Arab whose exceptional intelligence was attributed to their having shared Eden with Adam and Eve. Their hooves had no need of irons, he was told.

Amedeo's efforts as a vet had more mixed results. Borrowing instruments from the Italian doctors, one of his first jobs was to caponise a dozen chickens. He bluffed his way through the operation, but then one by one his patients expired until none were left. His credibility somehow survived when he then explained to his customer that Sana'a's high altitude discouraged this operation, and the cockerels were best left entire. He had more success curing a mule of haemorrhoids. But his greatest triumph was when he was sent to Ma'rib, the ancient capital of the Queen of Sheba, where the cattle were dying mysteriously. As soon as he arrived, Amedeo realised that it was *mandef*, the fly-borne sickness that had depleted the horses of the Spahys di Libya on the Eritrean lowlands. The only cure was to get them off the grass, where flies spread the disease, and feed them hay. As soon as the cattle were moved, they stopped dying. A grateful Imam gave Amedeo a bonus of fifty thalers and an old British gold sovereign for this service.

* * *

From his arrival, Amedeo was treated differently to the other European refugees. His allowance was far higher, and he could go where he wished in the city and even beyond it, while the Italian and German sailors had to be accompanied by a Yemeni guard and were never allowed out of Sana'a.

After some months, Amedeo was summoned by Ahmed, the Saif al Islam ('Sword of Islam'), the Imam's son and heir, who lived in Taiz, three days' camel-ride from Sana'a. Ahmed held his own court there, close to the coastal provinces so he could keep an eye on the troublesome *shafeit* population, whom he had subjugated with some severity. Ahmed was curious to meet the Arabic-speaking foreigner, who had commanded a cavalry regiment in war.

Surrounded by a heavily armed coterie, Ahmed welcomed the Italian cordially and invited him to tell of his adventures. They took to each other immediately, and the prince invited Amedeo to sit beside him while they ate. Politely, he scooped up in his hand the choicest piece of meat for his guest. While his father was elegant and refined, Ahmed was short and stocky with alarmingly bulging eyes and a fierce reputation. Inevitably their talk turned to the war. Ahmed could not understand why the Italians, who had so impressed him with their conquest of Ethiopia, had been defeated by the British. Mussolini's reputation of supposed infallibility had spread to the Yemen, and Ahmed even knew some words of an Arabic song written in praise of the Duce. Amedeo firmly told him that, in spite of the loss of Africa Orientale Italiana, the war was going well for the Axis powers, for so it seemed in 1942. He was struck by the prince's keen intelligence, grappling to understand the modern world with his classical Arabic learning. After talking for a while, Ahmed announced that he was tired and would now sleep. As he waited with the others for the prince to rise after his *siesta*, Amedeo played chess with his vizier, fitting seamlessly into the court at Taiz, just as he had in the labourers' shack in Massaua. At the end of his visit, Ahmed asked the Italian whether he would not prefer to stay with him rather than return to Sana'a.

'*Maulana*,' Amedeo replied, 'My lord, it would be ungrateful of me to leave the Imam after everything he has done for me, now that he needs me for various tasks.'

The reply satisfied the prince. They would in any case soon meet again, and Amedeo went back to Sana'a, having made a powerful friend.

After a year, Amedeo's life in the Yemen had settled into a routine. His chances of reaching Italy by sea or land, before the war's end, seemed very remote. For the moment, he could do nothing but wait and there were many worse places to be at the beginning of 1943 than in the neutral Yemen.

The Axis victories had ended and those of the Allies were just beginning. But these seemed abstract events in comparison with the marriage of the Italian female doctor to a colleague, the birth of the Hansens' second daughter and the awful death of the older girl from diphtheria. Madamin and her husband were devastated, and everyone, irrespective of nationality, felt their loss. The German sailors dug her grave outside the walls of Sana'a, Dr Petrie led the prayers, while Amedeo played Chopin and some hymns on his harmonium.

No one received any personal news from Europe, nor was it possible to send letters from the Yemen. But a chance encounter in northern India was to end Amedeo's isolation from Bice and his family. A British officer, who had lately arrived from occupied Eritrea, was scrutinising the list of captured Italian officers when he noted the name of Landolfo Colonna. Amedeo's subordinate at Amba Gheorgis, had fought until the last with General Nasi at Gondar. The British officer, who spoke Italian, was curious to meet a member of the illustrious Colonna family, who had provided the Papacy and the Spanish empire with some of its greatest captains.

When Landolfo talked about life in the fort before the war, he mentioned Amedeo, supposing that the extraordinary *Tenente* Guillet must be long dead. The British officer corrected him. It was well known at the military command in Asmara that he had escaped to the Yemen.

A month or two later, Principessa Colonna in Rome wrote to Beatrice Gandolfo in Naples.

> I have just received a letter from my son, from whom I had asked for news. He tells me: 'Of Guillet one knows that, after Asmara was taken, he got away to the Yemen. The news is certain, coming from a very reliable source.' I congratulate you with all my heart.

sano e salvo nello Jemen!
Ricevo ora una lettera di
mio figlio, al quale avevo chiesto
notizie, in cui mi dice:
"Di Guillet si sa che dopo la
presa di Asmara è scappato
nello Jemen. La notizia è sicura
presa da fonte sicurissima!"
Mi congratulo di tutto cuore

Some time later, a letter arrived at the Missione Medica via the Red Cross in Aden, the first ever to do so from Italy. It was from Bice, expressing her love, enormous relief that Amedeo was still alive and demanding news. Sending a reply was far more difficult. There was no reliable contact between the Italians in Sana'a and Aden, and Amedeo doubted whether the British would help him, of all people. However, one day an Arab officer from Iraq arrived at Sana'a. Amedeo begged him to send a letter on his return to Baghdad. He was not optimistic that it would ever arrive.

## TWENTY-FOUR

# *Giulio Cesare*

Somewhere on the decks above him Amedeo could hear the cheers. They were faint at first and then grew louder as they echoed down below the water line. He could not catch what the British soldiers were shouting, just something about 'Musso'. In the minutes that followed he could almost feel the ripple that went through the ship as 2000 Italians on board took in the news. It began slowly at first, but was then taken up by everyone. The Red Cross ship *Giulio Cesare* reverberated to the sound of the *Marcia Reale*, that was Italy's old national anthem.

It was 25 July 1943 and the ship that was repatriating Italian civilians and wounded servicemen from Eritrea had just heard the BBC news that Mussolini had fallen. The day before the Grand Council of Fascism had voted with nineteen votes to seven to end the regime. Old comrades from Fascism's earliest days had turned against the Duce to save Italy from disaster: Grandi, the former ambassador to London, had moved a motion handing government to the king. De Bono, De Vecchi and even Ciano voted in favour. But the commanding presence at the meeting, it was said, was the shade of Italo Balbo. After twenty-one years in power, Mussolini had been slow to grasp that this was the end. When he was driven away from the Villa Savoia after meeting the king, he discovered that he was under arrest.

On board the *Giulio Cesare*, Amedeo tried to make sense of the garbled reports that reached him in the sanatorium, where he was hiding. For the moment, Italy was still in the war, with Badoglio as prime minister. Even though the Allies had landed on Sicily on 15 July, the German alliance was firm – except everyone knew that the man who had most wanted it in the first place was no longer in power. At the Canaries, Amedeo hoped to learn more news, hearing that the governor was his former Carlist commander in Spain, Captain-General Garcia Escames. But the governor could not risk meeting a fugitive stowaway of the British. Instead, he sent a couple of bottles of Tio Pepe to the sanatorium, with an affectionate letter by way of apologies. Amedeo had crossed half the world to return to Italy, but he had no idea what he would find when he got there.

It was thanks to the British that he was at last returning home. When the *Giulio Cesare* arrived in Massaua in the spring of 1943 to take mothers and children, the old and invalid, and a number of badly wounded soldiers back to Italy, the British extended the invitation to the tiresome Italian refugees who had made it to the Yemen. The authorities were keen to bring to an end this independent and unsupervised community. A motor launch would arrive at Hodeida to bring them back to Massaua. Almost everyone wanted to leave, except the Italian doctors, but Amedeo somehow doubted whether the British invitation extended to him, or whether he could trust them even if it did. If he ended up in their hands, the likelihood was that they would pack him off to a prison camp. Yet if he was ever to get back to Italy, the *Giulio Cesare* was his best chance, far better than trying to reach Turkey through the Suez Canal, or by land.

Amedeo explained to Imam Yahia that he wanted to leave, and asked whether he would help him cross the Red Sea to Massaua. Once there, he would take his chances getting on board the *Giulio Cesare*. The old man was displeased to hear this, for he had grown fond of the Italian and did not want to see him leave. He tried to dissuade him. Had Ahmed Abdullah forgotten how much the British had wanted him little more than a year before? If he joined the others on the British vessel at Hodeida he would certainly be arrested. Possibly shot. But the Imam could see that the younger man's mind was set. If he had to leave, he said, then of course he did so with his blessing. He asked only that Amedeo write him a note saying that it was his wish to go.

'I will not have it said that I have sent away a friend who was in need,' the old man told him, then rose from his divan, placed a hand on Amedeo's head and kissed it.

A little sambuk took Amedeo across the sea in four days, leaving him at the bay to the south of Massaua where he and Daifallah had waited for the smugglers a year before. The shacks in Al-Katmia had been rearranged slightly, but he managed to find Salah, who wept when he saw his young protégé, now plump and prosperous, return after his time in the Yemen. A bed was found for him, and Amedeo was assured that there was plenty of work at the port, where the big ship was taking on supplies for its journey.

But with half the Italians in Eritrea trying to smuggle themselves on board, the *Giulio Cesare* was tightly guarded. Carabinieri were checking the papers of all who were authorised to travel, while the women, Amedeo discovered, were being sorted out by Signora Maiorani, the wife of the Gruppo Bande's lawyer. He took care to ensure that she did not see him around the docks.

Fabio Roversi Monaco, a colonial civil servant and ardent Fascist, was one of many prepared to go to extraordinary lengths to get on board the *Giulio Cesare*. At first, he was simply going to bribe a British doctor for a false medical certificate, but he abandoned this idea, he wrote disgustedly in his diary, when he discovered that the man was taking the money and then not honouring the deal. Desperate measures were called for. Refined, delicate looking and with a clear skin, Roversi decided instead to pass himself off as a woman. He shaved his legs, paid meticulous attention to his dress and silk undergarments and then presented himself in make-up and tottering high heels in front of a British lieutenant. With typical Anglo-Saxon diffidence, the officer looked away from the gaudy creature in front of him, and issued the travel permit.

'Not even the lowliest Italian NCO would ever have reached quite such a summit of obtuseness to endorse with an official stamp so obvious a disguise,' Roversi wrote, witheringly.

As it happened, there was not enough room on the ship for all the women; Roversi's hard-won permit was rescinded and he had to try something else. As the date of the *Giulio Cesare*'s departure loomed, a handful of Italian POWs even resorted to swimming over to the ship at night across Massaua's notoriously shark-infested harbour. British sentries arrested them as they tried to climb on board. The most extraordinary escape attempt was made by a man who sucked up the spittle of a patient with tuberculosis and then expectorated it into a kidney dish while being examined by a British doctor. Confirmed as tubercular, he got his pass. Roversi was luckier. With the connivance of an Italian medic, he took the identity of a TB patient who was on the point of death.

While the Europeans were being closely scrutinised in Massaua, almost no attention was paid to the native dockers at the port. Carrying a bag of potatoes, Amedeo managed to stow himself on board, waiting until dark to find a hiding place beside the winding gear of the ship's anchor. By extraordinary coincidence, he was discovered there by the *Giulio Cesare*'s captain, who was alone. Seeing the campaign ribbons of the First World War on his chest, Amedeo confessed who he was and admitted that the British were after him. The old officer's fellow feelings were aroused, and he returned a little later to bring a thermos of coffee, a blanket and some European clothes. Once the ship cast off, he had Amedeo discreetly moved to the lunatic asylum beside a sanatorium.

In a ward full of madmen, Amedeo quickly recognised a fellow bogus patient, Angelo Silvestri, an officer in the Alpini whom he had met several times during the fighting at Keren. Over several months Silvestri had convinced doctors that he was mad, having rehearsed the symptoms of schizophrenia to perfection. But among the fifteen or so patients in the asylum, most of whom sat for hours blankly staring at the wall, only Silvestri raved and thrashed about whenever the British doctor did his rounds. A burly Italian sailor, who knew he was sane, would restrain him, hissing quietly to 'Angelino' that he would kill him next time he put on a performance if he did not remember to remove his shoes before kicking out.

Roversi would visit them in the asylum or walk with them on deck at night when the healthier patients were brought up to take fresh air. The captain, whom he had befriended, encouraged Roversi to do so for he was worried that Silvestri would really lose his mind spending two months in the company of lunatics.

'Absurd dreams in Silvestri's ward, where in the evening the indomitable Guillet speaks to us of his projects,' Roversi wrote in his diary. 'The Azebu Galla are in open rebellion; the Tigre is finding the Abyssinian yoke intolerable; the old Eritrea is a powder keg with the fuse lit, already prepared by Muntaz Ali. It would be enough to parachute in a few decisive and expert men, with arms and thalers, and a genuine explosion would send the English flying! Childish dreams, considering the events which in the meantime were maturing in Italy, but not for us, who were in complete darkness about everything.' (*Africa come un mattino*, a cura di Fabio Roversi Monaco, Tamari Editori, 1969.)

At Gibraltar, the British guards at last disembarked, and Amedeo could wander the ship at will. Mid-way across the Tyrrhenian Sea, the accompanying British patrol boats were replaced by Italian ones. On 2 September 1943 after a voyage of 51 days, the *Giulio Cesare* docked at Taranto in southern Italy.

Amedeo Guillet was finally home five years after he had left.

Even before landing he had made up his mind not to go to Naples or Capua. However much he wanted to see Bice and his family, he had to report to army command in Rome first. Italy was on the brink of collapse. Sicily was almost in Allied hands, and another landing was expected at any moment on the Italian mainland. American parachutists were set to take Rome, some said, while others believed the German army was poised to invade from the north. After three days travelling on the barely functioning railway, Amedeo arrived in Rome. The marshalling yards beside the station were a smouldering scene of destruction: the Holy City, for so long spared from Allied air raids, was now a target.

He made straight for army headquarters in the Via XX Settembre, where he was greeted with amazement. Some of his acquaintances had heard that he was alive and had escaped to the Yemen, but none were expecting him to arrive in Rome, least of all at that moment. Equally astonishing to his superiors was what Amedeo now proposed. The talks with Roversi and Silvestri on the *Giulio Cesare* were not wild fantasy. He wanted to return to Eritrea immediately. If he were only given enough thalers, a doctor, medicines and a quantity of heavy machine-guns and mortars, he was sure he could foment a rising that would push the British out of the colony. The occupiers had grown complacent, he argued, and there were only a few Sudanese troops controlling the entire country. If he could eject them, it would take another full-scale invasion for the British to return again. Would they really want to go to all that trouble, when in their hearts they had already decided to hand Eritrea to their friend, the Negus?

It would have been understandable, in this moment of national crisis, had the proposal been rejected out of hand. Senior officers were forever in meetings with Badoglio and the king, and the word at headquarters was that plans to ease Italy out of the war were far advanced – though how this was to happen without provoking a German invasion, no one seemed to know. Eritrea was a very minor consideration. Yet Amedeo persuaded General Aldo Remondino, of the Regia Aeronautica, that the chiefs in the colony were poised to rebel whether Italy helped them or not. The general gave his full backing to Major Guillet's plan – for Amedeo's long-waited promotion had been issued two years before, although he had been unaware of the fact. Remondino had been greatly impressed by Colonel Amedeo Paradisi's 30-hour flight from Italy to Asmara in May 1942. To the bemusement of the handful of British officers running the colony, Asmara had been showered with leaflets saying that the Patria had not forgotten Eritrea and that the tricolour would soon return. The aeroplane then disappeared in the direction of the Sudan for the long flight back. It had been an epic journey that Italo Balbo would have appreciated, but it also showed that Amedeo Guillet's proposal to make a one-way flight to a long abandoned airfield near Adi Abo in the Tigre could be done. Silvestri was eager to take part, a doctor volunteered and it only remained to find a pilot.

Once he knew that headquarters was taking his proposal seriously, Amedeo begged those who knew him to keep his return secret from his family and Bice. If he were to see them and announce that he was leaving for Africa again, he would cause unbearable pain. Nor was he sure that he would be able to leave them all once more. But he had to return to Eritrea. He felt he owed it to everyone in the Gruppo Bande who had been killed, to Togni, to Gebreyesus Geremeddin at Azzega, and the other Eritrean chiefs, and above all to the Duke of Aosta, who had given him, at thirty-one, a brigadier's command.

While he hurried on with his preparations, Amedeo discovered that his brother Giuseppe was in a hospital in Rome, having been wounded in Greece. He agreed that if Amedeo was determined to return to Africa he should do so without contacting the family. Once he had left, Giuseppe would explain Amedeo's decision to their parents, and to Bice.

A plane and a pilot were found, and the Treasury agreed to part with a quantity of gold and silver coins. Approval for the distribution of honorary title to the chiefs was sought. Then, to Amedeo's astonishment, he woke up on 8 September to discover that Italy was no longer at war. Tiring of what they perceived as

Italian procrastination, the Allies had announced the armistice a week earlier than agreed. The fighting, at least against the British and Americans, was over. A sense of unreality descended on Rome. German officers and civilians, so visible the day before, vanished from the streets. When Amedeo went to headquarters, he found it closed. Remondino could not be contacted. Like every other senior officer, he was trying to work out what to do.

By pre-empting the armistice, the Allies shattered the Italian chain of command and no plan was in place to resist the inevitable German invasion from the north. Armies in Greece, Yugoslavia and southern France were left floundering without orders. Hardly believing his luck, Field Marshal Albert Kesselring drove south finding one city after another falling into his hands with barely a shot fired. Several generals in northern Italy wanted to stop the Wehrmacht, but none had orders to do so. Outside Rome, the cavalry regiment of the Lancieri di Montebello made a quixotic stand to prevent the Germans from entering, but were cut down. Less than an hour before German forces took over the capital, the king and Marshal Badoglio abandoned Rome, taking a ship from Pescara to Brindisi in the south. Princess Jolanda remained in the city, which was left under the command of her husband Count Calvi di Bergolo.

In the confusion of the days that followed, some units that had fought beside the Germans, in Russia or the Balkans, found it ignominious to abandon their former allies. But most rallied to the king, from whom there was a complete and unaccountable silence. In Slovenia, the Italian army was rounded up by the Germans, while those who escaped were hunted down by Tito's partisans and hurled alive into the notorious *foibe* – the crevasses in the Carso. In Montenegro, some Italian units actually joined the partisans, although many of them starved to death in the winter of 1943–4. Only in Corfu and Cephalonia did an Italian army of 10,000 men under the Venetian general, Antonio Gandin, forcibly resist the Germans, confident that either the king in Brindisi or the Allies would send help. None came. Instead they were pulverised by German artillery and the Luftwaffe, and forced to surrender. Before he was shot, Gandin threw away the Iron Cross given to him by Field Marshal Keitel, and his officers were led away to execution, defiantly singing the 'Hymn of the Piave' from the First World War.

In a matter of days, fifty-one Italian divisions had been dismantled by the Germans, twenty-nine had been partially disarmed and only three remained intact in southern Italy. It was a débâcle from which the authority of the kingdom of Italy's military caste never recovered. A deeply distrustful German army now occupied most of the country, inclined to treat Italians as it had done the Poles. To the south, the Allies landed at Salerno the day after the armistice; a week later they had taken Naples and advanced north until meeting heavy German resistance on the Volturno, around Capua. Meanwhile, Mussolini had been freed from his prison in the Appenines by a daring parachute raid organised by the SS; many doubted, Amedeo among them, that the ex-Duce was overjoyed by his liberation.

At this critical point in the war, Amedeo was dressed in shabby civilian clothes with no identity documents. It suddenly dawned on him how vulnerable his own position had become. His badly injured brother was in need of medicines, which could only be bought on the black market for cash. He managed to get some form of identification from the Associazione dei Mutilati, the wounded soldiers' organisation, and borrowed money from Prince Prospero Colonna.

But with Rome likely to become a battleground in days, everyone in the capital seemed paralysed with indecision. Giuseppe told Amedeo that he had to leave for Brindisi. The king needed all his friends now. The sheer mess of the armistice – perhaps an impossible task – was being blamed on him, not on the Allies who had announced it unilaterally and earlier than agreed. Communists and socialists heaped opprobrium on the king by saying that he had

*Above* The surrender of the Duke of Aosta at Amba Alagi, 19 May, 1941.

*Right* Lieutenant Renato Togni, with the horse on which he was killed charging the British tanks at Keru, January 1941.

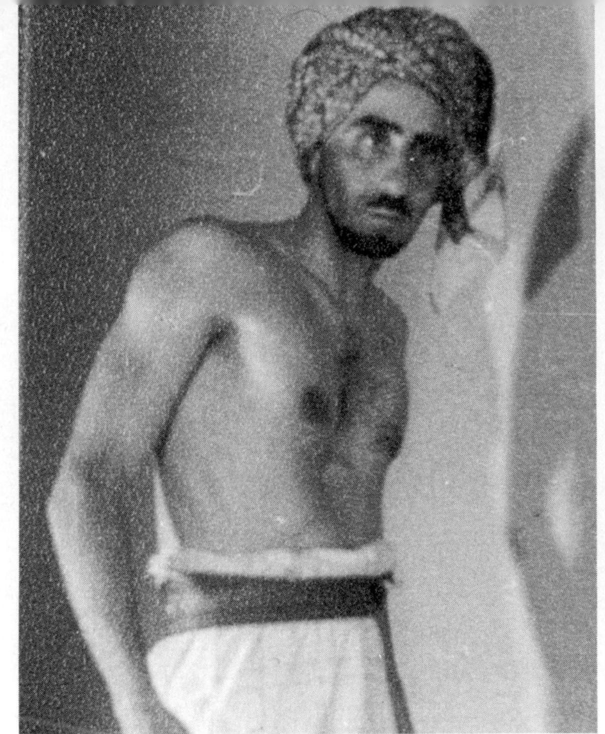

*Above* Daifallah the Yemeni, with whom Amedeo set out to cross the Red Sea. The photograph was taken after the war.

*Above right* Amedeo as Ahmed Abdullah, photographed by his friend Orlando Rizzi at the farm in Dorfu.

*Right* A rare photograph of Ahmed, Imam of the Yemen, given to his dear friend 'Ahmed Abdullah' before his departure as Italian ambassador to Jordan in the 1960s.

*Above left* Major Max Harari riding the captured Sandor at Asmara, autumn 1941.

*Top* Major Max Harari leaving his office in Asmara.

*Above* Sandor's hoof.

*Far left* Captain Lory Gibbs, who never adequately explained why he opened fire on Amedeo and Khadija on the road to Ghinda.

*Left* Captain Sigismund Reich.

Amedeo and Beatrice finally married, at Naples on 21 September 1944. An air-raid siren sounded during the service.

*Left* Torre Crestarella.

*Right* The Italian ambassador with a live cobra he captured in the embassy gardens, New Delhi, 1971. The secretaries fled in terror when Amedeo showed off his find – though Bice was, disappointingly, unmoved. She had grown used to such surprises during her husband's diplomatic career.

*Above* Amedeo, ambassador to Morocco, accompanies Italian foreign minister Aldo Moro in an inspection of the guard of honour, 1969. Moro was later to be murdered by the Red Brigades.

*Right* Sir Reginald Savory (right) meets his old adversary from Mount Cochen in London, 1976.

*Below* Amedeo with horsemen from the president of India's bodyguard, whom he trained to ride in the Caprilli fashion. The Sikh on the left is Mohinder Singh, who witnessed Amedeo's cavalry charge at Keru, on the Eritrean Lowlands on 21 January 1941.

ERITREA, MARCH 2000

*Right* Amedeo embraces an elderly *ascaro* and fellow veteran of the Second World War in Africa at the Catholic cemetery in Asmara.

*Below* The *comandante* visits the grave of Renato Togni, his friend and second-in-command.

*Below right* Amedeo stands at the pass of Ad Teclesan, where he destroyed three British light tanks. The track beside him may belong to one of them or, more likely, be the handiwork of his successors in the Eritrean People's Liberation Front.

*Top* The palace of the Italian governors on the waterfront at Massaua, which was the scene of bitter fighting with the forces of Ethiopia's Dergue during Eritrea's war for independence. Massaua was liberated after a women's battalion – who made up 30 per cent of the EPLF fighters – stormed across the causeways that link the city. Eritrea was finally recognised as an independent country in 1993.

*Below* The palace as it was in 1941, in a photograph taken by Max Harari.

Ahmed Abdullah, the water-seller, returns to a shack in Al-Katmia, outside Massaua, where he hid from the British during the autumn of 1941.

Back in Ireland in a pub in Trim, with the daughters of the author, Anna and Emily.

abandoned his people by 'fleeing the capital'. It was an absurdity widely disseminated at the time, which became an unshakeable belief in post-war Italy, that the king should have stayed in the capital and faced the invaders. Had he done so, he would have become a prisoner of the Germans and the country would have been left without legitimate government and become simply the occupied territory of opposing armies.

The two brothers parted. Three days later a German officer and one of the new style neo-Nazi Fascist officials came to ask Colonel Guillet where his loyalties lay. Giuseppe answered honestly that, as a regular army officer, he would support the king. His doctors applauded his courage, but made sure he left that night to find refuge with the Colonnas in Trastevere. Amedeo, meanwhile, filled a rucksack and headed for Termini station, finding it full of Germans arriving from the north. He abandoned his plans to catch a train and began walking south by night. When he reached the Volturno, battle was raging and all the bridges had been blown, including, Amedeo discovered with pain, the magnificent thirteenth-century bridge outside Capua built by Emperor Frederick II, the *stupor mundi*, to link his kingdom of Naples with the lands of the pope.

A stray Carabiniere policeman, whose beat had been turned into a battlefield, told Amedeo that Capua was deserted. Barone Guillet and his family had long since left. He did not know where.

Amedeo crossed the river by pulling himself over the water on a makeshift raft buoyed by oil drums, and continued trudging south until one morning he walked straight into a British patrol. The company commander questioned him briefly and then sent him under escort to the now pro-Allied Italian command at Naples, where his identity was confirmed. Preparations were made to have Major Guillet taken to Italian army headquarters in Brindisi.

In little over a week the war had taken a different turn. It was intolerable that the Germans be allowed to fight what was now their war on Italian soil. Neutrality was impossible. In a policy of co-belligerence – 'changing sides', as many Allied troops preferred to put it – the legitimate government in Brindisi, supported by the army and the overwhelming majority of the Italian population, allied with Britain and America and declared war on Germany. Mussolini, meanwhile, proclaimed the Italian Social Republic in the north at Salò, supported by Farinacci, Starace and Graziani, among many lesser names. It was Fascism returning to its populist, street-thuggish roots, repudiating the past twenty years of compromise with 'Victor Savoy' and the forces of conservatism.

With Communist partisans settling old scores, unconcerned whether they shot Fascists or monarchists, Amedeo's nightmare in Spain had been realised: Italy had fallen into civil war.

## TWENTY-FIVE

# *Sua Maestà*

The king was standing in the centre of a small functional office, which in happier times had been that of the municipality in Brindisi. He turned when Amedeo was shown into the room, and walked towards him, smiling slightly with his hand outstretched. Amedeo bowed low, and took his monarch's hand. When he looked up, he expected to see the king much altered from when they had last seen each other, during the first anniversary celebrations of the declaration of the empire six years before. He seemed a little older, but otherwise unchanged. Foreigners had turned his kingdom into a battleground, Rome was occupied by the enemy, and some of his family were prisoners of the Germans. But if Vittorio Emanuele III were crushed by these disasters he gave no impression of it. Instead, he seemed as always: dignified, implacid, a little remote. Throughout his forty-three-year reign, he had tried to do his duty, within the limits of his character; within the limits of the hand that nature had dealt him. There had been times when his people had loved him, and he had done his best to follow their wishes, not least in the establishment of the Fascism regime. More often he had been under-estimated and derided, yet time and again, this shy, awkward man had displayed reserves of strength no one had expected. He may have disliked his public role, but he knew how to perform it, and, for better or worse, he would do his duty, as he saw it, to the end.

Amedeo felt emotion well up within him, and tears pricked his eyes. All his life he had loved and revered this man; they were the feelings he had grown up with, passed to him by his father and family. For the Guillets, the Patria was the king, who embodied all that was decent and clean in Italian public life. Yet for years Fascists had treated him with ill-concealed disdain, and now he was a pariah to the left. Amedeo wondered whether it would be here, in the little municipal office at Brindisi, still filled with land registry files and records of local births and deaths, where the Kingdom of Italy would end. The Allies kept their distance, making it all the easier to repudiate a man, and perhaps a throne, that would embarrass them. British liaison officers appalled the Italians at headquarters by presenting themselves to the king in shirtsleeves and shorts, offering him arguments as though ultimata. 'Very old, pathetic and a bit senile,' had been the verdict of Harold Macmillan, the future prime minister.

Vittorio Emanuele's expression softened as he scrutinised the face of the sunburned major, seeking to recognise the features of Baron Guillet's boy. He could recall names and faces as meticulously as he could catalogue his vast collection of ancient coins. But the man before him was not the youth Jolanda would accompany out riding and invite back to the Villa Savoia. The face was scarred and etched with lines that told he had seen too soon life's suffering. Like so many other young men.

'My dear Guillet, everyone has been telling me the most remarkable stories about you,' the king said.

He sat down, offering Amedeo a chair, and asked after his mother and father. He expressed his sadness when the young man replied that he did not know where they were, now that there was fighting around Capua. The king fondly recalled Uncle Amedeo, much missed in these difficult times, and Uncle Ernesto, whose son, a fighter pilot, had been killed over El Alamein. So many of the best had died in this disastrous war, the king said.

Amedeo was the first Italian officer to return from Africa Orientale Italiana since Asmara fell in April 1941, and the king was eager to hear at first hand about the campaign. He began nervously at first, rushing ahead of himself and stumbling over his words. But the king's quiet interest put him at ease. For an hour and a half Amedeo spoke freely, recalling the preparations of the Duke of Aosta and Frusci, the British invasion and how the Gruppo Bande had charged the enemy at Keru.

They talked of the errors of the lowlands campaign, the pointless enlargement of the Italian front ordered from Rome, the British counterattack, the defeat at Agordat and the heroic stand at Keren. In Italy the battle had been down played, as Fascist propaganda highlighted the reversal of fortune in the Western desert with Rommel redeeming Graziani's shambles at Sidi Barrani. The king was struck above all by Amedeo's open affection and respect for the Duke of Aosta.

'I always knew that boy would turn out well!' the king said in Piedmontese. They were silent for a moment, recalling the cleanest of all the leading figures in Italy's disastrous intervention in the Second World War.

When at last Amedeo had finished, the king rose and smiled at him fondly, and they again shook hands.

'Welcome home, my boy,' he said, holding his arm.

At that moment, Amedeo saw the old king of the First World War – *il re soldato* – who had held the line at the Piave when all seemed lost. Deeply moved, he walked out into the corridor filled with the unfamiliar uniforms of Italy's new allies and out into the sunlit courtyard.

Brindisi was full of old friends, but Amedeo declined their invitations to lunch, preferring instead to sit alone in the threadbare little park opposite the municipality. In mid-afternoon he was tracked down by a captain who told him that Marshal Badoglio, the prime minister, would also like to see him. With General Taddeo Orlandi, the unsung hero of Italy's war of liberation, Badoglio was trying to gather up the pieces of his scattered armies. Amedeo was asked to prepare a list of 300-odd officers captured by the British in east Africa whose immediate release would help the war effort. But Badoglio also wanted to hear of the young major's exploits in Africa.

For a couple of hours they talked together, with the marshal eager to know everything that Amedeo had done, even during the conquest of Abyssinia in 1936. They spoke nostalgically of those days and the great hopes for the empire, of the immense pride Italians felt in it. They discussed the Duke of Aosta as viceroy, and how he was transforming Africa Orientale Italiana, and the mad folly of Mussolini in going to war, even though Badoglio himself had warned him time and again of the true condition of the army.

'Everything we did, every *lira* spent and every drop of blood was done for nothing,' said Badoglio, his voice faltering. 'All those brave men – the duke, Lorenzini, those who fought on with Nasi at Gondar – were wasted. They're just pages of a history no one will ever read.'

The marshal was almost weeping as he said these words, and Amedeo, too, was deeply moved – the more so as he had never felt any particular warmth towards Badoglio. Astute, cautious and seemingly unmoveable from the centre of Italian power, the marshal had not been popular with the Guillets; the ambition had been too obvious, and so too were the pretensions of a self-made man from the lower rural middle classes of Piedmont. But as Badoglio reviewed the ruin of the Patria, which he had done his best to prevent, Amedeo felt great sympathy for him. The man who had conquered Ethiopia, who still carried the mocking title of Duke of Addis Ababa, suddenly looked very old. For the second time that day, Amedeo felt the tears in his eyes.

## TWENTY-SIX

# *Liberation*

The British truck pulled up outside the Italian command in the piazza in front of the palace of the Bourbon kings of Naples. On the opposite side of the square, American GIs were sitting in the sun at Gambrinus, the city's most exclusive café, drinking beer and resting their boots on the plant pots. The soldiers in the truck watched them enviously. Their leave over, they were on their way up to the new frontline at Monte Cassino. The corporal at the wheel irritably sounded the horn a couple of times. No one liked leaving Naples. And they liked it even less to be kept waiting by an 'Eyetie' major, whom they had been told to take as far as Capua. The horn blared again just as a short, sunburned figure emerged from the courtyard, walking past the sentries. In heavily accented English, Amedeo greeted the British soldiers cordially, who nodded unsmilingly, and then he climbed into the back, finding a place to himself by the tailgate.

It took a couple of moments for him to notice that the soldiers' attention was focused on the other side of the square. A waiter in white was remonstrating excitedly with drunk GIs, who were sitting at a table with some local prostitutes. Amedeo watched impassively. He had seen similar scenes a hundred times since he had arrived in Naples three weeks before. But not in Gambrinus, where in former times Uncle Rodolfo and Aunt Luisa would have a drink before the opera. The cost of Italy's liberation was going to be high, and the women of Naples were paying it on their backs. The whole city had been turned into a brothel by the liberating armies. In the narrow alleyways of Forcella or in the Quartiere Spagnolo, hollow-cheeked women sold themselves for a bag of flour or a tin of spam. Half-starved even before the Allies arrived, the great southern metropolis, unchanged in essentials since the time of the Bourbons, was suffering a cruel awakening. In a broken Europe, America and the modern world had arrived.

The GIs fascinated Amedeo. They were quite unlike any troops he had seen before, and he found them even more outlandish than the Allied women in uniform, sometimes in trousers, who strode confidently through the Neapolitan crowds. More like overgrown children than the soldiers of a conquering army, the Americans seemed to lack any sense of self-respect, making no effort to conceal their drunkenness or lust, still less inhibited by the presence of their officers. But they were generous, Amedeo conceded, sentimentally moved by the barefooted *scugnizzi* street urchins, who pestered them incessantly and pandered their sisters. Paid as much as a British major, the GIs doled out tins of corned beef, rice pudding or condensed milk from a seemingly inexhaustible supply. Having been fleeced by one family with a pretty daughter, a GI would be 'sold' on to another, led away in drunken stupor by a *scugnizzo* to spread his largesse of ration coupons, or dollars, or nylons.

The British soldiers, now standing in the truck, began to shout over to the Americans, laughing at them contemptuously and gesticulating. Gnarled, short men in ungainly uniforms that seemed to be made of woven cardboard, they seemed to Amedeo far older than the GIs, although there was probably no difference in age between them. To his eyes, they were less alien, even though the livid tattoos that covered their forearms made him think of the barbarians who had sacked Rome. Over at the bar, a fair-haired American had knocked over a table, and the women were looking anxious. As the British truck manoeuvred reluctantly out of the square, disappointed to miss seeing how this scene would end, a couple of American MPs in white helmets began walking towards the bar.

It was late afternoon by the time the truck pulled up at the steps of Capua's cathedral, where it brusquely deposited the Italian major and then sped off again in clouds of dust towards the north. Amedeo was pained to see that the fighting had disfigured his home town, damaging its ancient buildings with no respect to the glories of Capua's past. From where he was standing, he could see that his family's palazzo had been hit. A shell had burst through the wall of his father's study, bringing down the pedimented window. Through the gaping hole he could see the library shelves disgorging books, and even a couple of familiar portraits hanging askew on the walls. At the bar across the piazza, he was told that *baronessa* Guillet and her husband were living on the other side of the River Volturno, in the village of San Secondino. It was only three or four kilometres away, but the old men in the bar warned him that only Allied soldiers could cross the new pontoon bridge over the river.

A British sergeant and two soldiers were guarding the crossing and when Amedeo approached, the NCO demanded to see his papers.

'Where have you been fighting, sir?' the sergeant asked, noting the medal ribbons on his chest, which now included the Kingdom of Italy's highest, the Ordine Militare di Savoia.

'Africa,' Amedeo replied.

'Keren?'

'Yes.'

The sergeant drew himself up and saluted. 'Let the major pass.'

For many British soldiers who fought in both battles, the Italian defence at Keren was considered even tougher than that of the Germans at Monte Cassino, that was then raging fifty miles to the north.

San Secondino only had one, unpaved street and as he walked down it he suddenly heard a piercing shriek of 'Amedeo!' And then there was his mother, normally so reserved and dignified and called '*La Signora*' by the townsfolk of Capua, running towards him with her arms outstretched. He lost himself in her embrace, holding her tightly. She was thinner than he remembered, and her long black hair was flecked with grey. But she seemed content, apparently even happy in her reduced circumstances at San Secondino. At the small villa on the edge of the village she had her chickens and grew vegetables, and it seemed that in facing the challenge of survival she was fulfilled. As she fussed over him and issued instructions, he smiled to hear her pour scorn on the Germans, whom she perversely insisted on calling *austriaci*.

The *barone* was more miserable, stuck out in the countryside with only the peasants for company. He was going out of his mind with boredom, he confessed to his son, and agriculture had never been his passion. In old age, he was becoming cranky, his son had to concede. At the height of the fighting on the Volturno, when everyone else in San Secondino was cowering in the network of cellars below the village, he had insisted on sleeping in his own bed at the villa. A German battery had been set up in the courtyard and continued firing throughout the night. The old veteran had marched out in his pyjamas and told them to keep quiet. The Germans had laughed at him, but an hour or so later the guns had, in fact, packed up and left.

For all his misgivings about the Duce, which the *barone* had held even when the dictator was at the height of his popularity, he had never imagined that the Patria would be brought so low. The country was again a battlefield for foreigners, almost as though the unification of Italy had not happened at all. Whatever the future might bring, he felt he had little place in it. The only comfort was that his two sons had rallied to the cause of the king.

From his parents Amedeo discovered, as he had expected, that Bice and the Gandolfos were living in their villa at Avella, deep in the countryside not far from Avellino. Vietri had been seized by British Commandoes during the Salerno landings, and the

Gandolfos' Torre Crestarella had narrowly escaped German artillery fire, whose shells fell in the sea. After a couple of days with his parents, Amedeo borrowed the bicycle of the housekeeper, filled a rucksack with some food and a change of clothes, and set off for Avella fifty miles away. It took the whole morning to cycle from Capua south past Caserta, where the great palace of the Bourbons was the new Allied headquarters, and then in the afternoon he turned inland through the hills. There had been no fighting in this part of the country away from the Naples plain. Amedeo pedalled laboriously past woods of chestnut and oak, and through villages where the fields were filled with crops. He had been to the Gandolfos' eighteenth-century villa many times, and knew better than to knock at the front door, which he had never seen opened. Around the back, a little iron gate opened on to a pleasant courtyard, filled with wallflowers and with a well in the centre. His hand was shaking a little as he reached for the rope of the outdoor bell, and rang it. Rosa, the oldest Gandolfo sister, came down to open the door, gasped her surprise and embraced him. Bice was upstairs with their grandmother. The old lady was ailing and had better be spared the excitement of Amedeo's sudden return, Rosa explained. She led him down a corridor to a little-used drawing room filled with faded, heavy furniture where he could wait.

Half an hour passed before he heard the clack of shoes on the marble stairs, and he rose to meet her. For a moment Bice paused in the doorway to look at him and then she ran the last few paces. There were tears in her eyes as she threw her arms around him. And then she kissed him in a way that she had never done before.

To be alone, they went into the garden, where they sat on a stone bench asking questions and then not waiting for the answer as they held each other in their arms. Bice was exactly as she had been when he had last seen her, waiting in the mist as he boarded the flying boat for Tripoli, and he had made that unfortunate remark about Penelope and Ulysses.

'You had a lot of courage to wait for so long,' he told her.

'I had to know for sure whether you were ever coming back,' she replied, and he felt a spasm of guilt that he had ever doubted the strength of her love for him.

Having left the two alone for more than an hour, the Gandolfo family could not resist joining the couple in the garden. Uncle Rodolfo, dressed for the country in a suit of Scottish tweed, enfolded in his arms the younger man, whom he had long thought of as a son.

'You made us wait, but welcome, my boy. Welcome!'

Amedeo was overwhelmed and his replies to eager questions were brief and flat. He was grateful for the few moments when the focus was off him, and the others talked amongst themselves. He looked over to Bice, his senses in turmoil. Both were relieved when, after dinner, they were left alone again. In the garden they had hardly spoken to one another, but Amedeo had to tell her of Khadija. He had not, he believed, betrayed Bice, for his feelings for her had remained constant. But he had to explain to his future wife that for a long while he had lived with another woman, who had cared for him with no thought for the future, and whom he had also loved. He told her of how they had come together at the fort of Amba Gheorgis, how the bond had developed between them, and of Khadija's loyalty to him even in moments of extreme danger, and during those long months after the Italian defeat when he had been a fugitive.

Bice listened without interruption, and bowed her head. He told her of how Khadija had felt so proud of fooling the Sudanese sergeant at the farm at Dorfu, which she considered their home, and of how he had upset her by saying that they were to leave the next day. He recalled the last time he had seen her, when he had disbanded his men near Ghinda, and how he had wept when she left.

'What a wonderful girl,' Bice said, looking up at him through her tears. 'I wonder whether I would have been able to do what she did.'

Amedeo took her in his arms and pressed himself against her long reddish blonde hair, and breathed deeply. He suddenly felt very tired. He had only travelled from Capua that morning, but it seemed as though he had come from much further away. As though on cue, the first tell-tale shiver of a malaria attack ran down his back. The next morning Bice was ministering to him again, preparing the boiled-up lemon juice.

They waited until Rome was liberated before they married. The celebrations were, Amedeo would say, of 'Franciscan simplicity'. Only a handful of friends and relatives could attend in Naples on 21 September 1944, and all the bride and groom had to offer by way of hospitality were a few cakes and glasses of vermouth. Bice had changed before the service at Santissima Ascensione a Chiaia, in the Gandolfo's war-damaged palazzo. After putting on her wedding dress, she edged her way around the gaping hole in the drawing room where a British naval shell had made a neat hole that went down seven storeys. In the church, the air raid siren sounded, but it was followed quickly by the all-clear, before the priest had ushered the guests out of the door.

At last man and wife, the couple were driven by a fellow officer to their honeymoon at the Torre Crestarella at Vietri.

# TWENTY-SEVEN

# *A Bracelet*

ASMARA, DECEMBER 1945

The Sudanese sentry beside the white metal gates of the Villa Roma drew himself up and saluted as the army Jeep pulled into the drive. It circled the ornamental fountain and crunched the gravel as it came to a halt beside the whitewashed portico. The delegation from Rome, two civilians from the Foreign Ministry and one army officer, had arrived at the residence of the British military governor. Surrounded by a cluster of officers, Brigadier J. M. Benoy came out on to the steps to greet his guests, who had flown in courtesy of the United States Air Force. Brigadier Benoy shook the hands of the civilians, but the man he was most curious to meet was the thirty-six-year-old major with several layers of medal ribbons on his chest.

'Welcome back to Asmara, major,' the governor said, shaking his hand and then leading him and the others into the villa's large drawing-room. The last time Amedeo had been in the room was the night that Asmara passed from Italian to British rule, and he had arrived to comfort Signora Frusci, sitting hunched in her cardigan and incessantly smoking. The glistening art deco mirrors were just as he remembered, and the woodwork and furniture. But the portrait of the Duke of Aosta on the far wall had been replaced by a photograph of George VI.

Amedeo had no idea how the British in Eritrea would react to the return of the man they had once hunted so assiduously. When he had been invited to take part in the delegation, whose task was to organise the repatriation of Italian civilians from the former colony, he had urged the Italian Foreign Ministry to find out whether the British in Eritrea were still looking for him. He had been surprised by the response. A telegram had come back from the Foreign Office in London saying that 'the authorities in Asmara were well aware of the honourable part Colonel Guillet had played in the recent hostilities', and they looked forward to receiving him.

Far from being suspicious or circumspect, the British in Asmara could not have been more welcoming to a man who, a few years before, had been looting their convoys and derailing their trains. A car would be placed at his disposal, and Brigadier Benoy invited him to ride any of the twelve horses that his Italian predecessors had left behind in their stables in the governor's palace gardens.

Amedeo had only one request. As the others talked among themselves, he explained to the brigadier in halting English that during the two months of his assignment it was very likely that his former soldiers would want to meet him. He could not turn them away. The governor applauded his sentiments, and reassured him. Far more of a headache, these days, was the imprisonment of Zionist terrorists, who had been removed from Palestine to Eritrea. The prospect of the Gruppo Bande reforming in the centre of Asmara did not bother him in the least. The largest conference room of the Hotel CIAAO, where the Italians were staying, would be a good place to receive his men, the governor suggested.

'The only thing I ask is that you don't talk politics,' Brigadier Benoy told him, adding: 'Especially not concerning the future of Eritrea.'

It was strange how the threads of his life seemed to have come together, Amedeo reflected as he walked through the formal gardens of the Italian governors' palace above the city. Less than a month before in Rome, he and Bice had been out riding early one morning at the cavalry centre at Tor di Quinto. It had been their habit, even before the war came to an end, to arrive on the earliest tram, work a couple of horses in the big manège and ride the smaller cross-country courses or hack over the steep, sandy hillocks topped by spreading pine trees that characterised the Roman *campagna*. Amedeo would then go to work in the offices of SIM, the Italian military intelligence service, with whom he had served since his meeting with the king and Badoglio in Brindisi.

That morning as they were putting away their horses, Amedeo was struck by a huge, familiar head looming over a stable door. None of the grooms seemed to know the horse's history. He asked Bice to run her hand over its quarters, where she would find a little cross of white hairs. She asked how he knew, patting the spot where Amedeo had cut its skin in Tripoli years before. It was Ariosto, the horse he had bought in Germany, and on whom the Duce had unsheathed the Sword of Islam. Mussolini had been so pleased with the giant Hanoverian that he had brought it back to Rome. It now belonged to an American admiral, the grooms told Amedeo, and in a few days' time Ariosto was to be shipped to the United States as booty of war.

On a Sunday afternoon shortly afterwards, Bice answered the telephone in their apartment in Piazza Mazzini, near the Vatican. A Major Harari wanted to speak to him, she told Amedeo. The name was faintly familiar, but he could not immediately place it. Most of the Allied liaison officers he had known had returned home in the months immediately after the end of the war. But then he remembered. He was back at the farm at Dorfu just after the British soldiers had searched it, and Orlando Rizzi was talking to him anxiously of the head of intelligence at Asmara. Major Harari was the man he should fear, Rizzi had said. He was genial and courteous, but shrewd: it was he who was pursuing Amedeo halfway across Eritrea.

The voice on the other end of the line was that of an urbane and educated man, speaking perfect, almost accentless Italian. He had always wanted to meet Amedeo Guillet, Harari explained, as there had been no occasion to do so in Eritrea in '41. An hour later, Amedeo was cradling a Campari soda in a hotel bar in the centre of Rome when a tall, good-looking man, immaculately dressed in a civilian suit, strode towards him with his hand outstretched. A mutual acquaintance had told Harari that Amedeo Guillet had survived the war, and was living in Rome. His own duties as the military governor of Capri had come to an end, alas, and he was preparing to return home to Cairo in the next few days. But, before he did so, he had to meet the man he had spent the best part of a year trying to capture.

After a few more drinks, Amedeo invited Harari to his house for dinner. Bice received the British officer politely, but remained distant, and for all Harari's polite attention, she had a wary, animal look in her eyes. The teaching of the *Soeurs du Sacré Coeur* in Naples had not prepared her for entertaining a man in her house whose sole qualification as a guest was that he had tried to capture or kill her husband. She sat listening to the two talk about those distant times in Africa, and the absurdity of a war that had ushered in a modern world that neither man was convinced would prove to be a vast improvement on the old one. After the suicide of Europe, only the Americans and the Communists seemed to count now.

Harari was not the first enemy officer from Eritrea he had encountered, Amedeo told him. Just after the liberation of Rome, he had been staying in the Hotel Anglo-Americano, off the Piazza Barberini. He had given his name to the *portiere* to collect his post, when a British captain standing at the desk had spun round to face him.

'I think we may have met before,' he had said. Abruptly, he demanded to know whether Amedeo had been the man riding a camel on the road to Ghinda, accompanied by a few others including a woman, when a British officer had opened fire. Amedeo confirmed that, indeed, it had been him.

'Thank God for that!' replied the stranger, ignoring Amedeo's astonished look. 'I was right to open fire after all!'

Amedeo, too, was curious to meet this officer, who had shot at him even though no words had been exchanged. Over a drink in the bar, he asked Captain Lory Gibbs how he had known that he was not just an innocent civilian. Gibbs would say only that as soon as their eyes met he knew whom he was looking at, and had reached for the gun.

Harari was intrigued to hear this story, and he recalled Gibbs fondly. But a far more dangerous enemy Amedeo had made was Captain Sigismund Reich, who seemed to view the Italian's guerrilla activities as a personal affront. Reich seemed little changed, Harari said. Only recently he had heard a story doing the rounds how Heinrich Himmler, no less, had expired in Reich's arms after swallowing cyanide, but had given him his watch before doing so. An able man, brilliant even, but quite unhinged, and Amedeo was fortunate, indeed, not to have fallen into his hands.

'I did everything I could to catch you and, had I had to, I would have shot you without a second's hesitation,' Harari told him. 'But in my heart I admired you for fighting on as you did, and for never surrendering even though the cause must have seemed hopeless.'

It was late when Harari took his leave, and as he did so he bent over Bice's hand, but she withdrew it and, instead, kissed him.

'How strange life is that two good men should be set to kill each other,' she said.

More than twenty years later, when Max Harari was again staying with Amedeo and Bice Guillet, now among his closest friends, he left behind a present on the desk in the study. Inside, Amedeo found a pale horse's hoof, meticulously shod in the Italian fashion and mounted in silver with the inscription in Italian: 'Sandro. Barbary grey. 12 years old. Max Harari, Asmara. June 1942.' There was also a photograph of the grey Arab stallion, Sandor, looking out of his stable, on which Harari wrote the words: 'To Amedeo in memory of the wonderful animal that was the cause of our friendship.'

* * *

They came in groups of five or six at first. Then tens and twenties. And in all Amedeo must have re-encountered 80-odd of his former soldiers. They would gather outside the Hotel CIAAO – for the time being still the *Cooperativa Italiana Alberghi Africa Orientale* – and wait for their former *comandante* to emerge. As with Gebreyesus Geremeddin, the old chief whom Amedeo visited at Azzega, he discouraged any talk of the political future of Eritrea. He was a guest of the British, with the specific task of repatriating those Italians who were to return home, as well as pleading the cause of those with a right to remain. His war – Italy's war – against the occupiers was at an end. But he would do what he could to help them in other ways. Almost everyone in the Italian community was pleading with him for a favour on behalf of some relative or other, so he was well placed to find twenty to thirty of them jobs with local farmers and industrialists. Brigadier Benoy also helped, finding work for several with the British authorities.

It was a disappointment to Amedeo that none of the former officers of the Gruppo Bande were in Eritrea. Instead, they were scattered around the British empire, or had already been sent home to Italy. Battizzocco had been the last to be released, he later discovered. He had been imprisoned in the Sudan with Fascist functionaries of the colonial administration, who had threatened him with retribution when he refused to apply for party membership. But once the Italian armistice was declared, the Fascists overnight proclaimed themselves life-long social democrats, and were separated by the British for early release. When it was Battizzocco's turn, he told his captors that he had nothing in common with such scum, pointing to the turncoats. For another eighteen months, until the war's end, he remained incarcerated with a handful of intransigent, albeit honest Black Shirts.

But Orlando Rizzi and the lawyer Maiorani were still in Asmara, and they celebrated Amedeo's arrival at a large reunion dinner. Relations between the British and Italians in the colony had improved after the armistice, and become cordial during Italy's 'war of independence' against the Germans. In addition, Eritrea's economy had boomed with the unlimited wartime demand for its produce, such as Birra Melotti, which was now exported all over British East Africa. Yet underlying everything was the deep fear of the 60,000 Italian population living there that one day the British would hand the country over to the Ethiopians. At the dinner, Maiorani embarrassed Amedeo by toasting his return with '*Viva L'Eritrea Italiana!*'

A few weeks after his arrival, Amedeo drove his Jeep down to Massaua, and then headed south over unmade tracks through the desert. Accompanied by the chief of the Assaorta tribe, which had provided the IVth Toselli with its recruits, he carefully skirted Arkiko, where he and Daifallah had deceived the villagers, and drove on towards the Buri peninsula.

The little bay of Sayed Ibrahim was as he remembered it five years before. The old man welcomed his visitors and they sat under the lean-to by the seashore and drank *gishir*. Sayed Ibrahim did not recognise the European officer dressed in uniform. In time, the conversation turned, as it probably did with all the old man's visitors, to that strange bright night during the war between the Christians when he had been on his way to Barasol to sell fish. Two men claiming to be Yemeni pilgrims – although they certainly were not – had lain in ambush intending to kill him, but had, instead, fallen to their knees and pleaded for his aid. They were, the old man decided, messengers of God, sent to test his faith and he had saved them.

Amedeo sat listening in silence. He had intended to thank the sharif for having saved his life, but he could not shatter his innocent illusion. After they left, Amedeo asked the chief to build a concrete wall around the old man's well, for he had been complaining that the mud bricks around it kept collapsing.

'What shall I tell him when he asks who has paid for the work?' his friend asked.

'Just tell him you received a letter – from a grateful Yemeni.'

* * *

Two months had passed since the Italian mission had arrived in Asmara and its work was nearly over. The three emissaries from Rome had managed to steer tactfully between the conflicting interests of the Italian community and the British authorities, who wanted to reduce Italian numbers in the colony. Instead, they congratulated themselves for having obtained residence rights for 800 more than had originally been foreseen. It remained only to tidy up a few final details, and then, their task completed, they could all return home.

For Amedeo, only one matter still rankled like the dull ache of an old wound. He had met many of his soldiers, and thanked the chiefs who had helped him on the run, and he had been to see Sayed Ibrahim, who had saved his life. But he had made no effort to find Khadija. In his suitcase, wrapped in tissue paper, was a gold bracelet with a diamond that Bice had given him before he had left. It was a family jewel, not one that she had bought, and she had made Amedeo promise that he would give it to Khadija once he arrived in Eritrea.

He had refused at first, trying to reason with his wife. How would it look if he, of all people, arrived back in Eritrea and the British discovered that he was seeking out his former mistress? He was taking part in an important mission for the Foreign Ministry. There would be other occasions when he would be able to return to Eritrea and then, perhaps, together they might be able to find Khadija and . . . Bice had cut him off.

'She is the woman who risked her life for you, who cared for you and who suffered with you,' she told him. 'You must find her and thank her. And you must thank her from me.'

One morning, as Amedeo was leaving his hotel to go to work, he was stopped by a former soldier. It was Togri's former orderly, the only survivor of the Lieutenant's desperate charge. Khadija had arrived. She had crossed over the border from the Semien and reached Asmara the night before. Amedeo felt confused, his irritation fanned by a weight of guilt that he was reluctant to admit.

He could not see her now, he replied brusquely. He was on his way to meet the governor. The British, he explained – peculiarly reserved and diffident concerning women – would view him with contempt if they learned that he had sought out a local woman. He unburdened himself of all the feelings he had rehearsed before with Bice, falling silent only when he noticed the soldier's perplexed and uncomprehending face. To a veteran of the Gruppo Bande, one of those who had fought to the end, it seemed extraordinary that the *comandante* felt ashamed of Khadija, who had always been at his side.

Amedeo looked at the man, sensed his embarrassment and felt his own. It was not the feelings of the British that worried him; he was more anxious about his own. He did not know how he would behave if he were to see Khadija again. For three years they had shared their lives completely, and he knew her as well as it was possible to know another human being. He had always told Khadija that one day they would part, but half of him had hoped that that day would never come. Many times when the British were looking for him, and he had shed his former self, he had been tempted to disappear into her world, and they would live as husband and wife. But Bice and the Patria had pulled him back.

'Don't worry about the British, *comandante*,' said the soldier, understanding only that Amedeo did not want to be recognised. 'They have long since taken up all the old habits of the Italians, eating pasta at midday and then having a *siesta*. In the afternoon heat, you won't see a single European on the streets of Asmara.'

A few hours later Amedeo came out of his hotel again, following the soldier at a distance. They crossed the main Corso Italia by the cathedral, passed the Friday Mosque and entered Asmara's native quarter. The soldier stopped at an alley, checked that all was clear, and then pointed to a faded blue door. It was a *tejeria*, where Eritreans, whether Muslims or Copts, would settle down to get mildly drunk on mead. A young girl opened the door and led Amedeo down a dark corridor to the back.

Khadija, her head wrapped in a white shawl, was sitting on a rope bed, waiting for him. She looked up when he appeared in the door. All his love for her returned and he ran forward to clasp her. As he held her in his arms and kissed her face, Amedeo shook with tears.

For what seemed like hours, they sat on the *angareb* holding hands, and saying nothing. Finally, Khadija asked whether he was married. When Amedeo replied that he was, she sighed.

'So I have not harmed anybody.'

'And are you married?' he asked.

'No,' she replied, looking away. 'I had my chief.'

She was living with her father in the village in Semien, where they had first met. He was old now and so she ran the tribe, helped by Asfao.

Amedeo told Khadija how moved Bice had been on hearing of her and of all that she had done for him. He took the bracelet wrapped in tissue paper from his pocket and handed her his wife's gift. Khadija took off the paper and turned the gold bracelet over on her lap, where it shone brightly against her *shammah*. She bowed her head low, and teardrops fell to make widening circles on the white gauze.

# *Epilogue*

AL-KATMIA, ERITREA. 16 MARCH 2000

For the first time, the large embassy Mercedes, with a pennant of the Italian tricolour on its bonnet, hesitated to follow. All afternoon it had been trailing reluctantly behind the battered Toyota 4×4 through the bomb-blasted ruins of Massaua like an idle dog forced out for a walk. But faced with the chasm of a broken drain its nerve seemed to falter, and the vehicle slowly crunched to a halt. The embassy first secretary and the military attaché, both in sharp suits, ties and the latest shades, sprang from the back and watched in mute protest as the old Toyota disappeared down the labyrinth of narrow sand tracks that serve as streets in the shanty town of Al-Katmia. As though he had been trying all day, Ahmed Abdullah al Redai had given his minders the slip at last.

At the wheel beside him, delighted at the diplomats' discomfort, was the impish figure of Tewolde Andu, a veteran of the Eritrean People's Liberation Front and mayor of what remains of Massaua after forty years of struggle against Ethiopian occupation. Making himself understood in a mixture of Arabic, English and Tigrinian, and relishing what little Italian his father had taught him as a child, he was taking the *generale* back to where he had lived as a water-seller sixty years before. In Asmara, we had been alerted that Tewolde, though an engaging and hospitable host, was *un po' bizzarro* – an eccentric. But he had met his match in the 91-year-old Italian sitting beside him, who seemed to know every corner of the mayor's city, even the least salubrious. Through the open window the old man watched with mounting excitement as life in Al-Katmia unfolded before him. He scrutinised each passing face, almost as though expecting to see Salah leading his donkey down the street, laden with water skins, or Daifallah the Yemeni waiting at the entrance of one of the shacks. Each of these timber structures seemed indistinguishable from the other, roofed with sheets of corrugated iron, and surrounded by high fences of brushwood and straw. The use of plastic bags in their construction was an innovation on the old man's day, as were the gaudy T-shirts worn by the children. But otherwise Al-Katmia was exactly as he remembered it.

Tewolde Andu came to a halt in an open space where children were kicking around a ball. Amedeo pulled himself out of the car, replaced his trilby and set off with rickety but brisk strides towards the nearest shack. His back was bowed by age, the shoulders uneven – thanks to another fall from a horse when he was well into his sixties – and the gnarled hands, whether in summer or winter, in County Meath or Rome or Al-Katmia, were enclosed in little brown cotton gloves with the fingers cut off. His face was a ploughed field of lines, with hillocks of melanomas testifying to a life lived under an unforgiving sun, but the grey-blue eyes were vivid and bright. A tall, grey-haired Eritrean in his seventies scrutinised the outlandish new arrivals from the entrance to his courtyard. He and Tewolde Andu exchanged a few words, and we were invited in.

The man's wife, elegant in her spotless white *shammah*, was bent over an open fire in the corner making the evening meal. Pots and pans were stacked on a makeshift shelf beside her and hanging from a branch were some maize, chillies and a few onions. To the side was an *angareb* rope bed, and a few hens clucked around our feet. A dozen children and curious passersby pressed in at the entrance, eager to discover the cause of the commotion, for very few strangers came to Massaua, let alone Al-Katmia.

Crushed in uncomfortably at the back were the two Italian diplomats, who looked as though they had jogged all the way.

'Don't you recognise Ahmed Abdullah, the old water-seller?' Tewolde Andu asked, relishing the bemusement his words caused. The elderly Eritrean studied Amedeo closely and, for a moment, seemed to nod approvingly, as though in recognition that he had done well after leaving Al-Katmia all those years ago. Tewolde told Amedeo's story, and again the old man nodded. The time of the Italians was part of his youth. It was long ago, almost forgotten, and the only period in his life when Eritrea had seemed at peace. He was sorry that he could not help Amedeo in his quest to find the old shack he shared with Salah, the water-seller. The shifting sands of Al-Katmia had long since moved on, and too much had happened in the past 60 years.

No part of Eritrea has been left unscarred by the long struggle for independence, and nowhere more so than the country's principal port. Earlier that afternoon we had driven into Massaua over Werner Metzinger's narrow causeway to the islands on which the city proper stands. At the end of it were three large Russian tanks on a makeshift plinth, standing as a permanent memorial to the day when Massaua fell to the EPLF in 1990. This vital bridgehead had been stormed at heavy cost by a battalion of women, who made up a third of the EPLF forces. The houses all around were still pockmarked with bullet holes, and cratered by shells. Many were just heaps of rubble. The white palace of the Turkish and then the Italian governors, which Amedeo had first seen when he arrived with the Spahys di Libya in 1935, lay in ruins by the seafront. The elegant horseshoe balustrade of the steps was in fragments on what was once the lawn and the cupola caved in like a broken egg. Of the red shield of Savoy, which ships were once able to see against the brilliant white of the palace from several kilometres away, there was no trace.

The sun was going down as we sped along the desert road out of Al-Katmia. In fragmentary Tigrinian, which Tewolde duly embellished, Amedeo had been telling his listeners how he had fought the British at the great battle of Keren, which all had heard of, and then hidden from them in Al-Katmia. To survive he had sold water in the city, leading a donkey over a nearby hill to a well that doubtless no longer existed.

'But it is still there,' the elderly Eritrean interrupted. Everyone used to get water from the well whenever Ethiopian bombing broke the mains supply. It was along the track that led to the burial ground of the Italian soldiers. Amedeo embraced our host in farewell, and the swollen crowd that now surrounded the Toyota parted to let him through.

Amedeo saw it first. We pulled off the road beside an old piece of Soviet artillery, the barrel of which had exploded, leaving the remains looking like a blown flower. At the foot of a stony, barren hill, which Amedeo recognised as the short-cut back to Massaua, was a scruffy *zeriba* bush and, just beyond it, the circular stone wall of the well. The old man climbed out of the car and, steadying himself on my arm, approached it with tears in his eyes. The rope grooves in the stone and the ledge where he had stacked his goatskins were exactly as he had described them in his study in Ireland. He closed his eyes for a moment, took off his hat, and bowed to kiss the wall of the well. We sat down on it saying nothing, as the red sun sank behind the mountains of Asmara.

Much had happened since Amedeo's mission to Eritrea in 1945. Shortly after his return, he had been promoted to colonel, aged thirty-seven, in recognition of his exceptional abilities. During the 'war of liberation' in 1943–45, he had again distinguished himself. He infiltrated the first meeting of Palmiro Togliatti, on the Communist leader's arrival in Naples from the Soviet Union. In the latter stages of the war, he used a laisser-passer of the celebrated partisan chief, Walter Magnoli, to retrieve the crown jewels of the Negus, so that Italy, not the Allies, would return them to Haile

Selassie. Cunningly, he used the same safe conduct to remove the compromising archives of the War and Foreign Ministeries from the communist brigade 'Garibaldi'. But unique film footage discovered by Amedeo of the trial and execution of Ciano and De Bono, who had voted for the Duce's dismissal, was handed over to the Americans. It was not returned and has never been seen again. As one of Italy's most decorated soldiers, and one untainted by Fascism, few doubted that had Amedeo stayed in the army he would have reached the top. But he resigned his commission in June 1946 after the plebiscite that abolished the Italian monarchy; after seven centuries, it also brought to an end the long rule of the Savoy dynasty.

It had been a dubious vote, won with a slender majority, that set the tone for the future divisions in postwar Italy. The day after the plebiscite, Amedeo presented himself at the Quirinale to inform Umberto II of his decision. The king, whose reign had begun a few months before after the abdication of his father, was chillingly disapproving. 'Far more important than me personally is Italy,' he said, pouring scorn on such gestures. 'If all the best officers leave the armed forces the country risks falling into the hands of the communists and their Soviet friends.' To prevent this, Umberto II released army officers of their oath of allegiance to the crown after the referendum. 'I will forgive you,' the king said. 'But tell your brother that if he, too, resigns, I won't even reply to his greetings.'

Coming from a man shortly to be banished from ever returning to Italy, the king's words carried great weight. Giuseppe Guillet did, indeed, remain in the army, where he became a lieutenant general, while Amedeo pondered an uncertain future. He had been attracted by the idea of becoming an anthropologist at a university, or, perhaps, finding some work in the Middle East. Instead, he decided to serve the new Italian republic by entering the Foreign Ministry. Given his prestige and his connections, and the good opinion he had earned in dealing with the British in Eritrea a few months before, he could have entered the ministry through a high-level recommendation. But Amedeo, as ever a Don Quixote, insisted on completing the public examination.

His first posting was to Cairo in 1950, then at its most lively and a delightful contrast to the austerity of postwar Europe. Max Harari provided Bice and Amedeo with an introduction, and a friendship that would be life-long took form. In the course of his duties. he came to know King Farouk and the royal family, especially Prince Abdel Moneim, who became regent after Farouk's abdication in 1952. He also met the originators of pan-Arabism, such as Gamal abd al-Nasser, who would shortly unleash passions that would transform Egypt and the Middle East.

Of the coming men, Amedeo was close to Mohammed Naguib, first president of Egypt, and Zakaria Moyeddin, a future prime minister. But he was fondest of Anwar al-Sadat, who was kept in the background by Nasser. Amedeo was again struck by the curious connections he had made in his life. During the war, Sadat had been the contact of two German spies brought to Cairo after a daring journey across the desert led by Lazslo de Almasy, 'the English Patient'. Amedeo had met him briefly in Budapest, as his brother, Janos, was a close friend. He would listen to the great explorer tell of his searches for the lost army of Gambyses which, according to Herodotus, had marched into the desert and vanished. In the remote massif of the Gilf Kebir, Almasy had found the prehistoric cave paintings of swimmers, and it was through these mountains, in the southern Sahara, that he brought a patrol of the Afrika Korps to deposit the spies south of Cairo. 'Operation Condor' was an epic 1500-mile journey, and though the spies were quickly captured by the British, Almasy was awarded the Iron Cross. In Cairo, Amedeo learned that after the war the explorer had been arrested in Budapest as a Nazi sympathiser, but that the Egyptian royal family had bribed Hungarian communists to secure his release. Almasy, however, had died of dysentery in Salzburg in 1951, before taking up the post of director of the Desert Institute in Cairo. Many years later his reputation as a great lover of women, owing to the success of Michael Ondaatje's novel and the film of *The English Patient*, caused hollow mirth among those who remembered him in Cairo, for the love of his life was a young officer in the Afrika Korps.

Throughout his career, Amedeo never neglected his equestrian interests, and they helped ensure that he did not become a diplomat who seldom left the embassy, but instead enthusiastically joined local society. With Max Harari's help, he set up a large riding establishment at Mena House, not far from the pyramid of Cheops. Riding in the desert, especially at night under a full moon to the pyramids of Saqqara eighteen kilometres away, became the popular pastime of influential Egyptians and the diplomatic community. Humphrey Trevelyan, the British ambassador, paid tribute to Amedeo in his memoirs, and his name appears in various accounts of this last phase in the Arab romance.

In the years 1952–54, the Yemen decided to open diplomatic relations with the outside world, and the Italian Foreign Ministry seconded Amedeo from the Cairo embassy to be the minister-representative in Taiz. Imam Yahia had been murdered in 1948, and Ahmed, his son, was now ruler. In a letter to her mother, Bice described their first journey to the Yemen, which began with a flight to Aden. ('I am amazed at the amount of alcohol that the English are capable of drinking even in early morning!' she noted.) From Aden it took eleven hours to drive over unmade roads to Taiz, through the territories of various chieftains, past caravans of camels and through a desert fortress which served as the frontier. Finally, they arrived at the city, with its white mosques and tower houses; a sentry in flowing robes and carrying a rifle kept guard on the wall above the gates. For the next six years the city was to be their home.

Wearing the morning coat and astrakhan hat that would be his formal attire in the Yemen, Amedeo presented his credentials to Imam Ahmed, who greeted him with the words, 'So, Ahmed

Abdullah, you have come home at last.' Their old friendship was renewed. In the years that followed, the Imam would rely on the Italian's advice more than any other westerner. From this vantage point, Amedeo was uniquely placed to witness the Yemen's attempts to face the modern world, and he would liken Imam Ahmed to Peter the Great of Russia, with all the qualities and all the defects of that figure. 'The personal influence of Sig Guillet, the Italian minister, continually grows . . .' noted the British representative, Christopher Pirie-Gordon, who became a close friend of the Guillets.

Alone among the foreign diplomats, technicians and Italian medical staff in the Yemen, Amedeo and Bice were instructed by the Imam to make their home in one of the tower-houses within the walls of Taiz. There were drawbacks to this honour, however, for the city gates closed at sundown, allowing no one to enter or leave. When the pregnant wife of their porter went into labour, the Italian minister and his wife were unable to call for help from the European doctors outside the walls. But Bice successfully delivered the baby girl on the kitchen table, cutting and sewing the umbilicus, while Amedeo fetched and carried. The following morning, like buses, four Italian doctors arrived all at once at the house.

Bice looked back on their time in the Yemen as the most magical period of her life. In the Fifties, it was a land emerging from the middle ages, of which alarming traces still remained. She was discomfited to be waited on at table by a servant weighed down by chains, who had in some manner offended the Imam's law. Her maternal heart was also moved when she discovered that in the ruler's castle above Taiz the sons of various tribal chiefs would be held as hostages – 'like a compulsory Eton', according to Pirie-Gordon. The arrangement ensured that the Imam could rely on the eventual compliance of recalcitrant chiefs. Curiously, the practice did not cause resentment, for many felt that it was rather chic to have been a hostage, confirming as it did that the young Yemenis came from good family.

For the education of their own sons, the Guillets sent Paolo, born in 1945, and Alfredo, three years younger, to an Italian boarding school in Asmara, which still had a sizeable Italian population in the Fifties. In the holidays they would cross the Red Sea and spend unforgettable days riding horses through the mountains or fishing in the Red Sea, escorted by Daifallah, whom Amedeo re-employed at the Italian mission. Once, when landing their sailing boat at Hodeida, Amedeo and Daifallah recognised the pirate captain who had left them to die in the desert more than a decade earlier. The temptation to have revenge was strong, and the Imam would certainly have given Amedeo the man's life had he asked for it. But hatred, Amedeo felt, devours those who succumb to it; the past was best left behind.

Margaret Luce, wife of the British governor of Aden, makes several mentions of the 'legendary character' Amedeo Guillet during these years in her published diary, *From Aden to the Gulf* (Michael Russell, 1987).

> 'The Guillets' house was given to Amedeo by the Imam. It is a completely Arabic house in the middle of the town, joined on to the house of the Arab owner of both, and surrounded by Yemeni families and their children, with all of whom Amedeo is on terms of the most cosy friendship. But I am not quite sure how Signora Guillet feels. She is rather young, and gentle and sweet, with red hair – their two sons are at school in Asmara. Amedeo is always rushing dynamically about, to Hodeida, or Sana'a and Aden and Asmara and even Italy, and she is left living alone in the middle of the suq. She has made the house as charming as it could be, and filled every little rooftop and open space with tubs of geraniums and poinsettias and hibiscus, while Amedeo has insisted on covering the wall with prints of 'The Earl of Derby's Fox-Hounds'.'

Mrs Luce was far less enamoured with the Yemen than Amedeo and Bice, likening the country to 'something out of the *Mikado*'.

She was much intrigued by the harem of the Imam, which she visited with some western women in November 1959 and met the wives and concubines within. 'One of them was quite pretty in a flashy vulgar way, and sits chewing gum and smoking all day long.' The youngest wife, aged twenty-three, was half-English, being the daughter of a Yemeni who somehow made his way to Hull, where he worked as a docker. He married an Englishwoman and brought his three daughters back to the Yemen, whereupon the Imam insisted on having the eldest one as his wife. The other two joined their sister in the harem to keep her company. Mrs Luce observed:

> 'They now, not surprisingly, want to go back to Hull, and sometimes smuggle pathetic letters to Christopher Pirie-Gordon, who can do nothing as they are legally Yemeni subjects. But Signora Guillet says that the eldest one (only twenty-three now) and the Imam's first wife, who is quite old, are very great friends, and are the two wives who are most seriously fond of the Imam. The half-English one was the only wife who was any real use in trying to dissuade him from his morphia [to which he became addicted during his illnesses], and is not afraid to tell him what she thinks. Perhaps that is just why he won't let her go back to Hull.'

Equipped with a classical Arabic education, Imam Ahmed attempted to come to terms with the modern world, trying to make sense of the competing and equally incomprehensible ideologies of American liberal democracy and Soviet Communism. Because of its strategic position, the Yemen was wooed by both the superpowers during the Cold War. An additional complication was that after Nasser's coup in Egypt, a wave of Arab nationalism, which the Soviet Union exploited, swept over the Middle East.

Amedeo tried to keep the pernicious influences of both East and West in balance or at bay. When the Soviets built the port at Hodeida, it was thanks to him that the first vessel to enter was a US warship. Similarly, when the Russian ambassador had some success with influential Yemenis by introducing them to the novelty of Soviet propaganda films, he encouraged the American representative to screen a western for the Imam at the palace. The ruler and his wives watched the film in amazement and at the end he asked for the whole thing to be shown again.

Numerous Yemeni students and pilots were sent to Italy to study, and when the Imam fell ill with a heart condition, he was treated in Rome, reassured that Ahmed Abdullah would be able to arrange all.

The Yemen's most problematic diplomatic relations were with Britain during this time, partly because of its links with the Saudis, but mainly because Aden provided shelter for Yemeni dissidents calling for the Imam's overthrow. At one point, diplomatic relations between the two countries almost broke down on this issue, but owing to Amedeo's intercession this was avoided. Sir Ashley Clarke, the British ambassador in Rome thanked the Italian government in 1961:

> 'the help given by Minister Guillet, who has been extremely useful, and not only on this occasion . . . With almost twenty years experience of the Yemen, and thanks to his personal relations with the Imam, quite unique of their kind, he has been able to give advice whenever required . . . thus avoiding a break in Anglo–Yemeni relations which would have prejudiced not only the interests of the United Kingdom, but also the free world.'

On two occasions, Amedeo was called to the United Nations in New York to share his unequalled expertise of the area: he was returning to the assembly after having a coffee when, to his joy, he witnessed Nikita Khrushchev's shoe-banging episode.

In July 1962 Amedeo was appointed ambassador to Jordan. He took his leave of Imam Ahmed, who disguised the sadness he must have felt in an almost off-hand manner, too proud to display emotion. Amedeo was beginning to feel hurt at this treatment, when the Imam beckoned him to a window at the palace in Taiz.

Below, standing in a courtyard and held by a groom, was a beautiful Hamdani colt, one of the finest Arab horses in the world. Amedeo called the horse Nasr, and his grandson, Akbar, is today kept in the field beside his house in Ireland.

In September 1962 Imam Ahmed died and was succeeded by his son, Al-Badr. Amedeo travelled down to Sana'a from Amman to represent the Italian president at the funeral, although he would have attended anyway to mourn his friend. As a guest of honour he was lodged in the Al-Magam royal palace. The night of the funeral, he was awoken by the sound of cannon fire. He looked out of his window to see tanks crushing through the intricate archways of the square in front of the palace. The Imam's bodyguard, all of whom were to die, kept up a furious but ineffectual barrage of small arms fire. The tanks then fired volley after volley into the far wing of the palace where Badr had his quarters. All of a sudden the Imam and a few followers, half-dressed and loading their weapons, burst past Amedeo in the corridor. They made their escape through his window, jumping down into the garden below. In the excitable news reports that followed, both the Imam and the Italian ambassador were reported killed. Amedeo had done his best to mislead the rebels by saying that the Imam was under the heap of rubble at the other end of the palace. Nasserite officers, for the tank crews had been trained in Egypt, had staged the coup, aided by the Soviet Union. Three days later, a well-armed Egyptian division landed at Hodeida to 'keep the peace' and Russian-piloted MiGs were deployed against those who remained loyal to the Imam. Many of Amedeo's closest Yemeni friends were murdered in the days that followed the coup, people whom he had known since he had first arrived in the country in December 1941. For the next ten years the Yemen disintegrated into civil war, and the Arabia Felix that had been his refuge turned its back on a thousand years of political independence under the Imamate. In 1992 Amedeo made an emotional return to the Yemen, accepting an official invitation, and was gratified to witness its renovation.

His ambassadorship in Jordan lasted for six years. It was a key posting in the Middle East, on the frontline between the Arab world and Israel. In the time he was there, Amedeo befriended King Hussein, a man whom he greatly admired. His own reputation in the Yemen had preceded him, and his fluent Arabic and knowledge of life in the Middle East greatly impressed the monarch. Until Hussein's death in 1999, they remained in regular contact, and Amedeo is still close to Jordan's royal family, and an intimate friend of Prince Hassan, the king's uncle. During this ambassadorship, Amedeo had to organise the visit of Pope Paul VI to the Holy Land, the first ever by a pontiff, which was fraught with possible complications. It passed off smoothly.

But the Arab–Israeli conflict overshadowed everything. When Germany made payments to Israel to atone for the Holocaust the entire Arab world was indignant, for what of the Palestinian refugees, they demanded, who had been forced from their land because Europeans had murdered the Jews. With feelings running high, German and American citizens had to leave Jordan, and it was left to Amedeo, as dean of the diplomatic corps, to organise the emergency airlift. Not long afterwards, the Six Days' War broke out, with Jordan losing the West Bank and Jerusalem. Amedeo obtained emergency humanitarian funds from the Italian government, and Bice's role in helping the Palestinian refugees made a strong impression in Amman. It was during these years that Amedeo came to know leading British public figures who visited Jordan, such as Julian Amery, Duncan Sandys and, with greater warmth, Christopher Soames ('in appearance a typical Englishman, but with a mind as sharp as a Neapolitan's').

In April 1968, the Guillets were transferred to Morocco, King Hussein insisting that a Circassian groom of his bodyguard accompany Nasr, who was transported by ship. Extraordinarily intelligent, the horse was capable of doing complicated dressage movements, responding to voice prompts even when not mounted, and the stallion's fame spread throughout the Arab horse world. An Italian TV documentary was devoted to him.

It was King Hassan II of Morocco's custom to celebrate his birthday at his villa at Skirat on the coast, to which ambassadors and leading figures were invited. Amedeo enjoyed these occasions, as they were informal and involved horse riding, swimming and golf and then a leisurely buffet in the gardens. He was lying on a divan by the pool waiting for the birthday ceremonies to begin in 1971 when suddenly he heard the sound of shots. Some ambassadors thought it was a folkloristic display by the Bedouin, but the distinctive sound of automatic fire disinclined Amedeo to share this view. It was a coup. Soon bullets were ripping through the tents in the garden, guests and waiters were scrambling for cover, some lying wounded or dying on the lawn. Amedeo felt someone slump against him and turned to see a high Moroccan functionary fall shot in the chest, his bloody hand making a perfect print on the Italian's shirt. The Greek ambassador was about to flatten himself on the ground, until Amedeo stopped him. The soldiers were firing from above on the wall surrounding the gardens; lying down just made the target bigger. He took the Greek's arm and together they ran towards the firing for the 'dead angle' beside the wall.

After a while the random shooting ended and the guests were rounded up and assembled on the lawn, where they were made to lie face down with their hands behind their heads. The soldiers called out names of prominent government figures one after another, then perfunctorily shot those who stood up in acknowledgement. But the coup ended on a bathetic note when the soldiers called out the name of a minister and a doctor with a similar name stood up. The coup leader, General Medbough, stepped between the soldiers and their intended victim telling them he was not the right man, and was shot dead by mistake. Meanwhile, King Hassan had gathered the soldiers sent to seize him in the villa. They had been deceived by the coup's leaders that their actions were to save the king. The coup attempt at Skirat failed by a hair's breadth, but of the 800 guests, 100 were killed and 200 wounded. The Belgian ambassador was among the dead, and three other ambassadors were wounded.

A month after Skirat, Amedeo and Bice were again on the move to their last diplomatic posting: New Delhi. He arrived as ambassador just in time for India's war with Pakistan. Among the correspondents who arrived to cover the war was Oriana Fallaci, the maverick feminist writer then at the peak of her fame, who insisted that the new ambassador fix an interview with Indira Gandhi. Bice could not resist teasing Amedeo, worn down by his demanding 'new girlfriend', who seemed no less determined than India's prime minister. Amedeo established close relations with Indira Gandhi and her family, including her daughter-in-law Sonia, who is also Piedmontese.

In the early Seventies, many of India's highest army officers were veterans of the campaign in Italian East Africa, and Amedeo was an honoured guest at various regimental reunions, including that of Skinner's Horse and the Rajputana Rifles. In another of those peculiar coincidences in his life, his driver at the Italian embassy was Mohinder Singh, the Sikh corporal who had witnessed his charge at Keru. From this shared experience, Mohinder and the ambassador became very close.

As before, Amedeo proved himself to be an untypical civil servant of the Italian Republic. On a couple of occasions, embassy staff were alarmed to see the ambassador returning from the garden to their offices carrying a cobra that he had captured in the flowerbeds. Bice had become used to such surprises, for Amedeo had taught himself to capture snakes between two forked fingers, and he had had to catch a number of them in their tower house in Taiz. To the uninitiated, however, and doubtless to Amedeo's glee, it was an unsettling experience.

His love of horses again meant that he involved himself to an unusual degree in local life. When the Indian army learned of his reputation, they asked him to school the president's bodyguard in Caprilli's 'forward seat', as they still jumped obstacles in the British hunting style of the Twenties. Amedeo staged an international showjumping competition beside the Red Fort in Delhi and invited over one of the most celebrated practitioners of Caprilli's method: Piero D'Inzeo, the world champion Italian showjumper. In 1973, he also organised a 'torch-light tattoo' at night in front of the president's palace, in celebration of the bicentenary of the mounted bodyguard that had once served the British viceroys. It was a highly prestigious event, staged in front of numerous international guests, with ample scope for disaster as riders performed the spectacular exercises once taught at Pinerolo, like jumping between four unfortunate soldiers seated at table as though at dinner.

Bice, too, won the good opinion of Mrs Gandhi, and many in Delhi admired her for her efforts on behalf of the Tibetan refugees, who had poured into India. 'Most ambassadors are forgotten a few months after they leave,' Mrs Gandhi told Amedeo. 'But I doubt whether you will be.' And so it proved. Four times, after their departure, he and Bice were invited to return to India.

In August 1975, the Guillets retired to Ireland, where they had bought a Georgian rectory in Co Meath at the beginning of the Sixties. Horses were one of the main attractions, but so too were the peace and tranquillity. Or, as Amedeo once put it: 'I am weary of the world, and so chose to live on its periphery.' Bice would sort out the garden – the first one that was truly hers in her adult life – while Amedeo spent his time painting, playing music and, his chief passion, schooling his horses. Every winter he rode with the Meath Hunt and the Tara Harriers, and though an exotic and highly individual character, he fitted into Irish country life with his usual tact and generosity, teaching his neighbours' children how to ride.

Meanwhile, army friends in India had passed the word around in England that the man who had led the charge at Keru was alive and living in Ireland. In the mid-Seventies there were a number of reunions with his former adversaries. The gunners of the Surrey and Sussex Yeomanry invited Amedeo to a dinner in March 1976; the surviving officers of the 4th Indian Division did the same later in the year. Among others, he befriended Brigadier Robert 'Bobby' Popham of the Sudan Defence Force, and Colonel H. A. Hughes. Lieutenant General Sir Reginald Savory, who had led the fighting on Mount Cochen, was his host and later became a friend. At the dinner, the British general presented Amedeo with a silver plate, with the shield and cross of Savoy, that he had taken as a souvenir when he had been military governor of Asmara. Was it true, the Englishman asked, that Amedeo really intended to kidnap him, as he had been informed? 'Perhaps,' the Italian replied.

When attempts were made to force Sikhs to wear crash helmets on motorcycles in England, Sir Reginald appeared in a Manchester courtroom as a witness for the defence. At Keren, he told the court, Sikh turbans were found to be sufficiently protective to stop a bullet; indeed, when they were unravelled flattened lead was often found inside. Naturally, he forwarded a press cutting of the case to his fellow veteran of Keren in Ireland.

Just before he died in 1977, Sir William Platt invited the 'man on the white horse' to meet him in London. He spoke frankly to Amedeo of his anxiety that the Italians might have held on at Keren. It had been a very close call, the former commander of the British invasion force admitted. 'Had I been judging military manoeuvres,' said the old general, 'I would have given the victory to the Italians.' It was Amedeo's sincere belief that both Platt and General Carnimeo, had inspired the most heroic qualities in the men under their command.

By this time, a number of books appeared in English which referred, in passing, to Amedeo's war, particularly the charge at Keru. Anthony Mockler, in his meticulously researched and outstanding work, *Haile Selassie's War* (OUP, 1984) writes of the charge:

> 'It had certainly shaken the British and proved to those who doubted that Italian officers knew how to fight and how to die . . . But though the advance of the invaders was held up, the retreat of the defenders was chaotic and disorganized. Had it not been for Guillet and his horsemen, almost all the Italians would have fallen into the hands of the blocking column behind Keru.'

Later, when the Italian front crumpled at Agordat and the Eritrean lowlands were lost, Mockler acknowledges Amedeo's role:

> 'Lieutenant Guillet and his horsemen were again the last to leave, holding out until the end and then escorting the whole garrison down the railway line, avoiding the road and its trap. So, of the 15,000 troops there, less than 1,000 were taken prisoner.'

There were several published first-hand accounts of Amedeo's action at Keru, including Peter Cochrane's *Charlie Company* (Chatto and Windus, 1977), *The Desert and the Jungle* by Sir Geoffrey (GC) Evans (William Kimber, 1959) and *Spearhead General*, Sir Frank Messervy's ghosted autobiography by Henry Maule (Odhams, 1961).

Of all his former enemies, Amedeo remained closest to Max Harari. Divorces had diminished his fortune, which disappeared altogether with the confiscations after the Suez Crisis. But Max, happily married to Jane, had rebuilt it with spectacular success taking employment at Wildensteins, the international art dealers. Most years he would visit the Guillets at their various postings or, later, in Ireland, or they would come to find him in his large house in Northamptonshire. He died in 1987, and had a memorial service at St James's, Piccadilly. Lory Gibbs, the officer who had shot at Amedeo and Khadija on the road to Ghinda, died the same year. The two former adversaries had met several times with their families in the Middle East, where Gibbs had worked in Saudi Arabia.

Captain Sigismund Reich, better known as David 'Storm' Rice after the war, became a professor at the School of Oriental and African Studies in London. He committed suicide in 1962.

All the former officers of the Gruppo Bande Amhara a Cavallo are now dead, the last to fall out being Guido Battizzocco, who died in Rome in 1998. Orlando Rizzi died in Asmara in 1968; while Angelo Maiorani, the Gruppo Bande's lawyer, was killed in 1958 by *shifta*. Mohammed Daifallah died of stomach cancer in Hodeida in 1960.

For sixteen years Amedeo and Bice enjoyed a quiet retirement in rural Ireland, returning to their apartment in Rome to keep in touch with friends. It was there that Bice Gandolfo-Guillet died in 1991.

Amedeo continues to divide his time between his houses in Co Meath and Rome. A particular trial has been supervising the repairs of the family palazzo in Capua, which was damaged in the 1981 earthquake. Until he was eighty-six, he rode to hounds following their hair-raising chases across the Meath countryside, where every field division is a wide ditch. He still keeps two horses, and was recently given two delightful, but time-consuming, Arab fillies – a rarity in Ireland. He rides occasionally, and once in the saddle the aches and pains of age and old wounds disappear. As for the problem of his cataracts, 'the horse can see perfectly well for me'.

Amedeo was at home in Rome in summer 1999 when he was telephoned by an anxious official at the Farnesina, the Italian Foreign Office. President Isaias Afwerki of Eritrea was on a state visit to Italy, when he had surprised his hosts by asking whether he might meet Amedeo Guillet, for the man was a legend in his country. From this encounter came the invitation to visit Eritrea in March 2000 and, like Sancho Panza following Don Quixote, I accompanied him.

President Isaias, who had led the Eritrean People's Liberation Front in the last stage of its long war with Ethiopia, welcomed Amedeo in what had once been the Italian officer's club in Asmara. His offices were next door, in the former army headquarters where De Bono and Badoglio had planned their invasion of Abyssinia, and where Max Harari and Sigismund Reich had sought to put an end to the activities of Lieutenant Amedeo Guillet. President Isaias proved to be a generous host. In spite of the tension with Ethiopia, which erupted into full-scale war six weeks after our departure, Amedeo could go wherever he liked. A car would be put at his disposal, and also a former Soviet gunship, in which he could fly down to Keren and the Sudanese border.

But first a meeting had been organised for the surviving Eritrean *ascari* who had fought for Africa Orientale Italiana. There could not have been more than a couple of dozen waiting in the crystalline winter sunlight in Asmara's Catholic cemetery. Some were dressed in frayed European suits, others were in white cotton; all wore medals, with the green, white and red ribbons of the Italian tricolour. A Carabiniere from Italy stood beside them in full dress uniform, holding a wreath in a white-gloved hand, and when Amedeo appeared at the end of an avenue of cypress trees, reviewing a guard of honour of the modern Eritrean army, he snapped to attention.

Padre Protasio Delfino, an Eritrean priest from Asmara's cathedral, led prayers beside Christ on the Cross, surrounded by the tombs and statues of the Italian dead. Some of the *ascari* had been in the Penne di Falco Cavalry (the 'falcon feathers'), others were infantrymen of the IVth Toselli, but none, sadly, were veterans of the Gruppo Bande Amhara a Cavallo. Amedeo singled out the oldest among them, who at 94 was three years his senior, and embraced him 'as I can't embrace you all'. Some women in the crowd of *vecchi coloniali*, the 800 or so Italians who have hung on in Asmara, dabbed their eyes with their handkerchiefs. After the ceremony, we walked through the cemetery pausing at the tombs of the Rizzi family, and a large edifice for the dead of the

Gondrand massacre that Amedeo had witnessed with the Spahys di Libya in 1936.

Asmara had changed hardly at all in the past 60 years. The fabric of the city, frayed and tatty after the years of Ethiopian dominance, was still as Amedeo remembered it, right down to the Bar Vittoria, the Pizzeria Napoli and the art deco Tagliero Fiat garage. The governor's palace had been gutted, however, and not far away was the so-called 'tank cemetery', a seemingly endless junk yard of rusting Soviet war materiel, as well as, incongruously, the Italian governor's railway carriage from the turn of the century. The acres of twisted lorries and tanks were a powerful memorial to the scale of the EPLF's victory over their Goliathan enemy.

We stayed at the Villa Roma, the residence of the Italian ambassador, Antonio Bandini and his wife, Consuelo, who had meticulously restored it to its former glory. From the cellar, they had retrieved the portrait of the Duke of Aosta, in his white uniform of the Regia Aeronautica. It was one of the few items not looted by Cuban advisers during the war.

The days that followed evoked many memories. At the Ponte Menabrea, still with the inscription of '*Ca custa lon ca custa*' above the arches, Amedeo got out to scrutinise the road he himself had mined 60 years before, while at Ad Teclesan, he looked down from the road to where the Gruppo Bande had had its trenches. For a couple of hours we searched for the remains of the three British light tanks he had destroyed, which had still been on the side of the road in the late Fifties. A burned-out Soviet troop carrier and tank, its turret blown off, raised false hopes: they were the work of Amedeo's EPLF successors. But at a place where the new road widened, there was a single tank track with Roman lettering, rather than the Cyrillic of the Soviet equipment. It may well have been one of his, the carcasses of the old British machines having gone into the road's foundations.

But the highlight of Amedeo's visit was the journey to Keren and Keru. The old Soviet gunship heaved itself off the tarmac at Asmara's airport, then turned and headed north towards the mountains. An hour later it touched down outside Keren, where almost the whole town had turned out to catch sight of their illustrious visitor. Police cars, army lorries filled with soldiers and motorcycle outriders set off in convoy past the crowds, looping round the Girafiori roundabout, before halting at the Italian military cemetery. An Eritrean priest celebrated mass, marvelling at the folly of man that Italians and the British should find cause to fight each other so far from home. Afterwards Amedeo walked past the rows of tombstones, dazzling in the morning sun, to that of Lieutenant Renato Togni.

After inaugurating Keren's new hospital, Amedeo was invited by the priest to rest a while and take *gishir* under the trees near the sanctuary of the Madonna of the Baobab. The Baobab was a huge, hollow tree where four Italian soldiers had fled when the line broke at Keren. A British tank, seeing the men, had fired at the tree, making a perfect circle in its trunk, but leaving the soldiers inside unscathed. It has been a sanctuary ever since.

Once rested, we were back in the gunship heading towards the Sudanese border. We flew above the gorge of Dongolaas, the fulcrum of the battle of Keren, and then over the lowlands towards Agordat. Below was the stony brown desert, but with patches of green following the course of the sandy wadis. The four-span Ponte Mussolini, as it is still called, stood above the dried bed of the Barca river, where the advance of Messervy and Gazelle Force was crucially delayed before Keren. Over Mount Cochen, at Agordat, the doors of the gunship were opened, and Amedeo and General Kesete Berhane, designated his official companion, looked down on what had once been both men's battlefield. For Mount Cochen had been held by Cubans during the EPLF's war.

The landscape became flatter, and more sandy towards the Sudanese border. In the distance, at the end of the dead straight Italian road, was the distinctive rocky outcrop of the oasis of Kassala. Amedeo grabbed my shoulder, and I removed my headphones.

'There! The fort of Keru!'

Below were several old buildings, gun emplacements and trenches. And stretching away before it was the plain of Aicota where, for a day, the Gruppo Bande Amhara a Cavallo had stopped the British advance.

He is tired now. It's a dark November evening outside, and I can hear the rain on the windows behind the Georgian shutters. While I am writing these words on the dining room table at Kentstown Glebe, Amedeo has stretched out on the floor at my feet, covering himself with a blanket. His early habits have disinclined him to enjoy the comforts of his house. Throughout their marriage, poor Bice had to sleep beside her husband, who lay on a wooden board over his half of the mattress.

Amedeo has been talking all day, and as ever I am amazed at his memory for the smallest details: the Sword of Islam, the princesses in the Villa Savoia, Daifallah in the desert, the king at Brindisi, could all have happened yesterday. From below the table, I can hear his heavy breathing and occasional snores. In a couple of hours, Angela Lynch, his housekeeper for the past 25 years, will arrive to prepare supper. It will be an Irish version of pasta, followed by *spezzatino* or lightly grilled fish, and then a slice of her own *crostata*.

The mementoes of his extraordinary life are all over the house. Hundreds of photographs cover the walls and every available surface: Bice at Vietri, Paolo and Alfredo on horses in the Yemen, the Duke of Aosta, Uncle Amedeo, officer cadets at Modena in 1929, Mrs Gandhi, Piero D'Inzeo, Princess Jolanda, Imam Ahmed, King Hussein, Pope Paul VI, Umberto II.

We'll eat downstairs in the breakfast room, beside his array of tack and saddles, now creaky and gathering dust. Under a blanket somewhere is the Pariani saddle he used on Sandor at Keru. He will tell his favourite stories of his time when he was an ambassador, or lament the absence of the gardener/handyman who has gone off on a bender. He will ask me about my young mare which we bought together a year ago, and which I have called Khadija, or Kaddy. And maybe tomorrow he will give me a riding lesson, sitting in the middle of the sand school on a chair barking out instructions as he used to do at Pinerolo in the early Thirties.

After supper we will go upstairs to the drawing room, where Amedeo will play the piano, while I sip tea and let my eyes wander over the portraits and photographs I know so well. He plays from the heart, summoning up the great swelling arias of Verdi and Mascagni. They falter at times, for the left hand still bears the wounds of Selaclaca, and the right has a fingertip missing, chewed off by a horse. I can picture him as he plays, as a young subaltern in the mess, his olive-grey tunic buttoned at the neck with just a hint of white stock beneath.

After the arias, a little Schubert and always, at the end, Jacques Prevert's '*Les Feuilles Mortes*'.

'Because I am the last leaf to fall'.

Not yet, though. Not yet.

# ACKNOWLEDGEMENTS

The main source of this book and the man to whom I owe the greatest debt of gratitude is Amedeo Guillet himself, now in his ninety-third year. It has been a great privilege to have befriended him, and we have both, I think, enjoyed reliving the years of his youth together. Without his vivid descriptions of people and places sixty-five years ago, and his extraordinary memory for detail, this project would not have been realised. I must also sincerely thank him for his forbearance during the writing of this book. Having your life summed up in a biography, especially one written by someone of a different generation and outlook, has been an occasionally unsettling experience. It must have saddened him at times when reading the manuscript that though we agreed on so many things, there were others about which we would always differ. But with the humility and curiosity that characterise the man, he would always – perhaps after an initial explosive barrage – admit the possibility of an alternative view. In this, and in many, many other matters, he had much to teach the author.

I wish to thank Amedeo's son, Alfredo Guillet, an environmentalist in the Italian foreign ministry, who was cast in the unenviable role of UN peacekeeper at times, as the Abyssinian conquest was re-fought, the issue of mustard gas and arguments dragged on over the Second World War in Africa, and the plebiscite for the monarchy. Unfailingly patient and affable, as well as erudite, he never lost sight – as we were tempted to do – of the main goal. Having spent his childhood in Eritrea and the Yemen, and knowing many of the leading characters in this book, Alfredo's insight was invaluable.

I am deeply grateful to Vittorio Dan Segre, the author of the internationally renowned *Memoirs of a Fortunate Jew*, for his very generous encouragement. He, too, has written about Amedeo, whom he has known since the Forties, in *La Guerra Privata del Tenente Guillet*, but has always believed a fuller biography was warranted. For his courtesy and kindness, I must thank him.

I also thank Rosangela Barone, formerly director of the Italian Cultural Institute in Dublin, who helped Amedeo and kept him company as we worked together on this project. Owing to her efforts many documents and photographs were retrieved, and her comments on the text were meticulous and helpful, as one might expect of someone who has rendered Gaelic poetry into Italian. It was thanks to her that Amedeo's visit to Eritrea in March 2000 passed smoothly, and it delighted us both that she, too, had the opportunity to visit the places described in these pages.

There are many others I must also thank. President Isaias Afwerki of Eritrea kindly allowed me to accompany Amedeo Guillet, whom he had invited to visit his country. I thank Antonio Bandini, formerly Italian ambassador to Asmara, and his wife, Consuelo, for their generous hospitality during our stay at the Villa Roma. Among those in Eritrea whom we befriended, I would like to single out General Kessete Berhane, a veteran of the Eritrean People's Liberation Front, for his warm humanity and many kindnesses, and Alemseged Tesfai, a playwright and historian, for sharing his knowledge on the birth of the Eritrean national movement. I am grateful to Tewolde Andu, the mayor of Massaua, for his guided tour of Amedeo's old haunts in his city, and to Petros Solomon, war hero and the Minister of Fisheries, for his hospitality at the Albergo Torino on the Red Sea. All these EPLF veterans, whose lives have been overshadowed by war since childhood, were unfailingly generous and courteous towards the returning, ninety-one-year-old Italian *generale*. He must have seemed a figure from a very remote past.

Among the *vecchi coloniali* of the Italian community in Asmara, I would like to thank Fratell' Ezio Todini, for allowing me to visit his extraordinary library, that has survived the Dergue, the MiGs and the Cuba looters. My thanks to Giuseppe Cinnirella, an Asmarino from birth, for his local knowledge and pearls of gossip from life in the Thirties and Forties.

Colonel Douglas Gray, of Skinner's Horse, kindly shared his memories of the day the Italian cavalry charged out of the morning mist at Keru, and accompanied me in visiting their commander in Ireland. Jane Harari generously lent her photographs of her husband Max, while Professor Edward Ullendorff, formerly of the British Military Administration in Eritrea, cast light on the tragic and intriguing Captain Sigismund Reich; as did Geza Fehervari, one of his research students, who recalls his mentor displaying Himmler's watch while lecturing at SOAS. While I cannot expect Richard Pankhurst to sympathise with the views or activities of the character described in these pages – I am grateful for his encouraging curiosity.

I would like to thank Colonel Giam Battista Pollone, director of the Italian Cavalry Museum at Pinerolo, for kindly setting aside a day to show me around his exhibits and archives, as well as the magnificent Caprilli Manège. General Raimondo Caria, director of the Istituto Geografico Militare in Rome, and Dott. Armando Lazzarini kindly supplied maps and other research materials. I thank Paola Lorenzini and Anna Carnimeo for the photographs of their illustrious fathers.

John and Elizabeth Coveney, in Co Meath, have been extremely kind and hospitable during my visits to Kentstown. I am also grateful to Angela Lynch and Maria Pia Castagna, respectively, Amedeo's Irish and Roman housekeepers.

My warm thanks to Arabella Pike at HarperCollins for taking the book on, and David Miller, of Rogers, Coleridge and White.

Finally, I must thank my wife, Kym, for many things, especially her patience in putting up with my many absences in Ireland, Italy and Eritrea.

## THE HONOURS CONFERRED UPON AMEDEO GUILLET

MILITARY

Croce di Cavaliere dell'Ordine Militare di Savoia. Awarded by Vittorio Emanuele III, 8 March, 1944.

Gran Croce dell'Ordine Militare d'Italia. Awarded by President Carlo Azeglio Ciampi, 6 November, 2001.

Bronze Medal for Valour, Selaclaca, 25 December, 1935. Awarded by Italo Balbo in Tripoli, 1936.

Silver Medal for Valour San Pedro de Romeral, Santander, 14–25 August, 1937.

Cruze Blanca, for valour. Awarded by General Franco, 1937.

Silver Medal for service on the Aragon front with Spanish Moroccan cavalry and for capturing three bridges with the Fiamme Nere's Arditi, 15 March – 16 April, 1938.

Silver Medal for Valour in actions against Uvene Tashemma at Dongur Duba, Abyssinia, 6 August, 1939.

Silver Medal for Valour in the cavalry charge at Keru, 21 January, 1941. (Recommended for the Gold Medal for Valour by the Duke of Aosta, but this was superseded by the Ordine Militare di Savoia.)

Silver Medal for Valour in the defence at Ad Teclesan, and for destroying three British light tanks, 16 October, 1954. (Confirmed by Presidential Decree.)

Campaign medals in the war against the Allies, 1940–1943; and in the "war of liberation" against the Germans, 1943–45.

Five crosses classed Merito di Guerra, one con gladio – with swords.

Croce di Cavaliere al Merito Coloniale (Medal of a War Volunteer).

Cruze por la Unidad Nacionale Española, 1938.

Cruze del Sufrimiento de la Patria, for wounds sustained in the Spanish Civil War, 1938.

Cruze Blanca and Cruze Roja, for valour, Spain 1938.

### DIPLOMATIC

Grand Officer of the Order of the Nile of the Arab Republic of Egypt, 1954.

Grand Cross, with stars and stripe of the Order of Merit, German Federal Republic, awarded in recognition of services to German citizens in Jordan, 1967.

Grand Cross of the Kawkab al Urduni Order of the Hashemite Kingdom of Jordan, 1968.

Grand Cross of the Alawita Order of the Kingdom of Morocco, 1971

Grand Cross of the Order of St Gregory the Great, Vatican, 1964.

Cavaliere of the Grand Cross of the Order of Merit, Republic of Italy, 1975.

### OTHERS

Freedom of the City of Capra, June 2000.

# INDEX